Occupy

Critical Climate Change

Series Editors: Tom Cohen and Claire Colebrook

The era of climate change involves the mutation of systems beyond 20th century anthropomorphic models and has stood, until recently, outside representation or address. Understood in a broad and critical sense, climate change concerns material agencies that impact on biomass and energy, erased borders and microbial invention, geological and nanographic time, and extinction events. The possibility of extinction has always been a latent figure in textual production and archives; but the current sense of depletion, decay, mutation and exhaustion calls for new modes of address, new styles of publishing and authoring, and new formats and speeds of distribution. As the pressures and re-alignments of this re-arrangement occur, so must the critical languages and conceptual templates, political premises and definitions of 'life.' There is a particular need to publish in timely fashion experimental monographs that redefine the boundaries of disciplinary fields, rhetorical invasions, the interface of conceptual and scientific languages, and geomorphic and geopolitical interventions. Critical Climate Change is oriented, in this general manner, toward the epistemo-political mutations that correspond to the temporalities of terrestrial mutation.

Occupy
A People Yet to Come

Edited by Andrew Conio

O
OPEN HUMANITIES PRESS

London

2015

First edition published by OPEN HUMANITIES PRESS

Copyright © 2015 Andrew Conio. Chapters by respective authors except chapter 2: Protevi, John. "Semantic, Pragmatic, and Affective Enactment at OWS." *Theory & Event* 14:4 Supplement (2011). © 2011 John Protevi and The Johns Hopkins University Press. Reprinted with permission of Johns Hopkins University Press

Freely available online at http://openhumanitiespress.org/books/occupy.html

This is an open access book, licensed under Creative Commons By Attribution Share Alike license. Under this license, authors allow anyone to download, reuse, reprint, modify, distribute, and/or copy their work so long as the authors and source are cited and resulting derivative works are licensed under the same or similar license. No permission is required from the authors or the publisher. Statutory fair use and other rights are in no way affected by the above.

Read more about the license at creativecommons.org/licenses/by-sa/4.0

PRINT ISBN 978-1-78542-004-7

PDF ISBN 978-1-78542-014-6

Cover Art: Declaration Flowchart by Rachel Schragis, Copyright © 2011 CC-BY-NC-SA 3.0

Open Humanities Press is an international, scholar-led open access publishing collective whose mission is to make leading works of contemporary critical thought freely available worldwide. More at http://openhumanitiespress.org

Contents

Preface		9
	Claire Colebrook	
Introduction		23
	Andrew Conio	
1.	On Anthropolitics: From Capitalism and Schizophrenia to Occupy and Beyond	67
	Giuseppina Mecchia	
2.	Semantic, Pragmatic, and Affective Enactment at OWS	88
	John Protevi	
3.	Pack of Leaders: Thinking Organization and Spontaneity with Deleuze and Guattari	97
	Rodrigo Nunes	
4.	Resistance to Occupy	125
	Claire Colebrook	
5.	Preoccupations	158
	Verena Andermatt Conley	
6.	Minor Politics, Territory, and Occupy	172
	Nicholas Thoburn	
7.	September 17, 2011: Occupy without Counting	191
	Ian Buchanan	
8.	Negative Space War Machines	203
	David Burrows	

9. Occupy America and the Slow-Motion General Strike   225
   Eugene Holland

10. Savage Money   238
    Andrew Conio

Bios   269

Acknowlegements

I would like to thank Claire Colebrook for her generous and steadfast support during the writing of this book; the contributors, Andrew Stapleton, Sigi Jöttkandt and my many friends at Occupy and the Economics Working Group especially David, Tim, Clive, Mary, Ellena, Omar, Janos, Peter, Mike, Obi, Schlack, Nick and Vica whose commitment to finding ways to create a better world prompted the writing of this book.

Preface

End the Occupation, Long Live Occupy!

CLAIRE COLEBROOK

I

At the time of this book going to press, amidst all the diverging political theories and commentaries regarding how the twenty-first century might cope with the intertwined complexities of climate change, collapsing global finance, wars on terror that are also wars on freedom, potential viral pandemics and increasing disaster scenarios (with increased vulnerability to disaster for the less fortunate) one thing seems clear enough: end the occupation. The attacks by Israel on Gaza have not received unanimous condemnation; there are still those, especially in the United States, who – for all the disproportionate suffering inflicted on those trapped in Gaza – still see Israel as having some right to defend itself, and still maintain that conflict was instigated by Hamas and therefore not subject to any critique outside the right of Israel to 'respond.' Regardless of the competing histories, narratives, conflicting allegiances and complexities, it nevertheless seems clear that ending the occupation would be the best and quickest way to end widespread and ongoing violence.

Why does ending occupation, amidst all this complexity, appear to be such a clear and just thing to do? There are two identities – the State of Israel and the Palestinians in Gaza – both of whom can lay claim to having suffered displacement and both of whom can seem to ask quite legitimately for a territory of their own. In the ongoing demands for a stable and peaceful future, perhaps one would support a two-state solution, or perhaps there are other alternatives, but ending occupation seems an immediate imperative before anything else might be achieved, and occupation seems to be a simple and unqualified evil: a people were residing in a territory, and that residence was taken over from without. Even if one regards Hamas's reaction to occupation as terrorism (rather than a war between a funded military force and those who have to find other means) the overwhelming fact is that Gaza is occupied. It was 'originally' Palestinian territory by virtue of the presence of those who are now imprisoned in Gaza. Here we strike a small difficulty with the concept of original occupation, which perhaps needs to be thought of as 'prior' occupation. The state of Israel is not occupying land that is *terra nullius*. This might allow us to think of 'minor' occupation – whereby a people is formed by occupying a space, with the space becoming the place that it is by way of occupation. This would need to be contrasted with 'molar' or 'majoritarian' occupation, whereby a world map is already laid out with established nations and agents who then lay claim (or not) to the right to occupy a space. Occupation is – initially – a form of territorialization, a becoming who one is, or becoming 'a' people by way of assembling in a spatial zone. Taking away a territory is not only taking away a people's being – their right to exist and their existence – it is also the creation of a different register. Rather than an earth that is occupied by peoples there is a map of states, polities, geopolitics, markets, relations and nations that overcode and negotiate the distribution of peoples across the earth.

To follow Deleuze and Guattari on this question: occupying space is not something 'a' people does. Something like a people emerges through the occupation of a field, which in turn becomes a space. If this is so, then one can see history, geopolitics, capitalism and the war on terror as a problem of territorialization and deterritorialization. Most simply, capitalism deterritorializes in many different ways but one way is to generate a field of exchange, markets, finance, debts, and labor flows that preclude any territory from being simply what it is. The occupation of any space becomes overcoded by another virtual space – the world of capital, and arms industries – and nowhere is this more evident than in the US response to Israel, where the simple moral demand to end occupation is neither fully enforced nor fully articulated because of that other register of 'security,' which will ensure that global trade, militarization and force become a smooth operating system with no other imperative outside the system's own ongoing function or operation. This is capitalism's cynicism that allows for any belief whatever, and then allows for the market and exchange not only to operate regardless of belief but also to commodify belief by generating 'green,' 'feminist,' 'queer' and even 'activist' commodities (such as Jay-Z's marketing of 'Occupy All Streets' t-shirts).

Here is where – despite first appearances – Deleuze and Guattari's philosophy allows for a nuanced political (or micro-political) account of occupation. At first glance their thought would seem to offer nothing but a violent relativism of force: there is no such thing as a people or a territory prior to occupation. Something becomes what it is by forming relations with what it is not, and those relations become relatively stable, but always and necessarily subject to deterritorialization. When a territory – Gaza – is represented by a single body – Hamas – one set of relations (bodies in space) has been overtaken by another set of relations (political identities and allegiances), and this other strata or register then becomes reterritorialized on a single system (capital) that *quite like Deleuze and Guattari's own philosophy* acknowledges no essential territories or relations. But the difference resides in capital's reference of all relations and territories back to a global system of maintaining a global system. So, yes, there is nothing in Deleuze and Guattari's philosophy that grants anyone any right to anything; all identities and territories begin with appropriation and deterritorialization, becoming what and who one is in relations that are not one's own. Any attempt to grant supreme importance to a single territory – the United Nations (UN), the World Bank, capitalism, democracy – is a form of violence that precludes the very dynamism that brings anything into being.

But there are two modes of occupation: minor and molar. Minor occupation produces a territory through occupation so that a people or movement comes into being by way of assembling and taking up space. We might say that all indigenous peoples, by definition, are forms of minor occupation insofar as their being has no existence outside the taking up of space. The sequences is not, 'this is who I am and what I stand for, and therefore I have a right to occupy,' but rather, 'this is occupied space, and therefore this is who we have turned out to be.' In the Occupy movement that inspired this volume the logic of minor occupation was at work. Yes,

Wall Street was the site for a people – finance, banking – and yes, this site was overtaken and occupied by protestors. The logic was not, 'this is our space and we have a right to this space because of who we are what we represent and because we stand for humanity in general.' On the contrary, the occupation began and *then* certain motifs of proportion or statistics were made quite explicit: to say 'we are the 99%' is less a claim of identity, property and right and more a claim of assembling. And if Wall Street was based on a deterritorialized system of owning space because some system other than occupation was at work (real estate, property, colonization of space), the Occupy movement was based on 'higher deterritorialization.' Rather than right or ownership or taking back what was owed to 'us,' there was no 'us' or 'we' outside the event of occupation.

I would suggest that the same applies to Israel and Gaza: the Israeli defense force is adopting majoritarian or molar occupation, appealing to a narrative of nation, right, security, constituted peoples and property. Tragically, those abandoned in Gaza, cannot appeal to any straightforward conception of nation – but Gaza is where they are. All they have is their occupation of space, a space that has then been occupied by a force that does not simply counter-occupy but places the competing claims to space as some grand narrative of security, nation, legitimacy and right. It might seem quixotic, and violently so, to suggest that rather than respond with a counter-narrative of right and nation one imagines a world of occupation without right. Such a new earth would not set the occupation of a territory within a moral framework but would instead begin with occupation – the assembling across a space that generates 'a' people, and then enables certain narratives of rights to be formed *ex post facto*. Such a call for a radically immanent politics might be naïvely wishful, but here I would quote Isabelle Stengers and Philippe Pignarre who affirmed the possibility that was articulated at the Seattle protests (prior to the Occupy movements) that *another world would be possible*:

> Becoming the child of an event: not being born again into innocence, but daring to inhabit the possible as such, without the adult precautions that make threats of the type 'what will people say?', 'who will they take us for?' or 'and you think that is enough?' prevail. The event creates its own 'now' to which the question of a certain 'acting as if', which is proper

to children when they make things (up), responds. (Stengers and Pignarre 2011: 4)

II

Deleuze and Guattari once declared that it was not easy being Heideggerian. By this I take them to mean not that Heidegger was a difficult thinker (for then they might have said the same about Kant or Leibniz), nor that it was unfashionable to be a Heideggerian phenomenologist in the late twentieth century (for then they might have said the same about any of their more obscure commitments to less canonical figures, such as Raymond Ruyer or less politically tolerable writers such as Henry Miller or Ezra Pound). Rather, there is something intrinsically risk-laden about the possibility of Heidegger's philosophy that takes us to the heart of the relation between philosophy and politics, or the polity. Philosophy is possible by way of deterritorialization: the formation of the polity occurs when life's relation to the earth shifts in register and one can create concepts that are not extensive (regarding what there is), but intensive (or what one might be able to think). It is in *What is Philosophy?* (1991) that Deleuze and Guattari theorize the geopolitical conditions of philosophy, tying philosophy to an agonistics that can only occur among friends who can be genuinely combative at a conceptual level because they are occupying a terrain of luxury that liberates them from immediate material production. (A similar notion of philosophical agonistics was articulated by Jacques Derrida in *Politics of Friendship* (1994), where he quoted William Blake's 'Do be My Enemy for Friendship's Sake,' (Derrida 2005: 72)). If one is bound to another for reasons of state or diplomacy then relations are mediated by some external measure of justice or propriety, but if there is nothing at stake other than the struggle itself then the genuine force (of concepts) can take hold. Deleuze and Guattari argue that certain geopolitical forces need to have played themselves out and constituted a specific territory for philosophical agonistics to emerge.

Their theorization of the philosophical plane of concept-creation has got them into quite a bit of trouble, given that they tied their observation to a specific limitation of democracy with regard to the 'becoming of subjected peoples.' Here, they argue that 'Europeanization' needs to be distinguished from becoming, just as in *A Thousand Plateaus* (1980) they argue that there is no 'becoming-man':

> Why are there so many becomings of man, but no becoming-man? First because man is majoritarian par excellence, whereas becomings are minoritarian; all becoming is a becoming-minoritarian. When we say majority, we are referring not to a greater relative quantity but to the determination of a state or standard in relation to which larger quantities, as well as the smallest, can be said to be minoritarian: white-man, adult-male, etc. Majority implies a state of domination, not the reverse. (Deleuze and Guattari 1987: 291)

In this sense the 99% remains as a minority (as do those 'living' in Gaza), not because they are fewer in number but because their identity has no basis outside the assembling in common. By contrast, the becoming of 'man,' has an internal end or *telos* towards which history is oriented. Both the figure of European reason and 'man,' go through time in order to realize their proper potential, in order to arrive at their own freedom, liberated from any specified form. Such a conception of democracy as a becoming that is nothing other than its own unfolding – as free self-determination – needs to be differentiated from Deleuze and Guattari's theorization of becoming as always 'becoming-...' (becoming-animal, becoming-woman, becoming-imperceptible), where becoming is not a self-unfolding but always in a relation with what is not one's own. This is why philosophy and art, they argue, allow for a creativity that can only occur by way of 'a people that are lacking'; one does not write because one is a member of a polity, for it is writing and creation that occur only in the absence of an autonomous or proper becoming:

> The creation of concepts in itself calls for a future form, for a new earth and people that do not yet exist. Europeanization does not constitute a becoming but merely the history of capitalism, which prevents the becoming of subjected peoples. Art and philosophy converge at this point: the constitution of an earth and a people that are lacking as the correlate of creation. It is not populist writers but the most aristocratic who lay claim to this future. This people and earth will not be

found in our democracies. Democracies are majorities, but a becoming is by its nature that which always eludes the majority. The position of many writers with respect to democracy is complex and ambiguous. The Heidegger affair has complicated matters: a great philosopher actually had to be reterritorialized on Nazism for the strangest commentaries to meet up, sometimes calling his philosophy into question and sometimes absolving it through such complicated and convoluted arguments that we are still in the dark. It is not always easy to be Heideggerian. It would be easier to understand a great painter or musician falling into shame in this way (but, precisely, they did not). It had to be a philosopher, as if shame had to enter into philosophy itself. He wanted to rejoin the Greeks through the Germans, at the worst moment in their history: is there anything worse, said Nietzsche, than to find oneself facing a German when one was expecting a Greek? How could Heidegger's concepts not be intrinsically sullied by an abject reterritorialization? (Deleuze and Guattari 1994: 108–09)

How might we approach this argument regarding Heidegger, concepts, philosophy, shame, and a future 'people and earth?' For Heidegger, philosophy had at one and the same time covered over the essentially non-essentially nature of being, and the intrinsically inauthentic nature of authenticity. Because philosophy emerges in a leisured and aristocratic condition, freed from an economy of material production and occurs *amongst friends who have the space to be antagonistic,* it is capable of creating concepts. If you are genuinely my friend and we have the luxury of speaking in a manner of absolute war – because the conversation is in a different register from the day-to-day constituted demands of the body – then we can start to create concepts on a different plane: we might ask what justice *really is* only if the answer is not bound by immediate material consequences and institutions. It is only in the absence of political and material diplomacy that genuine friendship opens genuine agonistics. For Heidegger philosophers broke away from the everyday world of projects, concerns, meanings, and the ready-at-hand; and they could do so because that world of projects could be rendered inoperative by asking the question *not* of what this thing is for me, but what this thing or being is as such.

It is in a moment of disorientation, or a certain *loss of world*, that one might start to think not of a world that is always already human but an *earth* (the forces from which the human world are composed). We might say that what Deleuze and Guattari refer to elsewhere as the 'war machine,' or an agonistics that has not been captured by opposing sides (such as political parties, nations, identified groups or communities), is only possible when there is no actual war: in a state of war one holds on to who one is, where one is, what one stands for and what one believes. Doing so reduces the intensity of the war machine to stabilized terms and oppositions; the war machine would be destructive of such a terrain. In this respect Deleuze and Guattari's philosophy, like Heidegger's, is not at all easy because it abandons the negotiation of a field, abandons settlement among terms and instead aims for a 'higher deterritorialization': in both cases one thinks the relation between 'world' (constituted meaning) and 'earth' (the plane that renders such constitution possible but also fragile). Heidegger argued *both* that one can ask questions and begin to think only because one has a world (a horizon of meaning, concern, care, others, history and 'ownness') *and* that one becomes aware of the having of a world when the world breaks down. Authenticity is therefore not so much attachment to the projects and horizons that make us who we are, but a sense that while all we do and think emerges from the 'lifeworld,' what is truly worth thinking about is *that there is a world, and that it might not be.* This does not mean that living authentically is liberation from any identity, history, project or tradition, but that having a world or tradition is something one takes on with a radical sense of decision. We can only take up a free and decisive relation to a world that was not of our own deciding, *and nothing* legitimates that world other than that world itself. And here, of course, is where things start to become 'not at all easy' as a Heideggerian. One might not only say that there are certain material and geopolitical conditions for adopting one's world freely and decisively, and that for Heidegger these conditions were tied to a German National Socialism that aimed to eradicate anything that appeared as too inert or unthinking to embrace radical self-becoming. One might also point out, as Jacques Derrida has done, that a certain notion of contemporary politics, democracy and modernity as a lazy consensus and acquiescence to passively received political forms was crucial to Nazi anti-Semitic rhetoric that relied on refusing democracy as a contamination of the truly decisive freedom of spirit. Democracy, parliamentary representation, communication and politics in its day-to-day combative forms were (for the Nazis and twentieth-century fascism) the hallmarks of a world dominated by money and an unquestioning acceptance of the constituted field. As Derrida pointed out in his reading of Benjamin, the dream of a 'divine violence' that would annihilate the ongoing order of received law was perilously close to the National Socialist rhetoric of renewal and redemption through a form of cultural rebirth (Derrida 1994).

One might then go on, as Deleuze and Guattari do, and tie the Heidegger affair to a problem of philosophy and its aristocratic temper. Philosophy is *deterritorialization* or the production of a register different and distant from the constituted terms of a polity; it is the refusal of the plane of functions, communication and certainly of '*the* people.' Is it any wonder, then, that this notion of authentic and decisive *thinking* could so easily align itself with another territory – in Heidegger's case the German *Volk* who were not one populace among others but the privileged people for thinking world-creation?

Bearing that in mind, we might say that today it is not easy being Deleuzo-Guattarian, and not just because their thought is abstruse, out of favor (in the new materialist turns) or irrelevant, but because their celebrated rhetoric of nomadism and deterritorialization is a luxury that displaced persons without a territory, or whose territory is occupied, cannot afford. Worse, as their criticism of communication and democracy above seems to suggest, a certain privilege is attached to those who are not mired in literal and material antagonism but can occupy another plane, of pure conversation. One might suggest that their celebration of deterritorialized philosophy offers a glib dismissal of a certain mode of capitalist democracy – the democracy of free markets and imposed conceptions of the consumer-oriented private individual – but reinstalls a hyper-democratic prejudice: some traditions, such as Western philosophy, have at their heart the potential to distance themselves from any constituted tradition such that 'democracy' would not be a worldview or tradition so much as a critical mood or irony with regard to any tradition.

International interventions that impose, maintain or secure democracy are supposedly not undertaken for the sake of this or that constituted people, but for some abstract or virtual ideal of humanity in general.

Against such a reading of Deleuze and Guattari's rhetoric of deterritorialization and nomadism as yet one more way in which the West uses a concept of the universal to impose its own norms, presenting itself as the ideology that is no ideology, and – worse – of using concepts of nomadism and deterritorialization in a world where real events of displacement are life and death matters, I want to suggest that we think seriously about Deleuze and Guattari's claim for a new people and a new earth as a genuinely futural endeavor. It is not easy being Deleuzo-Guattarian precisely because such talk of a people to come, deterritorialization, the war machine and nomadism appears at best uselessly naïve and at worst as violently appropriative. How dare one celebrate at a metaphorical level a placelessness that is traumatically painful for many who do not have the luxury of the philosophical view from nowhere? Isn't such a strategy stupid, risky and far too abstract to be of any use in urgent political struggles? What we need – it might be said – is *not* abstraction and deterritorialization, but history, facts, distinction, and –more than anything – the affirmation of what is genuinely owed to a people who have had their land, their personhood and their conditions for living stolen.

At the time of this volume's going into production the world was witness to such violent occupation and literal deterritorialization. Despite pressure from the international community, and despite widespread condemnation in much of the press and social media, the Israeli defense forces continued to assault and wage war on the occupied territories. Originally conceived in the wake of the radical and revolutionary Occupy movements across the globe, this collection of essays could (it seemed in 2012) quite easily contest capitalist and supposedly liberal ideologies of property by celebrating radical potentials for becoming, dissolution, non-identity and a notion of movement without place or clearly defined ends. Indeed, one might say that the neoliberal rhetoric of ends, outcomes, success and even personhood had done much to precipitate the increasing reterritorialization of all political possibilities on market efficiency and corporate personhood. To celebrate a certain destructiveness without clearly defined ends, a certain non-productivity and even social dissension, dispersal and vagueness at the time of Occupy was both a timely response to those who accused Occupy of not being a clearly defined social movement, and provided a clear foil against the discourse of property and right that had allowed profoundly anti-democratic measures to be put in place lest the entire market and workforce be vanquished by an even more catastrophic crisis of the financial sector. But, today, as a people who need to see themselves *as a people with a territory and a history* are subject to warfare, displacement, carnage and dehumanization, what use would philosophical abstraction and anti-democratic distance serve? One might say – as Derrida's critics did in his claim that South African apartheid required a sense of the entire Western tradition's implication in national identity and apartness – that what is needed now is *not* a critique of territory, nations, identity, peoples and place, but an acute sense of facts, history, data, locatedness and immediate policy (McClintock and Nixon 1986).

But here we can say, with Deleuze and Guattari, that the immediate needs of molar politics – claims such as those of the women's movement, or today demands for a Palestinian state and the right of a people to exist – do not preclude micro-political analysis and imagination. And here is where we go back to philosophy and risk: if we do not hold on to ideas of a people being entitled to the territory that is the milieu of their history and identity, do we not risk riding roughshod and violently over what – within the milieu of world politics and history – is a legitimate and fundamental right of the Palestinian people to autonomy, life and liberty? Yes, that is true: to question notions of territory, of peoples, of nations and of democracy is to risk falling into a managerial bio-politics that would undertake any means whatever to preserve life as such regardless of historical and political complexities. But it is also a way of enabling a post-territorial politics or a politics of higher deterritorialization. It is the same rhetoric of territory, right, history, what it is to be a people – and the rhetoric of holding on to historical complexities, and specific conflict histories – that not only is appropriated by the state of Israel to defend violent attacks that are anything but defensive, necessary or responsive; it also allows for certain styles of reporting (where both sides are represented fairly, when the ultimate issue should be the violence *of sides*), *and* encourages 'who started the conflict' modes of reasoning. What stands for democracy – or the debates and wars between and among identities that are constituted in a capitalist milieu of geopolitical borders produced by markets, trade agreements, and histories of appropriative nation states tied to warring territories constituted by trade competition – needs to be displaced by a mode of thinking in which no-one has a *prima facie* right, whatever the history, to occupy. What needs to be thought are less the molar categories of 'the people,' and 'the nation,' and instead the micro-political potentials that might open a new people and a new earth.

Rather than think of molar politics and minor politics as an opposition, it might be best to think of oppositional narratives versus narratives devoid of scale. That is to say, one could start to approach the Israel–Gaza conflict through the history of anti-Semitism, the horrors of the Holocaust and the desperate need for state security as a response to terror, or one could adopt a history of the Palestinian people and Hamas and the insecurity of Muslim culture in a Middle Eastern zone increasingly tied towards alignment with the interests of the US, capital, energy markets and other affiliations that have little to do with the survival of the people who are supposedly represented by governments, parties and brotherhoods. Molar politics focuses upon 'a' history of nation and party formation, and geopolitical border disputes; such competing narrations enable debates over the proper nature of scale: should the Israel–Gaza conflict be framed by the specter of the Holocaust and anti-Semitism, or by the other history of displacement of the Palestinian people? Deleuze and Guattari's micro-politics is not opposed to the molar, but pulverizes any such identity: *any* nation, party, people or brotherhood has as its condition of emergence thousands of years of a taming of the earth (including oil and other lines of capital), and no dispute over borders has a natural or proper scale. Rather than the banal claim that beneath religious, political, tribal or ethnic conflicts 'we' are all human – which of course *is* the violent imposition of a humanity of recognition and would demand that we all become liberal and distanced from the affiliations that mark out our territories – Deleuze and Guattari see difference as multiplying rather than weakening in micro-political analysis. Neither the Israeli defense forces nor Hamas can contain the proliferation of differences and identities that both sides violently seek to 'represent.' So rather than a democratic politics that would negotiate one people versus another, or that would reconcile the rights of people over territories, one might think beyond persons, beyond the demos, beyond the polity. One might start to consider how the *earth* – not the world – might generate a people to come, a people without right, ownership or propriety. Such a call for a world in common without propriety, without identity and without nations and that would be beyond the world by thinking the forces of the earth would *not be easy*. It would risk, as so many people have objected with regard to Deleuze and Guattari's work, a celebration of statelessness and impersonal life precisely when the world's most fragile people are seeking a territory and state of their own. But we need to ask, today, both when climate change and environmental collapse have been ignored as viable political concerns because states are concerned with their own survival, and when – as the Occupy movement demonstrated, states represent corporations rather then people – whether the ideals of personhood and nation are not more risky. Do not concepts of right and nation risk generating higher degrees of catastrophe than a possible future where there are not territories and peoples, but a new people and a new earth, no longer bound by the macro-narratives of the world and polities.

The heightened Israeli violence against Gaza occurs just as the earth – not the world but the *earth* (or the geological strata from which philosophy and various forms of humanity formed itself) – is poised at a singular point or threshold that would render all human life in its current mode untenable. Rather than extending capitalist democracy – a democracy that represents persons as private consumers with the right to self-determination – perhaps a better path would be to intensify the forces from which diverse peoples emerge, beyond states, markets, territories and right. The assaults on Gaza and the use of the figure of Hamas to destroy the lives of civilians is perhaps one of the more violent and flagrant events that have allowed the borders of states, markets, nations and molar identities to reduce the complex differences of people who do not have a state or a territory.

If it is not that easy being Heideggerian or Deleuzo-Guattarian, then one might insist that such difficulties are minor – very minor – when compared with the struggle to live in the occupied territories. Rather than see the means of violence – the state – as a right that should be extended, a minor politics would intensify forces that are irreducible to the state, disentangling Judaism in all its forms from Israel, and differentiating Islam from Hamas and the Muslim Brotherhood, and – in turn – disentangling life and the earth from the striated space of East and West.

Works Cited

Deleuze, Gilles and Félix Guattari. 1994. *What is Philosophy?*. Trans. Hugh Tomlinson and Graham Burchell. London: Verso.

Derrida, Jacques. 1994. *Force de loi: Le 'Fondement mystique de l'autorité'* (Paris: Galilée). English translation: 'Force of Law: The Mystical Foundation of Authority'. Trans. Mary Quaintance. *Cardozo Law Review* 11 (1990): 919–1045.

Derrida, Jacques. 2005. *The Politics of Friendship*. Trans. George Collins. London: Verso.

McClintock, Anne and Rob Nixon. 1986. 'No Names Apart: The Separation of Word and History in Derrida's "Le Dernier Mot du Racisme"'. *Critical Inquiry* 13 (1): 140–154.

Stengers, Isabelle and Philippe Pignarre. 2011. *Capitalist Sorcery: Breaking the Spell*. Trans Andrew Goffey. London: Palgrave.

Introduction

ANDREW CONIO

I. A Political Ontology of Flow

Life flows. Societies, economies, and political systems channel flows to produce things, functional processes and systems. Processes congeal to make autopoietic and highly relational social structures. The language of painting or music can be used to describe social processes because society is a mobile composition of points, lines and rhythms. Out of flows, densities, contractions, planes and surfaces compositions emerge. Deleuze and Guattari call them assemblages, milieus or plateaus. Every society in history has operated on the basis of flows and distributions. Capitalism's coding and decoding, de and reterritorialization, provide the most fluid and mobile compositional template of them all. 'Capitalism … decodes and deterritorializes with all its might'; it is a non-territorially based axiomatic of flows, but its distributions are dysfunctional as they channel wealth and power into the hands of the few (Deleuze and Guattari 2000: 369).

Deleuze's politics cannot be thought outside of his aesthetics because he captures this struggle between flows that travel unimpeded to merge with other flows, or that diverge to create new tributaries, and those that are blocked or turned against themselves. Power is linked to the control of flows, and Deleuze's anthropological[1] intention is to capture the forces or systems that seek to control flows.

For Deleuze subjugation is not imposed from the top down – we are not simply repressed as we are conduits for or contractions of forces far in excess of the boundaries of the 'self.' Each form of capture, be it phallogocentrism, colonialism, or sexism, controls the flow differently, hence there can be no crude economic determinism. As Conley[2] observes, by:

> advocating an ever-unfinished, non-dialectical, and non-hierarchical model of constructive dissent, [Deleuze and Guattari] do away with the Marxian notion of class structure to consider social conflict in terms of mobile micro- and macro-cosms, ever shifting lines, rhythms and harmonics.

Under neoliberalism, as it reaches ever further into the fabric of life, capital determines far more than it ever did. The global economic and political elite is commandeering the human genome and the building blocks of life as well as the ontological and epistemological horizons of thought. The central paradox is that while capitalism seeks to command flows, capital itself is the strongest force of irrepressible desire to escape all limits. As neoliberalism tightens its grip, Deleuze and Guattari's *Anti-Oedipus* (1972) takes on even greater prescience:

> the prime function incumbent upon the socius has always been to codify the flows of desire, to inscribe them, to record them, to see that no flow exists that is not properly dammed up, channeled, regulated. (Deleuze and Guattari 2000: 33)

Such insights support Colebrook's claim that *Anti-Oedipus* might be recognized 'as one of the twentieth century's most important works.'[3]

Release, capture, flow, systolic and diastolic rhythms, and the processes necessary to control these pulsations are to be found in all things, in 'flows of women and children, flows of herds and seed, sperm flows, flows of shit, menstrual flows' (Deleuze and Guattari 2000: 112). The paths of flows are always machinic: mouth–breast, sun–photosynthesis, camera–lux–lumen, and the production of subjectivity itself is a machinic process. Production is primarily desiring production, far in excess of the economic system: 'social life is machinic [and] may be conceived as a global system of desire and destiny that organizes the production of production, the productions of recording, and productions of consumption' (Deleuze and Guattari 2000: 142). There are, however, two valences to all things – block or flow, production or anti-production. Anti-production is not necessarily the opposite of 'creative' production. In anti-production things slow, gain traction or assume a different meaning. Retraction, denial, and entropy are diverse dynamics to be found everywhere in all things, so diverse as to make it impossible to theorize an overarching code of 'lack' or negation. It's pointless to imagine that anarchy as pure free flow is good, and the state, strata or assemblages are bad. Instead, block/flow, open/closed, anarchy/system have to be placed in a positive correlation in the formation of static or regular inscriptions that in turn facilitate the maximum degree of openness in all things – while capitalism creates false antinomies and dysfunctional syntheses.

This collection of essays presents Deleuze's unique approach to politics, an approach that begins with a theory of life as flows, refrains and forces: 'the notion of flow ... constitutes the heart of an ontology that ... conceptualizes all processes in terms of exchanges of energy' (Garo 2006: 58). This may sound abstract and tangential to the urgent problems faced by the world today: the destruction of the ecosystem, worldwide immiseration, the return of the despotic Urstaat or 'empire' in the capitalist socius (Thoburn 2003: 91), and the multiple layers of control and robbery. The Occupy movement, however, created a new environment in which discussions that might once have seemed impertinent have been gaining a new traction. 'Occupy' is a synecdoche for belief in the revolutionary transformation of the capitalist system: a new heterogenic world of protest and activism that cannot be thought in terms of the state, liberal democracy, parliamentary systems, or the hugely compromised nongovernmental organization (NGO) sector. Nor can Occupy be conceived in terms of class war or vanguard politics. These conceptualizations do not articulate fully where power is held, nor from where revolution may issue. A philosophical vocabulary that would materially inhabit the conditions of our present global world order is needed because the different registers of ontology (the movements of the earth), the social (the people yet to come), epistemology (concept formation), and aesthetics are nevertheless activated on the one single plane that is at considerable remove from the conventional terms of state or royal politics as they are understood today. This book seeks to contribute to this process of thinking a single plane of matter, knowledge, politics and art through analysis and illustration, but chiefly through the production of tools and methods that Occupy and the political ontology of Deleuze and Guattari demand of each other.

The combination of precision and subtlety to be found in Deleuze and Guattari's concepts accounts for the worldwide multi-discursive interest in their formulations. Recent politically-engaged Deleuzian scholarship,[4] the financial crisis, and the emergence of widespread social conflict following the collapse of the self-certainties of the Blair–Bush era have made their work seemingly indispensible in the struggle to transform capitalism. Whilst Deleuze and Guattari have many mediators and interpreters in political theory, most notably Michael Hardt and Antonio Negri, readers are increasingly attracted by the force of Deleuze and Guattari's own conceptual apparatus and the ways in which it reveals the 'immanent' dynamics of capitalism in the 'the pure flow of deterritorialization, of money and labor brought together in a conjunction of flows which is actualized in private property' (Holland), and the axiomatics that hold this system in place. Also fundamental to their analysis is an understanding of economic production as part of a much larger field of desiring production that produces the subjectivities and social relations upon which the economic system ultimately depends. Deleuze and Guattari's political concepts have the capacity to resolve many of the contradictions left unaddressed by other accounts of the machinery of capitalism. For example, their presentation of the immiserating, sadistic, world-destroying tendencies of capitalism is no barrier to their appreciation for capitalism's dynamic potential and boundless creativity. Their formulation of capitalist axiomatics provides a way to understand how capitalist systems, supported by a war machine of stupendous proportions, have the appearance of inviolable natural laws, and yet are constantly modified by capitalism's own inherent dynamism, the pressure of the multitude, and outright resistance. Deleuze and Guattari share with Marx the view that capitalism is the handmaiden of its own eventual demise. The construction of the contemporary subject is such that it is both the measure of capitalism's capacity for freedom and its primary mode of capture. In sum: the brilliance of Deleuze and Guattari's thought lies precisely in their ability to capture the multi-dimensional nature of social and life forces in such a way that (through the construction of a matrix of extremely sophisticated concepts) bifurcations, contradictions, and dialectics do not become impediments to thought but rather opportunities to delve deeper into the underlying dynamics of existence and sociality.

The inconsistent reception of Deleuze and Guattari's works may be due in part to the fact that their ideas stretch across so many discourses – from cinema to anthropology, philosophy to literature, and across the sciences; it is easy to get lost amongst the plethora of innovations that cannot be mapped easily onto the existing conceptual terrain. That their works first entered the English-speaking academic world through literary studies, film, aesthetics and architecture partly contributed to the sense that it would also be perfectly possible to engage with many of their idioms without attention to their political implications, which can be as evident as they are elusive. The scope of their works reflects the fact that politics itself is as multilayered as it is aesthetic, as ontological as it is linguistic, registering the fact that everything is political, or indeed, as Deleuze and Guattari themselves insist, that politics precedes being.

This volume presents a series of experiments with such Deleuzian concepts as the war machine, the pack, the event, the assemblage, becoming-imperceptible, capitalist axiomatics and the minor and molecular, with three papers discussing a Deleuzo-Guattarian approach to economics. Theories from both the left and right ends of the political spectrum are subject to critique. Rodrigo Nunes, for instance, argues against the Marxist concept of the vanguard as a predetermined social form, arguing instead for a vanguard *function* and for multiple vanguards. In a typical Deleuzian thought experiment, he takes the concept of the anomalous, developed by Deleuze in relation to painting, out of its original context and deploys it to capture more fully the kind of social practices associated with the Marxist notion of the vanguard. The pack rather than the crowd, and the anomalous rather than the vanguard, are dynamic transversal expressions of social forces.

What makes Deleuze so perplexing and fascinating, and also of the greatest value, is that many of his novel concepts mark a radical break with established political ideas; they articulate something that cannot be said even in an hybridization of existing words. They do not engage with such notions as the rights of man, the social contract or constitutional democracy, and in diverse ways this volume will show how and why such concepts cannot be afforded foundational status in the task of articulating the concrete dynamics of the contemporary world. Deleuze and Guattari's concepts have a deliberate indeterminacy and abstraction, which demands that the reader/writer/activist *engage* with them, putting them to work. The failure to grasp this crucial point has, as we shall see, led to a number of misplaced critical readings of Deleuze and Guattari's political ontology.

II. Deleuze and his Critics

A series of critiques from Alain Badiou, Jacques Rancière and Peter Hallward has given considerable ballast to the idea common in left-wing circles that Deleuze and Guattari's ideas are shallow exercises in rhizomatic absent-mindedness – 'joyous thinker[s] of the world's confusion' (Badiou 2000; 10) lacking in substantive engagement with the urgent need for genuine revolutionary change. Giuseppina Mecchia, proposing the concept of 'anthropolitics as method and analytical category,' tackles each of these critiques in turn in, pursuing her argument that the *anthropos*, 'a dynamic, material figure of political subjectivity,' has the potential to bring about the revolutionary transformation of society. For Mecchia, Badiou's reliance on set theory and Lacanian discontinuities means that he has no account for the role of the kind of subjective encounters and commitments that led to and sustained the Occupy movement.

In her critique of Badiou's notion of 'truth' based on his conception of the event as 'rare' and knowable 'only retrospectively,' Mecchia draws our attention to the psychological, affective, and bodily commitments of the Occupiers – factors that were a fundamental aspect of their commitment to creating the event 'Occupy.' She points out that the emergence of informed, affirmative activists sufficiently committed to staging worldwide the most important political protests of recent decades cannot be understood according to Badiou's concept of the event as a truth that does not happen to things or to persons, but rather happens through them. For Badiou, events are politically and ethically of the highest significance. In response Ian Buchanan points out that whilst Badiou's event may be universal and thus generalizable it still 'requires our fidelity, we have to choose to believe in it and place it at the centre of our lives.' He explains that, for Badiou, the event gives rise to truth (it is truth's condition), whereas for Deleuze it gives rise to sense (it is sense's condition). Far from involving a multiplicitous dynamic interplay of cognitive, semantic and affective forces – of the type outlined by John Protevi in this volume – for Badiou the event 'moves on' and produces the subject who is also (again following Lacan) barred from her own subjective formation by the event itself.

Events are such an important feature of Deleuze's conceptual landscape because he is a philosopher of transformation. These transformations are changes in both matter and sense, both corporeal and incorporeal, so that when changes become infinitely extended and ongoing processes they also become events. Buchanan clarifies that 'events' are not necessarily matters of scale:

> the event for Deleuze and Guattari is not measured by a change in the state of things – a large crowd gathering in a public square in Cairo or camping out in New York City is not intrinsically an event in Deleuze and Guattari's thinking. It only becomes recognizable as an event if it brings about a transformation of thought itself, if it yields a new idea, a new way of acting.

For example, when the genocide of the American first peoples is properly understood, then America's whole sense of itself is undone. Most importantly, for Deleuze, matter is evental; as Verena Conley puts it: 'changes can occur *autopoietically*, unbeknownst to the subject, before she or he even opens to the environing world.' The inward rush of the sea has a sense, a 'life-sense' as Buchanan helpfully phrases it. We might talk of crowds contracting, expectations growing, balance sheets expanding, blood levels rising, global digital signals pulsating across networks around a Champions League football match. Organic or urban, in relation to the moon, the molluscs, the pier and the bather (Williams 2008: 8), sense is dispersed and flows in waves through and across bodies. The sea and the moon provide a picturesque example, but the application of the same concepts to the retreating, collapsing, rising, and dispersing of flows in the stock market helps us to understand that markets are only rational within the sublime irrationality of the capitalist economic system, that they are affairs of animal spirits which are most often wolverine as they hunt in packs. It is a Deleuzian commonplace that there is no difference in nature between the economic infrastructure and the libidinal economy: 'desire belongs to the infrastructure, not to ideology, desire is in production as social production, just as production is in desire as desiring-production' (Deleuze and Guattari 2000: 348).

Many of the features of Deleuze's embodied/engaged (schizoanalytic) subject are marshalled in Mecchia's third defence of Deleuze's work (after her considerations of Badiou and Rancière) against the criticisms of Peter Hallward, whom she contends recasts and radicalizes Badiou's critique of Deleuzian politics. Here Deleuze is again accused of aloofness, his vitalism is considered a major flaw, and his commitment to a particular theorization of the virtual is taken to have left his theory devoid of agency or of any sense of a determinant material force that might act upon the world. Stephven Shukaitis summarizes Hallward's argument: 'this results in a politics that can only lead out of this world, because the potential of the actualized world is always compromised in comparison to the virtual' (Shukaitis 2010). Ambrose phrases a pithy riposte to this contention:

> It is never merely a question of attempting to 'break out' of the world that exists, but of creating the right conditions for the exposition of other possible worlds, the heterocosmic – to 'break in' in order to introduce new variables into the world that exists, causing the quality of its reality/actuality to undergo modification, change and becoming. (Ambrose 2006)

There are significant problems, in particular, with Hallward's understanding of the virtual. In *The Logic of Sense* (1969) Deleuze shows that the incorporeal is as real as the corporal. It is not the case that the virtual is some kind of unreality outside of the 'real'; rather, the virtual is 'real,' just not actualized. As Buchanan says in his contribution to this volume: 'the virtual is fully real, as real as an idea, an image, and an innovation, is real. It is real because its effects are real.' Think of the infinite variety of forms the wheel has taken, from prayer wheel to clock to waterwheel and propeller. Deleuze and Guattari suggest that there is an infinite multiplicity of potential in everything, only a minuscule portion of which is actualized at any given time – a virtual multiplicity is always in reserve, still to come. Both Conley and Nunes detail the movement from pre-existing states of affairs (the domain of the possible, where what is possible is essentially a repetition of what already exists) to the domain of the actual where that which emerges is unconcealed, new. At some point something boils to the surface, a virtual something that neither Badiou nor Hallward can account for: 'a threshold is crossed and without things being brought into the realm of possibility – should be this or should be that – the event has already happened,' or as Conley puts it: 'occupation always begins with an event, a rupture, a sudden surge of affect ... that rises spontaneously, *autopoietically*. It begins with a preoccupation.' Whilst for Nunes the event is a rupture, it is not a magical flash in the pan; it neither comes out of the blue nor is it a unique isolated new fact, but emerges out of a flux of interweaved virtual potentialities. As well as providing a succinct guide to the main points of disagreement between Badiou and Deleuze, Buchanan highlights their different treatments of the event: for Deleuze the event is an 'irruption of immanence (the opening up of a smooth space in other words) [that] does not necessarily correlate with an idea of the truth.' Buchanan also offers a more nuanced reading of Badiou than do many other commentators, noting that Spain's *indignados* were possibly lacking the type of 'affirmative idea' that Badiou considers essential to political struggle – an 'idea' like truth able to 'awaken the force of History itself.' Buchanan, quoting Badiou, appreciates Badiou's potential to contribute to our understanding of how an event like Occupy Wall Street works:

> It ignites what he calls a 'truth process' – it makes apparent to all that 'human animals are capable of bringing into being justice, equality, and universality (the practical presence of what the Idea can do). It is perfectly apparent that a high proportion of political oppression consists in the unremitting negation of this capacity. (Badiou 2012: 87)

III. A Politics of Collective Affect

John Protevi describes how the occupiers were forced by the ban on bullhorns to invent the 'human microphone,' which created a shared corporeal bond and affective identification between them. A profound sense of shared identity emerged as language was reclaimed and turned into both joyous affirmation and resistance to the command of order words. For example, when leading members of the Corporation of London braved the OccupyLSX General Assembly to explain that 'the Corporation of London does many good things, [and] has a long history of civic engagement,' the assembly fell about like cartoon characters in unrestrained laughter. This collective public ridicule of the guardians of the Corporation chimes with how Protevi talks of affect:

> affect is "in the air," something like the mood of a party, which is not the mere aggregate of the subjective states of the party-goers. In this sense, affect is not emergent from pre-existing subjectivities; emotional subjectivities are crystallisations or residues of a collective affect.

Many occupiers felt that they had tasted a kind of utopia in the sense of release from the oppressive hegemony of Blair–Bush doctrine – a non-coercive joyous experiment in creating the democracy yet to come. The life-changing impact of Occupy on its participants was often understated, but what they did, as Holland notes, was to take 'truly democratic social relations to the very "heart of the beast".' Things like the General Assemblies, direct action (Occupy operating as a kind of phalanx in the heart of the city from which further actions could be launched), workshops, mutual solidarity networks and the human microphone were indeed exemplary, as Protevi says of 'direct democracy enacted but producing an intermodal resonance among the semantic, pragmatic and affective dimensions of collective action.' However, as Thoburn cautions, this kind of 'communism in miniature' must not be mistaken for the real thing: 'From a minor political perspective, the risk with this formulation is that Occupy turn inwards, valorizing its own cultural forms at the expense of self-problematization and an ever-outward engagement in social relations.'

Protevi also has a warning: corporeal affective collectivity is not necessarily a good in itself; affect, after all, also surged through the Nuremberg rallies. Working through such valences is an essential feature of Deleuzian scholarship. When does becoming a body without organs lead to impotence rather than genuine becoming? When is a rhizome a sign of idiocy and when is it a line of flight to a new creation? When is organization facilitative and when suppressive? One question Nunes seeks to answer is exactly the same as that which pre-occupied the Occupy encampments worldwide: how do you create open and porous democratic structures that avoid the leaderless, formless quagmire experienced at times by all occupiers? How might one enable structures that encourage a different type of democracy based on the principles of *distributed leadership*? For Nunes, distributed leadership is not only an accurate description of the actual processes in play at Occupy but also describes the process of avoiding the false binaries between organization and formlessness, unity and diversity, spontaneity or planning, in a manner that allows for the articulation of the greatest unity consiliant with the greatest diversity. Indeed, the distinction between pack and crowd that Nunes draws upon is useful for thinking about how Occupy worked according to both the logic of direct democracy and the logic of the pack, whereby leaders emerged, led, provoked, instigated, and sometimes forced issues through. The logic of the pack allowed for divisions and stratifications and was arguably *more* democratic than modes of consensus. It was certainly a pre-requisite for getting anything done.

David Burrows also points to the pack-like movement and the effectiveness of distributed leadership in his study of 'negative space war machines' operating alongside Occupy in London in 2011 and 2012. Nunes argues that far from solving the problem of representation the Marxist vanguard often vests itself with the imprimatur of 'historical necessity,' and in setting itself the task of expressing and organizing the revolutionary activity of the workers, can end up exasperating it.

The name 'Occupy' has become a synecdoche for a proliferation of new protest and political movements fighting a myriad of causes, from closing down tax havens to defending the rights of indigenous peoples, from resisting the decimation of the welfare state to critiques of big pharma. At its inception Occupy spilt into diverse working groups, led by experienced activists and charged with research, securing provisions, media relations, planning, education, and so forth. This created a profusion of self-organized vanguards, each leading their own area. The distinction Nunes draws between the crowd and the pack is helpful here.

In the former, equal status is afforded to all and the crowd is organized; it moves as one, chants together, and there is a uniformity of function. Packs are not secondary groupings emerging from the crowd; they are the elemental ground of the mass and are formed out of alogical orders, consistencies and compatibilities. As was seen first-hand at Occupy, packs or multiplicities continually transform themselves into each other, and cross over into each other, through processes of alliance or contagion. As Deleuze puts it: 'Schools, bands, herds, and populations are not inferior social forms; they are affects and powers, involutions' (Deleuze and Guattari 2000: 241).

In their different ways Nunes, Protevi, Conley and Mecchia each find solutions to the problems inherent to the tendency to objectification, or the ways in which historically sedimented practices impede becoming. Protevi captures the process as follows:

> You don't combat [the shame of unemployment] by trying to change individual people's minds, one by one, with information about unemployment trends; you combat it by showing your face, by embodying your lack of shame, by putting a face on unemployment or homelessness. You thus counteract the existing collective affect by creating a positive affect of, shall we say, joyful solidarity. Shame isolates (you hide your face); joyful solidarity comes from people coming together.

For Nunes, in the body of the collective one gains access to the complex process of becoming-imperceptible, which, far from being an act of self-denial is a 'becoming-more' through allowing oneself to be exposed, to take a risk, and to trust that one can be formed by and, can help form, collective assemblages. Nunes shares with Conley a concern to place becoming-collective at the heart of the process of undoing subjectivation. He outlines how 'becoming-imperceptible should be understood as becoming more realistic about oneself and the real potentials and limitations to a process.' It requires the shedding of selfhood (*the* vanguard, *the* revolutionary), undermining pre-given divisions (self/other), finding differences that exist in potential, and the capacity to create new continuities. The sense that the novel and spontaneous is diffused in a web of practices and sensibilities that have been a long time in the making is shared by

Thoburn, who also places the evental quality of life at the imperceptible center of processes of social formation: 'the ungraspable and often highly seductive character of a formation whose directions remain unmapped, indeterminable, full, as Deleuze has it, of *virtuality*.'

For Deleuze, only some of the virtual potentials existent in the world are actualized as we are moulded by macro and microscopic affects and sensations that pass through us and which can be cosmological in extension.[5] We must think of contraction and dilation, release and flow, rupture and slice, entropy and clamor, as pure intensities: the world floods through us in a cacophony of multiplicities and singularities fused in an indeterminable concoction of affects and percepts across multiple landscapes of psychic, social and physiological geographies in the backwards and forwards of time in multiple durations.

IV. Deconstruction and Occupy

In her contribution, Colebrook discusses the continued relevance of deconstruction, addressing a body of work that has considerable traction in contemporary political philosophy, and whose influence may be seen in the refusal by contemporary political activists to adopt an unassailable and inviolable stance of purported truth from which to declare the correctness of their position. Colebrook discusses the difficulties inherent in claiming either a pre-existing place of purity, innocence or natural justice, or a futural justice yet to come from which resistance to an invading or occupying force might be mounted. Implicit in the language of Occupy, explicit in its structure and *modus operandi*, and suffused throughout its culture, was the question, how do you criticize capitalism without setting yourself up as the uniquely privileged defender of an imagined purity or innocence against some evil external power? More specifically, how do you defend a cause or mount a critique without repeating the same binary oppositions that sustain capitalism and which substitute underlying terms of exclusion and dominance for other equally determinant terms? How do you create change without being either fascist or Leninist, or naïvely accepting capitalism's claim that its leading terms such as freedom, equality, democracy and autonomy are somehow not complicit in the violence inherent in their constitution? These are the reasons Occupy steadfastly refused to assert a claim to a single overarching 'truth,' knowing that one claim to truth is a potential violence against another. Diversity is a strategy, a methodology and an objective; any attempt to impose a master narrative is seen as a type of violence done to the myriad micro-struggles represented in the lived struggles of the movement's members. The question often put to the occupiers, 'What exactly do you want?', is thus viewed as illegitimate, an attempt to delegitimize, belittle and close minds.

Colebrook explores the relevance of the works of Jacques Derrida and Paul de Man to these debates, and in so doing outlines the weaknesses in some interpretations of the deconstructive approach to politics (which saw deconstruction contributing to a politics of nihilism, relativism and cynicism), whilst highlighting some features that remain not just pertinent but necessary. First, in line with many of the arguments in this volume, and with its repeated theme of embodiment, Colebrook outlines how deconstruction arose out of both developments in the history of ideas and Derrida's 'tortured' response to the Nazi occupation of France, where the occupation of language and citizenship led to a sense that the material occupation of a territory and the immaterial occupation of language and subjectivity were violences of the same order.

For Colebrook, what began in material, historically specific circumstances provided the impetus for what became deconstruction's quasi-transcendental claim that neither the self-authoring presence of the citizen/subject nor language's representational certainties, nor indeed any binary opposition between inside or outside, innocent or contaminated, can be cited as non-compromised or non-complicit sites of resistance uncontaminated by the very logic of exclusion they were fighting against. Paul de Man, whom Colebrook says captures 'deconstruction's conception of politics at its most rigorous,' shows how there is no place where language and the real can find a seamless relation. Each side of the binary, the beautiful soul and totalizing power, resists a transcendental structure of impossibility and undecidability. Both are party to an oppositional dialectic or binarism and are marked by the failure to accept the *a priori* 'truth' of the never assimilable, ungraspable 'outside,' which places all claims for truth under erasure. This is true of any type of Marxism that might seek to ground resistance in some kind of 'system of *techne*' or authentic relation between the purity of labor and lived conditions that afford a 'practical and transformative relation between humans and their world.'

For deconstruction, to mount a position of resistance based upon a Marxist logic of production, value and expropriation, or liberal ideas of the sanctity of the individual or the rights of man, repeats a failure to admit that we are constituted through resistance to the truth of the impossibility and undecidability inherent to any attempt to claim truth. The Nazi occupier and resistance fighter, the capitalist apologist and the protester who seeks the 'pure' ground for the perfect argument or the ideal society, all deny the abiding force of the indeterminable and *différance*: one is already complicit, determined within the domain of difference that enables one to think. The insecurity that this creates is the motivation behind all 'presentness.' The idea that we might create coherent signs and narratives of this world, that we might resist the distance between signs and the world, that we might create a pure presence, center or ground, *is ideology*.

This stance, however, led in part to a widespread sense of deconstruction's political irrelevance: if truth cannot be theorized, and if truth claims are necessarily founded upon a denial of their own indeterminacy, then the ground upon which a critique of capitalism might be staged merely floats on a sea of differences; if difference leads to the impossibility of securing either a ground or a center, does this not amount to a form of compliance with capitalism's own anti-foundationalism? Colebrook however reminds us that in the 1980s and 1990s deconstruction did offer an important and necessary critical response to the illusions of capitalism when notions of autonomy, freedom, and liberal self-determinism acted as ideological balustrades. For her, there was 'nothing at all valid in the notion that post-structuralism's critique of representation plays a role in nihilism, relativism and capitalist cynicism.'

However, deconstruction's role in undermining both the illusions of self-consciousness, autonomy and integrity and the idea that these terms might provide the basis for a critique of capitalism has only limited currency in our age. Nine-eleven effectively marked the end of capitalism's own now insubstantial rhetoric, as individual freedom was progressively sacrificed to the demands of debt, surveillance and full spectrum dominance. Such concerns have been overtaken by an era in which 'market, choice, opportunity, autonomy and equality in the market place are now caricatures unable to conceal a logic of market ruthlessness.' We are now in the grip of a flagrant neo-feudalism that no longer even pays lip service to liberal ideology. We need to look elsewhere to explain how certain axioms have come to dominate and overtake the previous configuration: 'how did capital manage to escape difference and allow one axiom to overcode all others?' (These questions are further attended to by Holland and myself).

For Colebrook, instead of attempting to find a putative place of otherness we should think within system, *techne* and difference, critiquing capitalism from within. There is no outside to capitalism; becoming minor within a pre-existing language, economy and ontology is not only theoretically valid but can create a series of heterogenic economies and political systems, and a return to multiplicities of difference. In response to the question 'what do you want?' Occupy answers: ongoing reflection, an authentic relation not to life but to becoming minor and a revitalized commitment to difference.

V. Subjectivity and Aesthetics

Deleuze and Guattari oppose notions of an originating, proprietorial or intentional subjectivity. It is not unreasonable to say that their entire oeuvre amounts to a profound and relentless anti-humanism, where humanism is the conception that humanity somehow stands above or straddles 'life' or nature. In fact, 'life' precedes, envelopes and supersedes all that human beings are – 'the lived body is a paltry thing in comparison with a more profound and almost unlivable power of life' (Deleuze 2003: 44). Deleuze and Guattari do not claim that their model of trans-monadic becoming supersedes or supplants the present system, but rather that it is already what we are. We are already packs; the body is impressed with bodies of knowledge, medical bodies, juridical bodies and a myriad of collective assemblages of enunciation. Perception is already cinematic and memory photographic.

Nunes brings these themes neatly together by highlighting the correlation between event and subject taking place at Occupy. '[The] subject is not an autonomous, sovereign agent, but the way in which the event expresses itself. It exists to the extent that it affirms the event, as much as the event exists only because it expresses itself in this subject.' '[T]he event creates a new existence, it produces a new subjectivity' (Deleuze and Guattari 2003: 216), but not as an external cause; it is *in producing such transformations* that the event 'events'. That the subject is 'crafted by' rather than master of events is also crucial to Conley's argument. As Guattari asserts, changes can occur *autopoietically*, unbeknownst to the subject, before she or he even opens onto the environing world.

For Conley, Occupy presents an opportunity to revisit the promise of new forms of subjectivity outlined in *A Thousand Plateaus*, a work which, for her, marks a significant turning point in Deleuze's political thought. After the exuberance, almost delirium, of *Anti-Oedipus*, and after the defeats of the left and capitalism's resurgence, a more sombre and pragmatic approach was needed. As Conley notes, *A Thousand Plateaus* is far from being the vague and indeterminate series of loose assemblages of ideas it is sometimes taken to be, but is rather a series of 'territories held together by affective intensities made possible as a specific moment in history from which, in the "present" (for the authors in the aftermath of 1968) they think and write'. There is something so consistent about Deleuze's approach that it almost amounts to a methodology: from the indeterminate ground, the flux and flow of change, consistencies emerge; depending on the context these are fashioned as territories, assemblages, milieus or plateaus. Conley attunes us to the subtlety of Deleuze's use of plateaus to describe the creation of territories or planes of consistencies out of the profusion of complex multilayered social dynamics, semiologies and intensities. She writes of shifts in subjectivity, changes in relations and expectations, the dynamics of voyaging smoothly with awareness, of crossing thresholds, of the making of rhizomatic connections that happen way beyond the egotistic and outside of the world reduced to systems of economic, juridical and scientific signs. She affirms that in voyaging one can invite change by shifting to a new subjectivity, perspective or language, or taking a line of flight, and she finds plenty of evidence of such 'soft subversions' effected by artists, educators, and cultural creators. Considering the slippery nature of desire, Buchanan (2011) notes 'that changing the composition of desire is itself revolutionary, and as recent events have shown the transformation of desire on both an individual and collective level … is not something that necessarily requires planning.' Conley also asks, most positively of all, whether Occupy has not also put the dominant discourses of 'state', 'democracy', 'space' into variation: is Occupy another plateau?

In keeping with the spirit of this volume, Thoburn explores Deleuze's concepts not in order to illustrate or represent the themes and issues of Occupy but to create a dialogue between the two with the aim of facilitating their further development: 'It's a recursive relation, for reflection upon Occupy's themes or problems should also help extend Deleuzian concepts, lending them a contemporary vitality.' For Thoburn, the minoritization of politics has found expression in the shift away from identitarian and representational politics as part of long-term changes in the structure of capitalist development and the concomitant production of the multitude. The minor brings contestation, argument and problematization to the fore. This is exemplified by Occupy's single most important statement: 'Let these Facts be Known – the Declaration of the Occupation of New York City.'

> Let's acknowledge the reality: the future of the human race requires the cooperation of its members. Our increasingly interconnected world obscures the underlying truth that all of our grievances are connected.

Adding extra dimensions to this and echoing the autonomist Marxist tradition, Thoburn draws our attention to how 'willed poverty' and a form of 'boundary limitation' are actively affirmed as a means of resistance by the multitude. He shows how the range of economic structures and plethora of social relationships thrown up by the push and pull between these co-determining dynamics offers no fixed route, system or structure. He also presents a warning that seeing the multitude in this way might mean avoiding perhaps the most urgent task of all: creating a strategically planned, coherently organized, well-prepared and organized body able to win a fearsome class war.

Thoburn also pursues a thought experiment by thinking of 'democracy' as a *grid* – a series of lines, intersections and spaces, something like a diagram, imposed upon the virtual multiplicities of the socius. He marshals Deleuze: 'Elections are not a particular locale, nor a particular day in the calendar. They are more like a grid that affects the way we understand and perceive things. Everything is mapped back on this grid and gets warped as a result' (Deleuze 2007: 143). For Thoburn, democracy imposes a 'status quo' that inherently excludes the problems of inequality and exploitation. This state of affairs is normalized and treated as a natural condition that liberal democratic systems are best suited to resolve, rather than being imbricated in the very structures that bring these iniquities about. The grid 'democracy' is thus a matrix of principles, ideals, and structures into which people are expected to fit even when the inner logic of the system results in unelected technocrats taking control of the levers of power, as in Greece and Italy. Indeed, the idea that an unproblematized 'majority' might somehow stand for the 'will of the people' is itself a form of dictatorship. It's not that Deleuze and Guattari are anti-democratic, far from it; rather, they seek a far more intensive democracy, a *becoming democratic* in everything everywhere.

To this end, Thoburn suggests that the grid 'Occupy' can be seen as a 'means *of multiplying points of antagonism.*' For example, the slogan 'we are the 99%' (asserting that the vast majority of humanity is suffering at the expense of the few), may have captured world-wide attention, but we should recall that Occupy London took down the talismanic banner 'Capitalism is Crisis' because it accentuated a single theme. The fact that Occupy distinguishes itself relationally – the 99% versus the 1% – means, writes Colebrook, that it does not present itself as somehow positioned in a pure outside, occupying its own self-referential ground. It is a relation, 'it labels a mass not an identity.' The 1% has no identity other than that of its situation within an already distributed terrain. In this way Occupy both reclaims capitalism's claim of universality – a system of the greater good – and names a number and not an identity such as 'the workers' or a 'class,' a 'vanguard' or a method of 'socialism.'

For Deleuze a majority is like a dictatorship, or a weapon, a false abstraction imposed upon myriad forces, identities and singularities; indeed, 'counting,' for Buchanan, even a headcount of a million protestors, is not the same as that which transforms history. A majority is false because it adheres to number and not the dynamic multiplicities evolving in the will of the people. For Badiou, the majority is an *empty set*, a set that is determined by force, the terms of which majority might count having already been decided. The question, 'Would you prefer a society in which all people share of the common wealth equally?' is positioned as nonsense.

Contrariwise, historical transformation involves rather the irruption of immanence and a change in consciousness irrespective of number. Buchanan provides two examples to illustrate how such transformation can be both conceptual and historical. An idea whose time has come is a clear manifestation of the minor, it 'isn't concerned with results, with counting in the here and now, what it awakens is the force of history itself.' A raggle taggle of disaffected anarcho-political activists who numbered no more than a few hundred placed into world-wide public consciousness the idea that we might imagine the total transformation of society.

Buchanan also writes of the creation of smooth space and the mobility it affords being the key resource in battles for territory, technology, minds and ideas. However, elsewhere he is careful, in employing Deleuze's exact phrasing, to caution against an uncritical valorization of the term:

> it all depends on a careful systematic use … we're trying to say you can never guarantee a good outcome (its not enough just to have a *smooth space*, for example, to overcome striations and coercion, or a *body without organs* to overcome organisations. (Deleuze 1995: 32)

Thoburn likewise observes that a kind of smooth space is necessary to undo the illusions of democracy, but he fills this with layers of antagonism. Hence, the grid Occupy seeks is to encourage a problematics of contestation and critique, and the development of divergent positions in an extension and intensification of the problematic in concrete circumstances.

As well as emphasizing the contested and conflictual modality of Occupy, Thoburn explores the aesthetic dimension of political struggle. He references Deleuze's anthropological/ethological approach wherein animal, natural and human traits are interlaced in a social form that is indispensably aesthetic. We find in Occupy expressions of territoriality that are not just markers and signifiers of boundary lines but have an expressive sensory quality. As in the numerous ethological examples employed by Deleuze – the musicality of birds, the color of fish scales, the zigzag of the stickleback – such expressions are essential features of the territorializing function. As Thoburn carefully details, the occupations of Zuccotti Park and the St Paul's Cathedral steps involved much more than a mere physical encampment, including songs, found objects, art brut, and countless slogans, banners and placards weaved together in a tapestry as affirmative as it was functional.

An aspect of pathos is crucial to this. The problem with representational and identitarian politics is that the few speak for the many; hierarchical structures are created and power becomes concentrated in oligarchies or elites. There is, by contrast, a humility to Occupy; its members are very circumspect about speaking for the movement or making claims on its behalf. Consensus is not just an aspiration but also a way of life, and the atmosphere is suffused with a sense of mutual aid and suffering. As Thoburn puts it, 'this quality of life – fragile, impersonal, damaged – is central [to] … lifting "suffering" to a level of aesthetic expression without losing any of its "struggle".' This fragility is an important part of Occupy's expression: the cardboard signs, the mocked-up soup kitchens – OccupyLSX became a highly efficient kitchen feeding hundreds from day one, prompting the highly unethical response of the police who shepherded the homeless and the destitute to the park – and the provision of care for people suffering from mental health problems. Fragility became Occupy's aesthetic, resulting in 'mutually sustaining encounters' between meaning and politics through sensory and expressive qualities, all coordinated and self-managed by a leaderless, grassroots movement.

VI. The War Machine and the Multitude

Each of the contributors in this collection takes a different approach to the conceptualization of those aspects of capitalism that they find most egregious. But they also address how capitalism's creativity can be harnessed, and what is to be done in the face of 'an appropriated and pre-accomplished *global* war machine' (Marzec 2001), the object of whose rule is social life in its entirety (Hardt and Negri 2000: xv). They ask which of Deleuze and Guattari's concepts have the capacity not merely to illustrate but to be applied *along with* Occupy's practical tools and methods, not least in various approaches to the question of space.

Buchanan for instance observes how smooth space amounts to a commons. He argues that Occupy opened up a new way, a new space, for thinking and acting, creating a 'radical break with the normal continuity of things, interrupting and causing a counter flow to the usual flow of daily life'. Articulating the increasing interest in the 'common', the commons movement and commoning at Occupy, he suggests that the common, conceived as 'social relations', can be understood as a smooth space. We must bear in mind that neither Buchanan nor Thoburn equates smooth space with a flattening or an absence of conflict. Buchanan borrows from David Harvey:

> The common is not to be constructed, therefore, as a particular kind of thing, asset or even social process, but as an unstable and malleable social relation between a particular well-defined social group and those aspects of its actually existing or yet-to-be-created social and/or physical environment deemed crucial to its life and livelihood. There is, in effect, a social practice of commoning. (Harvey 2012: 73)

For Hardt and Negri the common is the basis for the existence of the multitude; the two are indivisible since the common is:

> that which allows the multitude to "communicate and act together" ... the common does not refer to traditional notions of either the community or the public ... the common ... is what configures the mobile and flexible substance of the multitude' and 'social life depends on the common. (Hardt and Negri 2006: 9, 10, 212)

The common is a space that allows for the greatest degree of singularity, it is composed of 'a set of singularities – and by singularity here we mean a social subject whose difference cannot be reduced to sameness.' Beyond all else, the common is the virtual space of pre-individual singularities, where flows of affects and percepts, ideas and processes, and the 'ground of all human life' (Graeber 2012: 101) discussed by all the contributors to this volume, are to be found.

Thoburn foregrounds contested and antagonistic spaces in which smooth space is by no means without conflict or fragmentation – the opposite in fact. Burrows' chapter attends to Deleuze and Guattari's concept of the war machine specifically in relation to what he calls 'negative space,' and he joins Conley in stressing the importance of creating *vacuoles of non-communication* and of the more general 'artistic' strategies and tactics of the movement. Where Thoburn employs the notion of an ethno-aesthetic territoriality, for Burrows, Occupy is to be situated at the cutting edge of contemporary art practice. Like other contributors, he does not simply offer a Deleuzian reading of Occupy, but rather the production of a forced encounter between certain theoretical resources and the various material practices and events that took place across 2010 and 2011. His essay also considers the 'networked dividual,' the role of art education, and the merit of various literary, philosophical and artistic strategies of non-relation to capitalism in the construction of a singular reading of the war machine.

The term 'war machine' may be one of Deleuze and Guattari's most misleading, as it has nothing to do with war and what it designates might be better termed a 'metamorphosis machine' (Patton 2002: 110) or a 'mutation machine' (Holland). Indeed the war machine and the multitude should be seen as synonymous terms; as Tampio explains:

> Hardt and Negri's major contribution to Deleuzian political theory is an attempt to name the social body capable of actualizing Deleuze's vision. The concept of the multitude rephrases Deleuze's intuition of a war machine combating the state apparatus, the composition of a joyful political body, and the full social body without organs (2009: 387).

With the concept of the war machine Deleuze and Guattari are describing a process of mutation and change. Now that a war is actually taking place over our bodies, minds, and increasingly the planet and life itself, 'it is the state that has war as its object, and not the nomadic war machine' (Marzec 2001). What Hardt and Negri once saw as an 'acephelous supranational order' is increasingly becoming a system of outright control, wherein power is vested in a specific identifiable group of financiers, politicians, institutions and corporations. There is then a tension emerging between what we already know from French intellectual writing after May 1968 – which broadly accepted the idea that 'power is not simply a matter of coercion or repression ... the product or the expression of a powerful ruling elite exercising influence over a powerless majority' (Buchanan 2008: 21) – and contemporary conditions on the ground suggesting the emergence of a transcendent neoliberal war machine of debt and perpetual war against people, communities and life.

We should also be wary of investing in the notion of the sovereignty of an 'empire' or 'despot' as a terrifying behemoth, lest we both misunderstand it and create a monster that can only be challenged by matching *its* scale and *its* weapons, in turn affording it even greater power. Instead, we should think with Hardt and Negri:

> Empire creates a greater potential for revolution than did the modern regimes of power because it presents us, alongside the machine of command, with an alternative: the set of all the exploited and the subjugated, a multitude that is directly opposed to Empire, with no mediation between them. (Hardt and Negri 2000: 393)

Capitalism is, in and of itself, decentered and deterritorialized; it is endlessly creative. It creates fluid networks, multiple hybrid identities, and demands new subjectivities. Its axiomatics create borders and inhibit flows, and yet it also cannot tolerate borders; indeed, we might argue that capitalist production cannot tolerate the unproductiveness of racism, sexism and homophobia, and certainly decoding and deterritorialization have immense emancipatory potential. According to Virno (2004) the capitalist mode of production in the transition from Fordism to post-Fordism was driven by the multitude's demands for new socialities, new working practices, and the development of new desires, relations, sexualities and attitudes to hierarchy that have subsequently been capitalized.

Given the inherent dynamism of capitalism, it is hardly surprising that the multitude takes on equally amorphous forms of expression. But the multitude is not simply a consequence of new forms of production; it emerges from the autopoietic drive of the resourcefulness of life – of difference – as the driving force behind new forms of capitalist production. Its force also emerges from disjunctive and conjunctive accidents and unexpected collisions, which foster new potentials and multiplicities that are to be found simultaneously in-between and beyond.

The new phenomenology of the multitude reveals labor as the fundamental creative cooperative activity that goes beyond any obstacle imposed on it and that constantly re-creates the world. Labor – material or immaterial, intellectual or corporeal – produces and reproduces social life, and in the process is exploited by capital. This intermingling of capital and labor becomes the new ground for resistance. Here Hardt and Negri encapsulate their project: 'The creative forces of the multitude that sustain Empire are also capable of autonomously constructing a counter-Empire, an alternative political organization of global flows and exchanges' (2000: 53).

The war machine is irrepressible, autopoietic and endlessly resourceful; a perpetual and continuous act, it is the driving creative force behind capital that capital seeks to control through its axioms. It is essential not to underestimate the extraordinary potential of the war machine; for Deleuze and Guattari it is 'another species,' 'another nature,' 'another justice,' 'another origin' (1987: 352, 353, 354).[6] This aspect of Deleuze's political ontology is entirely in step with Occupy's *modus operandi*. Everything is to be questioned using weapons and terms specific to the particular circumstances, the kind of violence to be resisted, and the joy to be released across the entire social field – made in the moment for the moment without coda or rules. This is an astonishingly flexible method, requiring no authorization from a creed or hierarchy.

Whilst Conley speaks to the advancing multitude, those cultural producers that create new nomadic, rhizomatic identities out of new spaces, for Burrows the war machine's specificity arises from its performance of resistance. He examines a range of political actions (swarms, teach-ins, collective action), some of which he took part in, in terms of how they occupy space, or how they created 'four-dimensional spaces.' Burrows draws out the complexities of three different expressions of refusal united in their rejection of the exigencies of neoliberal capitalist production. Each of them says 'no' to alienation by, or participation in, the already legitimized spaces of political discourse or civil society. This saying 'no' also involves refusing the affirmative search for solutions or exploring grounds for compromise. It takes the form of developing other spatial dynamics beyond the enclosed, regimented and delimited spaces of the public and private, of the media, commerce and political institutions – breaking these divisions down and thinking transversally across them. As Holland remarks, rather than making demands on a supposedly democratic system, Occupy Wall Street (OWS) tried to instantiate and illustrate what true participatory democracy looks like. Burrows also positions art as the privileged ground for engendering a spirit of the collective and for opening horizons. In doing so, he addresses the various ways in which protests are able to challenge dominant subjective and discursive formations by experimenting with the production of negative space or vacuoles of non-communication. He notes that for Deleuze and Guattari the negative space is non-incorporable, non-subsumable, as the war machine operates to decompose rigid forms: 'The war machine is the surest mechanism directed against the formation of the State' (Deleuze and Guattari 1987: 357).

Burrows thinks through the various forms of saying 'no' and shows how in many circumstances refusal can be recuperated, accommodated, commodified and marketized; as he puts it: 'the crumbling edge of capitalism is also the cutting edge of capitalism.' He compares the quiet, steadfast, ultimately suicidal refusal of Melville's Bartleby with Nick Land's theorization of both non-compliance and the problems inherent to organization. The war machine Burrows describes is resistant, actively negative, and creates conflict not by answering power but by opening up a new space for experimenting with affirmation and negation. The creation of collectives as an art practice brings together the various complexities at work here, not least in the enactment of a new sense of space and time through a new alignment of actual and cyberspace. This is in step with those art practices that over the last 40 years have striven to be non-subsumable by the market. Burrows contends that becoming minor within the global art establishment parallels – many would argue leads – the new politics of our age.

Along with Mecchia, Holland measures how the term 'war machine' was developed in response to May 1968, but can be adjusted to the imperatives of Occupy. He highlights how the war machine creates role specializations, is horizontal in its organization, and 'operate[s] via contagion, enthusiasm, *esprit de corps*, and solidarity (Deleuze and Guattari

1987: 241–9, 267–9, 278, 366–7, 384, 390–93) rather than strict obligation or duty,' although, he warns, there is nothing 'that can be considered decisive' about this *modus operandi* in itself, since the Tea Party movement, and indeed the stock exchange, share many of these features of the war machine. Notwithstanding this caveat, when looking to understand Occupy's potential for social transformation the concept of the war machine provides an invaluable tool. Historical change does not come only through violent revolution or sudden ruptures but also through slow developments in thought, affects and perception, through the shifting and sliding of subjectivities and communities. As we are seeing today, the potential for a revolution in consciousness is observable in the exceedingly clear political bifurcation that is taking place between diametrically opposed political ontologies, the furthest poles of which being exemplified by Occupy and the Tea Party.

Refusal is also central to Holland's analysis. He suggests that a slow-motion general strike (a strike against everything) may be taking place in the widespread subtraction of our collective and individual experience from the machinery of neoliberal capitalist production. It is clear that vast numbers of people are either reduced to exhaustion and dismay by capitalism's rage against love, community, and social solidarity, or are enraged by informed analyses of climate change, wealth distribution, people trafficking, the prison–industrial complex, modern-day slavery and so forth, and emboldened by experience in resistance movements across the globe. It takes time to create new networks and new subjectivities, and taking back time is both the method and objective of many of these disparate political groupings. Holland leaves open the question as to whether this will prompt a sudden irruption of the political unconscious or will continue in slow motion. Either way, 'the hoary old reform–revolution conundrum' does not become an issue because neither is negated in the open-ended political utopianism of Occupy.

VII. Money and Debt: Towards a Minor Marxism

Anti-Oedipus is a difficult read. It is Deleuze and Guattari at their most infuriating and perplexing, and yet it may be their most prescient text. For Holland it provides an indispensible anatomization of how the conversion of wealth into capital and work into dependent wage labor is central to the development of capitalism, and charts a path through different conceptualizations of money, debt, control societies and capitalist axiomatics to arrive at what appears to be capitalism's essence, the conjunction of three flows of decoding consisting of:

> The decoding of land flows, under the form of the constitution of large private properties, the decoding of monetary flows, under the form of the development of merchant fortunes, the decoding of a flow of workers under the form of expropriation, of the deterritorialization of serfs and peasant landholders. (Deleuze 1971)

The conjunction of the deterritorialized flows of abstract capital and abstract labor and their reterritorialization in the form of private property forms the center of the many 'factitious reterritorializations of capitalism.' In turn, private property functions to alienate the wage laborer whose so-called free labor serves as their only property, removed from their material and incorporeal reproduction of worlds, selves and the socius. Only as a consequence of these conjunctions could capitalism stabilize and endure.

In *Anti-Oedipus* we find that whilst critiquing all forms of arborescent thought, particularly Freudianism and Marxism, Deleuze and Guattari assert that capitalism has an archetypal structure. At first blush this appears to be a contradiction, but we should consider the difference between seeking to determine the essential nature of a thing and analyzing a historically contingent organization of forces. Indeed, there is a mood of exhaustion in contemporary Deleuzian scholarship, and the proliferation of Deleuzian aesthetics, the various alibis for rhizomatic absentmindedness and the championing of the liberating potential of desire and schizoid expressivity. This reading (clarified in some detail in this volume by Mecchia) has led to attempts to articulate a more careful and coherent Deleuzian political philosophy, achieved not least by the works of Ian Buchanan. A useful introduction to the basic principles of Deleuze and Guattari's political, social and economic thought can be found in Buchanan's 2008 *Deleuze and Guattari's Anti-Oedipus* (88–116), which concerns a particular section of *Anti-Oedipus* (pages 139–262).

These pages outline the relation of Deleuze and Guattari's political ontology to psychoanalysis and Marxism, as well as their reliance on Nietzsche's anthropological account of the role of credit and debt in the formation of human societies and the development of consciousness.

To briefly summarize: *Anti-Oedipus* offers a typology of three interrelated social formations in terms of the regulation of flows by coding. In the primitive/territorial period, bodies, acts, symbols, territories and subjectivities are enacted together in everyday life, initiations, rituals and language. The despotic age is characterized by an overcoding by the state, money and religion, whereby finite porous bonds are overcoded on the body of the despot. Finally, in the civilized/capitalist age, overcoding is replaced by capital's 'most characteristic' and 'most important tendency' of decoding and deterritorialization. The capitalist social machine is fundamentally different from the primitive and despotic abstract social machines in that it functions not by codes but through decoding and deterritorialization (Deleuze and Guattari 2000: 34). It is the first society in history where the aim of production is not to serve another end (social bonds or overcoding), but serves its own purpose: production for production's sake. The 'essence of wealth' is no longer a concrete objective thing, but 'the activity of production in general' (Deleuze and Guattari 2000: 270). As I highlight, the key objective of a mappable number of super-corporations and political institutions is the takeover, domination and then destruction, through monopolization, of the market. Thoburn likewise notes that production in general does have a purpose – the self-expansion of capital, the maximization of 'surplus value' from the expansive potential of life.[7]

This system is held in place by axioms. First amongst which is that 'Man must constitute himself through the repression of the intense germinal influx, the great biocosmic memory that threatens to deluge every attempt at collectivity' (Deleuze and Guattari 1983: 190). Deleuze and Guattari's political ontology is a theory of the connectedness of all things in the great germinal wash of life: the same wash of life that is the force behind the multitude. Capitalism's first axiom is to replace this with the assertion of capital's immanence. This harnessing of life's plenitude, diversity and vital creative force serves not the good of all but the acceleration of capitalist accumulation.

Central to the transition from the primitive/territorial to the despotic epoch was the role played by the development of money. In the primitive/territorial age, goods were exchanged according to a system of barter.[8] Credit and debt were measured using various fungible, finite recording systems criss-crossing a palimpsest of social and familial registers which laid the foundation of the development of thought (where thought is taken to include shared beliefs, alliances and filiations, inherited myths, social practices, recognitions and scales of values, affects, soma, and so forth), and social obligations. Money was not introduced to facilitate barter but imposed by the despot to secure his power and exact tribute. This, along with the development of abstract labor and capital, laid the foundations for the development of capitalism. The conjunction of these great forces of decoding were exacted through the figure of money, which retained the imprint of its originative incarnation as a power of command.

My own chapter shows how money, while its infinite variety of uses may be impossible to fully theorize, should be understood in terms of the originative division, forged in the transition from the primitive to the despotic age, between its dual functions as credit and exchange. The self-same coin acts according to two valences as *credit*, which allows for accumulation, the extraction of tribute and the power of command, and *exchange*, which facilities both invention, creativity and the multitudinous expression of desire. Exchange money is 'impotent' and turns us into slaves of the social machine of production and consumption wherein all desires are decoded and recoded into the general equivalence of money: 'under capitalism, all the flows of desire, and all of the intensities of life become grounded on one single flow: the quantifiable medium of capital and exchange' (Colebrook 2006: 50).

There is then a profound ambivalence at the heart of money. It facilitates the creative potentials of unlimited exchange and it also allows for quantitative exchange as a substitute for the time-consuming, socially complex and never quite concluded palimpsest of different mechanisms of trade.

> Quantitative measurement as a substitute for rational value judgment confers supreme moral security and intellectual comfort: the Good becomes measurable and calculable;

> decisions and moral judgments can follow from the implementation of a procedure of impersonal, objective, quantifying calculation and individual subjects do not have to shoulder the burden [of decision making] anxiously and uncertainly. (Gorz 1989: 121)

However, these extraordinary freedoms are curtailed as money becomes the supreme, indispensible criteria and single measure of value of all things. These values and criteria are largely determined by the manner in which is money is issued and the purposes to which it is put. These ambivalences and contradictions at the heart of money are fundamental, and Philip Goodchild's project is to show how thinking and reason are grounded in the same processes. Looking across the epochs we can question whether the great advances in trade and social development would have been possible without the cooperation and coordination introduced by the single quantifying measuring scale provided by money. Likewise, would the industrial revolution have been possible without credit?

These contradictions may explain why money's other side, its 'power of command' and extraction through rent and tribute, remains unhindered and leads to chronic overproduction, breathtaking inequality and wastefulness of human potential, and an inescapable, incessant schiz-flow of creative invention and destruction rather than revolution. What is hidden is the simple fact that money's ability to facilitate the expression of life's potential is severely curtailed by its issuance as credit money by the banks. Indeed, the appearance of a primary equilibrium of prices leads to a belief in an underlying principle of equality that conceals entirely functional and fundamental inequalities. As Goodchild, one of the foremost interpreters of Deleuzian economic theory, notes:

> Since money is created as debt, and debt must be repaid in the form of money and more debt, and debt becomes the supreme principle of theoretical knowledge, practical conduct, and mutual trust, then this perspective of evaluation is not chosen but imposes itself. (2013: 53)

Taking up the challenge of making Deleuze 'relevant' to policy formation and institution building, I ask whether the practical policy formulations of the political campaign group Positive Money (whose agenda is to strip banks of the right to create money) might be read as classical political economic manifestations of Deleuze and Guattari's philosophical speculations.

Also assessing the fundamental importance of debt to the fabric of neoliberalism, Holland argues that credit money creates three decisive forms of dependency: the enforced selling of labor-power to capital; enforced consumption in markets whose exchange values are bogus; and the creation of psychological dependency, leading to a state of debt peonage. For Holland, a minor Marxism seeks to overturn these dependencies. Because money is imbricated in the very foundations of subjectivity, thinking and power relations, this is not a single-issue campaign but one that strikes at the heart of capitalist production and is a direct invocation to the multitude to express its collective agency and challenge capitalist axiomatics. Indeed, the importance of this cannot be understated in so far as the creditor and debtor relation is the primary machine for the production of the difference which arrests and plunders the plenitude of all other differences.

Debt servitude under neoliberalism has similar characteristics to servitude under the despot: it is '*a debt of existence*, a debt of the existence of the subjects themselves' (Deleuze and Guattari 2000: 197). As such, a debt strike has the potential to release a collective identity from servitude to infinite debt, sending lines of flight in unforeseen directions across oceans of repressed fears, unlocking desire and thought and allowing for layer upon layer of armor to fall. At stake in such a debt strike would be not only billions of dollars of social and private debt, but (to paraphrase *Anti-Oedipus* (Deleuze and Guatarri 1983: 180)), all the stupidity and arbitrariness of the laws, all the pain of the initiations, the whole perverse apparatus of repression and education, the red-hot irons and the atrocious procedures that breed man, mark him in his flesh, render him capable of alliance and form him within the debtor–creditor relation.

Both Holland's and my own essays in this volume discuss primitive accumulation in terms of an array of debts and obligations being traded according to a palimpsest of fungible relations before the demands of exchange facilitated by money. Colebrook reminds us of an essential but under-studied component to this theory: that the fabric of the socius in the form of obligation and mutuality, dependence and merit, was realized through the practices of theft and gift.

Deleuze and Guattari detail how in the primitive/territorial age the destruction of surplus production in rituals or potlatch not only used excess to create a filiative lineage of social adhesion but also allowed obligations to remain, as the absence of wealth held in reserve necessitated continued social dependency. Mecchia reports on Pierre Clastres' view that 'many world populations were not frugal and stateless because of scarcity and political primitivism, but as a consequence of an explicit political decision, notably the unwillingness to engage in labor contracts and political representations.' Celebrations and expenditure to demonstrate excess, along with enactments of rituals and inscriptions, are all forms of gift that are very different from just simply giving something away, or from messy reciprocal gift-giving; they are commitments to the social bond. Buchanan (2008) explains that the chief doesn't exchange his wealth for allegiance; rather, through these practices he converts wealth into allegiance. Gift is also a form of trade, and to give often implies a power relation as the gift bestows power in the form of reputation, rank and sociability, which implies its mirror in the form of allegiance. By giving, credit is accrued, but also life force is expended, and by expending is in turn increased; 'the gift is the spending of energy *not* for the sake of return, indeed one's force is increased the more one spends' (Colebrook 2006: 126).

To a large extent to steal is to be, and very often the gift is indistinguishable from theft as elaborate feasts and gift-giving become a way of converting goods into prestige and allegiance: 'to prevent this from becoming an exchange the ritual of gift giving must make the gift seem like a theft' (Deleuze and Guattari 2000: 203). Before there is an economy allowing for the exchange of property, and before there is anything like scarcity, need or interest, Deleuze and Guattari argue for a milieu of forces that is neither the rapacious world of capitalist acquisitiveness and theft, nor a benign moral nature attuned to social harmony and benevolence. Once social systems are formed from a war machine that is a play of forces *before interests and property*, then a milieu of rivalry, envy and rank inevitably follows precisely because of establishing the single force of the proper or of ownership.

In the primitive/territorial age inscription on the body was often the instrument for bonding the protocols of theft and gift: as Nietzsche says, when impressed through pain, things are remembered. The rites of inscription, tattooing, scarring, painting and piercing served many purposes; the tribe was bonded by attaching bodies to symbols, minds and the socius (the body and gaze and the tribe are assembled at once, collectively), creating lateral alliances that countered the power of filiation and lineage and extending filiations to the extensive allying relations of the tribe. These rituals, dependencies and alliances warded off the uncontrollable power of unleashed exchange.

In sum, the requirements of the socius were enacted through systems (machines) of inscribing and marking, rituals and the measuring of credit and debt, to which the practices of theft and gift were essential: theft and gift are a style of relation that preceded coding as mother, child, priest, and despot. As Colebrook points out, theft and gift were fundamental to the creation of stable points within the psychosocial fabric and for the formation of territories, which in turn is a pre-requisite for the creation of genuine difference and genuine exchange.

What is to be found in the primitive/territorial society is exactly what the term implies: territories rather than exchange, stable points rather than equivalences. In our age, territories are formed primarily through the possession of capital, land and political power. Before the emergence of the exchange of equivalences and accumulation of abstract capital through money, territories were assemblages of natural disequilibriums between alliances, filiations, and potentialities expressed through the 'powers to differ actualized in productive encounters.' Genuine difference and genuine exchange, as Colebrook points out, leads away from insecurity, moralizing and the fear of living a full and active life towards vitality and arousal; 'I steal therefore I become' and 'I give therefore I accrue,' are not forms of 'power over but power to' (Colebrook 2006: 134).

> Desiring life is intensive difference. A body is made up of powers to differ, and these powers are actualized in productive encounters. Theft and gift are precisely the processes that allow for these differences to be expressed. (Colebrook 2006: 134).

The requirement of the socius was therefore that potency, agency, leverage and force create relatively stable terms, and intensive difference is a pre-requisite for a genuine calculation to be made regarding who has taken what. Such calculation, as I show, is taken by Nietzsche to be the foundation of thought.

In the primitive/territorial epoch we see an assemblage of adjunctive and disjunctive relations and collective territorialization occurs when the tribe is marked by 'processes [that] allow organs such as the eyes, penis, breast or head to be experienced collectively' (Colebrook 2006: 144). This collectivism also leads to a proto-individualism, as only in a form of territorialization can the body take itself as an individual; and individual memory, or a sense of self existing in time, is dependent upon collective memory. As Holland, Colebrook and I all make clear, fundamental to this process is debt and the ability to live up to a promise. As I argue:

> Certainly, without rational thought, anticipation and prediction, man would not survive; but memory is more than that. It lays the foundation for the formation of will by the creation of a link between 'I will' and the actual manifestation of the will in action. In this way an infallible psychological law leads to predicable subjects who, in turn, provide the infrastructure for the social bond.

Also emergent from this process is accumulation achieved not through expropriation but as a result of harboring and storing and the process of exchange, which together form the conditions for a nascent capitalism. Economic and subjective differences, a 'this is mine and that is yours' or 'non-exchangeable and non-substitutable' singularities between two discernable persons, are pre-requisites for trading. The emergence of capitalism was a consequence not of determining laws of history, nor of an underlying human nature, nor of a law of struggle or economic production, but of a specific historically contingent assemblage of forces.

VIII. Deterritorialization, Reterritorialization, and Smooth Space

Deleuze and Guattari are often presented as being in thrall to the deterritorializing effects of capitalism. Fueling this perception, *Anti-Oedipus* presents the 'schizo' as a figure of revolution, freed from the shackles of the despot and capital as a signifier-scrambling agent traversing the strata in a mode of permanent revolution. As early as 1991 Eugene Holland attempted to dispel the resulting misconception of an absentminded, sensation-fetishizing Deleuze and Guattari by demonstrating how in *A Thousand Plateaus* this revolutionary schizoanalytic fever became more tempered. What is usually overlooked is that de- and reterritorialization are tendencies not oppositions. They are aspects of the same process; as deterritorialization creates a space for reterritorialization, reterritorialization leaves a vacuole in its wake: 'the *least* deterritorialized [element] reterritorializes on the *most* deterritorialized' (Deleuze and Guattari 1987: 174).

Capitalism's great potential and allure is precisely that it is the first system whose *modus operandi* is immanent to a process that constitutes the formula of all being. But capitalism does not merely 'deterritorialize with all its might'; its force is determined by axioms irrespective of the damage caused to the *oikos*, the planet and life itself. Occupy and Deleuze's philosophy seek not to restrain capitalism (and life's) fundamental tendency towards deterritorialization but to bring about new kinds of reterritorialization organized around much more rejuvenating forms such as assemblages, social machines, plateaus and smooth spaces.

If a motif can be discerned in the many vectors of thought and diverse positions that make up this volume, then it turns on the question of territorialization in relation to potentials of causality, agency and leadership as well as the necessity of resistance and antagonism. It is a question of how these might be realized in pragmatic formations in the creation of territories, negative spaces, new subjectivities and sensibilities, and in new ways of understanding economics, particularly in relation to debt. We should not just occupy empty spaces but, as Conley puts it, 'rethink and refashion space by means of new distributions,' maintaining a commitment to change 'though rearranging inherited configurations of life.' To occupy does not necessarily imply taking over a psychical territory or seizing the fort but can be pure movement in the form of cadences and rhythms, drawing lines or tracing diagrams. And for such change to happen something has to happen first: the 'preoccupation' of a myriad of micro spaces that have to be pried open to bring about new sensibilities in the formation of other intelligences. Preoccupation for Conley entails new modes of thinking, experiencing and perception which, when held together by affective intensities, create a new plateau: Occupy.

In *What is Philosophy?* Deleuze and Guattari note that 'the territory implies the emergence of pure sensory qualities, or *sensibilia* that cease to be merely functional and become expressive features, making possible a transformation of functions' (Deleuze and Guattari 1994: 183). Thoburn saw this happening first-hand at OccupyLSX, where sensibilia took the form of a struggle for ideas, gestures, placards and signs, information systems, a collective will to self-education, the immersion of subjects in shared ideas and in the deployment of new social technologies. These expressive, sensory qualities were manifested most clearly by the tent, where the experience of poverty, precarity, debt, and racism – as well as the spatial arrangements of the city, the gendered divisions of labor and the partitions of public and private – were all refashioned in a different type of dwelling and form of possession. For Thoburn, the tent expressed and created a territory at once:

> The tent undid patterns of behaviour, laws, sensory structures, and economic forms that determine that space as a road, stage for commerce and governance, or municipal park. But if the tent and tripod deterritorialize in this way, they simultaneously generate a *new* territory, they *re*territorialize into an Occupy camp or a street party.

Thoburn's interest is in how two different modalities of composition, 'the sensory or expressive quality of Occupy and its *meaning* or explicit *politics*,' formed 'a mutually sustaining encounter.' He likens this new form of territorialization to the art object, which for Deleuze is always a composition of material form and expressive qualities. The art object as 'monument' is a fabulation, rather than a representation or image, and this fabulation has to capture something of the struggle to live, to express the struggle for existence. In this way, artistic and socially progressive forms lift 'suffering' to the level of 'aesthetic expression.'

In a paper similarly concerned with aesthetics, Burrows writes of swarms, teach-ins and collective actions spearheaded by art students, made possible by the knotting together of 'the seemingly infinite, inhuman scale of cyberspace and communication technology with the space and time of occupation and protest.' This knot of cyber and physical space enabled individuals who may have previously felt atomized to discover the joys of collective action. For Burrows reterritorialization took the form of the creation of negative spaces in the various practices of saying 'no'; in this way he shows the versatility of the war machine, specifically how new collective assemblages created new space-times and the production of a negative space became the material of protest. The breadth and scope of the war machine is also drawn out by Holland, who reminds us of Deleuze's insistence that the war machine 'exists only in its own metamorphoses' (Deleuze and Guattari 1987: 366) or 'in specific assemblages such as building bridges or cathedrals or rendering judgements or making music or instituting a science, a technology' (Deleuze and Guattari 1987: 366).

Attending to the question of space, Buchanan addresses how, in rupturing the striated spaces of capitalism, Occupy instigated a change in sense and perception through the creation of smooth spaces. This amounts not so much to a change in the state of things, or redefining the map, as to the creation of a new way of being in space. For Deleuze and Guattari smooth space speaks not of a flattening, but of social relations where regularities, points, measurements and predetermined modes of being give way to openness, and where multiplicitous relations and differently accented rhythms create irregularities and constant itinerancy. For Buchanan, following Harvey, it is in smooth space that the new commons is to be found – not as a presumption of commonality but in terms of a regard for contingency and variation, where instability and incoherence is to be *worked through* in the manner of Occupy rather than concealed beneath conviviality or the false ideal of 'the public.' Buchanan stresses, partly in response to Badiou, that the 'Idea' in the form of an affirmation of what might be possible, rather than a state of *ressentiment* or anger, is essential to the creation of smooth space. Deleuzian analysis of social space concerns less how to create the conditions for universalizing concepts such as 'a public' than how to construct a place where genuine conflicts between ideas are given expression. We might say, as Thoburn does, that dissolving the passivity of consensus, antagonism and dissensus fosters a sense of alertness and empowers people and groups to embark on multifarious forms of resistance. In this sense, the smooth space of Occupy is a territory wherein further, deeper and more extensive conflicts are to be assembled.

Smooth space for Mecchia is nomadically itinerant, vibrant and open, but densities or refrains emerge within it to create points from which life may be processed or machines assembled. Smooth space contracts and opens, and conjunctions between forces emerge. Following such conjunctions, Mecchia addresses how de- and reterritorialization are played out in the figure of the subject. First, deterritorialization means taking apart existing egos as well as monolithic and totalizing philosophical and psychoanalytical theories and, most importantly, their ties to capitalist de- and reterritorializations. Second (or better concomitantly), it is necessary to reterritorialize in the figure of the 'anthropos,' understood as a 'dynamic, material figure of political subjectivity' that criss-crosses the striated spaces of social organization. For Mecchia the anthropos is both a method and an analytical category, the meeting place of which was given material expression at Occupy. It does this through a collective conceived not in terms of party structure, nor as subject to the demands of 'truth,' but as an assemblage of empirical, machinic processes that are transversal across striated spaces: 'neither man nor woman, rich or poor, powerful or subjugated – what constitutes this kind of collective organization is … one of the most powerful practico-theoretical figures for our understanding of the emergence of the Occupy groups.'

For Nunes also, binary oppositions such as 'openness against closure, diversity over unity, spontaneity over purposive organization, rhizome over arborescence, deterritorialization over reterritorialization' are all equally unreliable. Nonetheless, as tendencies, the drift towards either end of these poles is obvious. The crucial issue is how in any given situation these tendencies are to be balanced and to what purpose. For example, as Nunes notes, at one end of the scale, formlessness only serves to lay political movements open to irrelevance and capture, but he is also at pains to show how, at the other end of the scale, vanguard politics can no longer capture or mobilize new forms of political protest, or the emergent sensibilities of political collectives. For Nunes the 'twilight of the vanguard' has seen the emergence of multiple vanguards, collective assemblages and packs, all of which are experiments with political transformation in ways that retain the maximum degree of openness and mobility. Rather than universal forces of history or the endless struggle between capital and labor, the nature of event and the complexity of our times require new more mobile forms, thinking strategically about how to take on the war machine at its most abstract, precisely in the manner of Occupy.

For Protevi, Occupy created an environment for people to show their faces to each other, assume an identity, and challenge the 'crystallization of the collective affect of shame in the American air.' By showing their faces to each other in a new collective space the Occupiers sought to counteract existing stratified and homogenized affects 'by creating a positive affect of joyful solidarity.' Placing body next to body and becoming immersed in the shared expression of the chant are forms of vibrating and being in phase: an indissoluble togetherness capable of creating a positive intermodal feedback of percept, affect and sense.

IX. Conclusion

War machines, smooth spaces, packs, assemblages, plateaus, becoming-minor, transformations in subjectivity, the creation of new collectivities and forms of distributive leadership – all these ideas and processes are addressed in relation to Occupy in the chapters that follow. While there are many other aspects of Deleuze and Guattari's political ontology that could also be invoked and applied here, it is hoped that these are sufficient to demonstrate how their political concepts are relevant to this new neo-feudal age and to the type of sociopolitical movements that have emerged in response. Life flows, life is irrepressible, the question is always what social forms might be created to make these flows more malleable, open, flexible and more able to express the creativity that lies at the heart of human nature and life. This book articulates a shift away from the fetishization of deterritorialization towards fluid and open forms of territorialization as figures of potency, agency, leverage and force, in search of genuine difference. As Deleuze and Guattari say, everywhere, 'the depth of difference is primary' (1994: 51). The aim of politics is to release difference from its entrapment within the logics and axiomatics of capitalism. Capitalism is a difference-producing machine that cannot tolerate its own plenitude. In response, rather than following the Deleuze popularized in some circles of accelerated difference we need to find or invent, with Occupy, difference-affirming machines. Occupy's 'Let these Facts be Known' captures the myriad forms of minoritarianism that allow for contradictory, antagonistic, connective, rhizomic differences. Recognizing that our urgent times do not afford us the luxury of absolute deterritorialization or fantasies about an outside to capitalism, Occupy is intensely pragmatic – all of its groups and assemblies are charged with experimenting with questions of how to devise practical solutions to the problems of the state, democracy, economy and social relations. In the end, both Occupy and Deleuze are rooted in practical analysis, and both reject the stifling alternative 'reform or revolution,' because both understand that 'the question [of revolutions] has always been organisational' (2007: 143): the organization of flows into autopoietic and highly relational structures.

Works Cited

Ambrose, Darren. 2006. 'Deleuze, Philosophy, and the Materiality of Painting'. *Symposium* 10 (1): 191–211.

Badiou, Alain. 2000. *Deleuze: The Clamor of Being*. Minneapolis: University of Minesotta Press.

Badiou, Alain. 2012. *The Rebirth of History: Times of Riots and Uprisings*. London: Verso.

Buchanan, Ian. 2008. *Deleuze and Guattari's* Anti-Oedipus: *A Reader's Guide*. London: Continuum.

Buchanan Ian. 2011. 'Desire and Ethics'. *Deleuze Studies* 5 (Supplement): 7–20.

Colebrook, Claire. 2006. *Deleuze: A Guide for the Perplexed*. London: Continuum.

Choat, Simon. 2009. 'Deleuze, Marx and the Politicisation of Philosophy'. *Deleuze Studies* 3 (Supplement): 8–27.

Conio, Andrew. 2012. 'The Ontogenesis of Language'. *Journal of Literary, Cultural and Language Studies* 3 (2012): 44–62.

Deleuze, Gilles. 1971. 'Cours Vincennes 16/11/1971 (Deleuze / Anti-Oedipe et Mille Plateaux)'. Trans. Daniel W Smith. Accessed July 19, 2013 from: http://www.webdeleuze.com/php/texte.php?cle=116&groupe=anti+oedipe+et+mille+plateaux&langue=2

Deleuze, Gilles. 1990. *The Logic of Sense*. Trans. Mark Lester. New York: Columbia Univeristy Press.

Deleuze, Gilles. 1995. *Negotiations 1972–1990*. Trans. Martin Joughin. New York: Columbia University Press.

Deleuze, Gilles. 2004. *Francis Bacon: The Logic of Sensation*. Trans. Daniel W Smith. Minneapolis: University of Minnesota Press.

Deleuze, Gilles and David Lapoujade. 2006. *Two Regimes of Madness: Texts and Interviews 1975–1995*. Los Angeles: Semiotext(e).

Deleuze, Gilles and Félix Guattari. 1987. *A Thousand Plateaus: Capitalism and Schizophrenia*. Trans. Brian Massumi. Minneapolis: University of Minnesota Press.

Deleuze, Gilles and Félix Guattari. 1994. *What Is Philosophy?*. Trans. Hugh Tomlinson, and Graham Burchell. New York: Columbia University Press.

Deleuze, Gilles and Claire Parnet. 2007. *Dialogues*. Trans. Hugh Tomlinson and Barbara Habberjam. New York: Columbia University Press.

Garo, Isabelle. 2008. 'Molecular Revolutions'. Trans. John Marks. In *Deleuze and Politics*. Ed. Ian Buchanan and Nicholas Thoburn. Edinburgh: Edinburgh University Press.

Goodchild, Philip. 1999. 'Money, Gift and Sacrifice: Thirteen Short Episodes in the Pricing of Thought'. *Angelaki* 4 (3): 25–39.

Goodchild, Philip. 2010. 'Philosophy as a Way of Life: Deleuze on Thinking and Money'. *SubStance* 39 (1): 24–37.

Goodchild, Philip. 2013. 'Exposing Mammon: Devotion to Money in a Market Society'. *Dialog* 52 (1): 47–57.

Graeber, David. 2012. *The History Of Debt: Slavery, Money, and the Crucial Role of Violence*. Accessed September 28, 2013 from: http://www.pubtheo.com/page.asp?PID=1745

Hallward, Peter. 2006. *Out of This World: Deleuze and the Philosophy of Creation*. London: Verso.

Holland, Eugene W. 1991. 'Deterritorializing "Deterritorialization": From the *Anti-Oedipus* to *A Thousand Plateaus*'. *SubStance* 20 (3): 55–65

Holland, Eugene W. 2013. *Deleuze and Guattari's* A Thousand Plateaus: *A Reader's Guide*. New York: Continuum.

Holland, Eugene W. 2013. 'Deleuze & Guattari and Minor Marxism'. *The Selected Works of Eugene W. Holland*. Accessed February 28, 2013 from: http://works.bepress.com/eugene_w_holland/3

Hardt, Michael, and Antonio Negri. 2000. *Empire*. Cambridge: Harvard Univeristy Press.

Harvey, David. 2012. *Rebel Cities: From the Right to the City to the Urban Revolution*. New York: Verso.

Kennedy, Margrit I and Stephanie Ehrenschwendner. 2012. *Occupy Money: Creating an Economy Where Everybody Wins*. Gabriola Island: New Society.

Lazzarato, Maurizio. 2011. *The Making of the Indebted Man: An Essay on the Neoliberal Condition*. Trans. Joshua David Jordan. New York: Semiotext(e).

Marzec, Robert. 2001. 'The War Machine and Capitalism: Notes Towards a Nomadology of the Imperceptible'. *Rhizomes* (3). Accessed April 25, 2015 from: http://www.rhizomes.net/issue3/marzec/marztitle.swf

O'Sullivan, Simon. 2009. 'The Strange Temporality of the Subject: Badiou and Deleuze between the Finite and the Infinite'. *Subjectivity* 27 (1): 155–71.

Patton, Paul. 2005. 'Deleuze and Democracy'. *Contemporary Political Theory* 4 (4): 400–413.

Patton, Paul. 2002. *Deleuze and the Political*. London: Routledge.

Roos, Jérôme E. 2013. 'Autonomy: An Idea Whose Time Has Come?'. *ROAR: Journal of the Radical Imagination* (June 23).

Shukaitis, Stevphan. 2010. 'Deleuze and (Which) Politics. Review of *Deleuze and Politics*. Eds. Nick Thoburn and Ian Buchanan'. *Culture Machine Reviews* (September).

Tampio, N. 2009. 'Assemblages and the Multitude: Deleuze, Hardt, Negri, and the Postmodern Left'. *European Journal of Political Theory* 8 (3): 383–400.

Thoburn, Nicholas. 2003. *Deleuze, Marx and Politics*. London: Routledge.

Virno, Paolo. 2003. *A Grammar of the Multitude: For an Analysis of Contemporary Forms of Life*. Cambridge: Semiotext(e).

Williams, James. 2003. *Gilles Deleuze's Difference and Repetition: A Critical Introduction and Guide*. Edinburgh: Edinburgh University Press.

Notes

1. The anthropological view of politics sees the institutions and structures of political life as contingent. And the premises and principles that underpin these are far from taken from given but the subject of enquiry and comparison.
2. All references unless cited otherwise are to papers in this volume.
3. Claire Colebrook, endorsement for Ian Buchanan's *Deleuze and Guattari's* Anti-Oedipus (2008).
4. Most obviously: *Deleuze and Political Activism* (2010) edited by Marcelo Svirsky; *Deleuze and Marx and Politics* (2003) by Nicholas Thoburn; *Deleuze and Politics* (2008) edited by Ian Buchanan and Nicholas Thoburn (2008); *Deleuze and the Social* (2006) edited by Martin Fuglsang and Bent Meier Sørensen; *Deleuze and Marx* (2009) edited by Jain Dhruv; as well as numerous titles by the Deleuzian entangled Phillip Goodchild.
5. As illustrated in Deleuze (2008).
6. See also Marzec (2001).
7. As Anne Pettifor points out: real wealth should be seen not in terms of the tangible stuff (homes, money land) but in terms of the intangible stuff the economic power that wealthy people are able to exercise by virtue of the fact they have got assets, those assets enable them to borrow and leverage their wealth at a rate that is unprecedented in human history. For example the Glazier brothers bought Manchester United using very little of their own money, they used borrowed money. They had some collateral but the real collateral was Manchester United football team itself, and its supporters and its streams of revenue. They were about to purchase a football club and make others pay for the debt, through buying tickets, televisions rights, tee-shirts. Those revenue streams are paying down the debt incurred by the Glazier families is an exact example of how the rich are further enriched by the enforced indebtedness of others. See *Boom Bust* (June 5, 2014), RT America. Accessed April 25, 2015 from: https://www.youtube.com/watch?v=1Yqalvi5jUM
8. The first coinage by the Lydian or Phrygian despots in the Greek colonies on the Aegean around 680 BC, probably for fiscal, military and political purposes rather than for trade; coinage only acquired a use in trading between cities in the following century in the main Greek trading ports, such as Athens. (Goodchild 2008: 28).

Chapter 1

On Anthropolitics: From Capitalism and Schizophrenia to Occupy and Beyond

GIUSEPPINA MECCHIA

The events related to the Occupy movements caught many by surprise: how often, especially but not only in the USA, have we seen people occupying the streets and parks of major Western cities, in the very strongholds of global capitalism, expressing a radical opposition to their most profound economic and social determinations? As the persuasion exerted by the capitalist way of life became more globally widespread, one might have despaired that such a mobilization could still be possible. Even more striking was the pointed eloquence of the demonstrators, who performed an impeccable analysis of the financial crisis that started in 2008 and chose to bring it forth in deeply significant public–private spaces. From Zuccotti Park in New York City, just a few blocks from Wall Street, to St Paul's Cathedral in London, a few hundred yards from the London Stock Exchange, students, long-time activists and newly minted militants decided to take their message to the streets. Leaving the message aside for a moment, the mere appearance of these crowds was worth pondering: how could the protesters have materialized, both physically and psychologically? How could it be that in an age when our mental abilities and physical resources seem to have been completely coopted by economic imperatives, so many of us could suddenly break the spell? In other words, how does the subject of politics emerge – if only from time to time – from the dejection of every day drudgery and delusion?

Nothing less than a social psycho-philosophy of the subject could start to account for such an event, and this is the direction that I will take in this chapter. In the following pages, I will argue that Gilles Deleuze and Félix Guattari left us with basic elements of an ethico-political stance that can best let us understand the political discourses and practices that saw in the Occupy movements their most recent instantiation. In particular, their common work on schizoanalysis will help me propose the concept of the *anthropos* as a dynamic, material figure of political subjectivity. Defined as the psychosocial subject of the schizoanalytic unconscious, such a figure can help us conceive not only capital's current grip on global forms of life, but also and most importantly the limits of such a hold and the spaces that can still be reclaimed for *anthropolitical* projects of liberation and affective redirection.

Before going any further, a few words about schizoanalysis are in order. While the limits of this chapter don't allow me to go into the more technical details of their presentation, let us remember that Deleuze and Guattari introduced the concept in *Anti-Oedipus* as a political response to some contemporary trends in psychoanalytic thought. We should remember how, in the early 1970s, Lacan's pessimism about the movements of May 1968 – when he famously claimed that the students were simply looking for another master – was becoming increasingly influential in intellectual circles, and was later promptly adopted in the reactionary atmosphere of the 1980s. The Lacanian unconscious cares little about history and political change: deeply rooted mechanisms of physical and mental dependency internal to the human physiology and familial structures remain constant, and beside stoic acceptance and analytic lucidity, little or no space is left for any serious questioning of one's determinations. Political revolt is largely presented as an ultimately insignificant smoke-screen, behind which an immutable tale of suffering and neurosis continues to unfold. To this pessimist narrative – always liable to become a socially conservative political stance – Deleuze and Guattari opposed a revised version of the Lacanian unconscious, at once less chronically despondent and more politically satisfying. In the chapter entitled 'A Materialist Psychiatry,' we read that contrary to Lacanian orthodoxy, the productions of desire are real, and are borne by the machinic investments expressed by constantly created bodies and minds:

> If desire produces, its product is real. If desire is productive, it can be productive only in the real world and can produce only

reality. Desire is the set of passive syntheses that engineer partial objects, flows and bodies, and that function as units of production. (Deleuze and Guattari 2009: 26)

The task of schizoanalysis is then progressively made clear: intervening in the 'passive syntheses' that constitute the 'partial objects' of desiring production, responding to the suffering caused by deadly investments in oppressive and stunting processes – be it familial entrapments, capitalist cooptation or statist bureaucracies – with an effort to follow decoded 'schizzes,' defined as the desiring chains working toward the 'continual detachments' (Deleuze and Guattari 2009: 39) of 'disjunctive' moves against pre-determined, ready-made individualized significations. Refusing the normative call to individualization and the injunction to name oneself as attached to a specific desire, those who follow the schizzes resist filling the space of the 'I' understood as the isolated subject of a reified identity:

> There are those who will maintain that the schizo is incapable of uttering the word I, and that we must restore his ability to pronounce this hallowed word. All of which the schizo sums up by saying: they're fucking me over again. (Deleuze and Guattari 2009: 23)

Deleuze and Guattari are careful to contextualize their rethinking of the psychoanalytic unconscious in relation to a critique of capitalism, through the different social mutations of private property and accumulation, since 'it is this form that produces the capitalist field of immanence, "the" capitalist, "the" worker … [and that] produces a vast conversion of this world by attributing to it the new form of an infinite subjective representation' (Deleuze and Guattari 2009: 303). Only by perceiving one's 'subjective representation' as the result of an oppressive, even deadly, assignation can one try to redirect one's energies in a less nefarious manner.

The Occupy movements, in this respect, were profoundly 'schizoanalytic': supported by non-proprietary and anonymous cultural forces such as Adbusters or Anonymous itself, and by individuals whose identities of workers/unemployed/students/producers became the asignifying numeric symbol of the 99%, the people involved in these actions were able to defy and physically contradict – at least for a time – the capitalist subsumption of their mental and social energies.

On Capitalist Crises and Insurrectional Responses

Although I intend to formulate a critique of the present with a focus on the Occupy movements, there is no better introduction to my main argument than a very old quotation taken from *A Thousand Plateaus*:

> Doubtless, the present situation is highly discouraging. We have watched the war machine grow stronger and stronger, as in a science fiction story; we have seen it assign as its objective a peace still more terrifying than fascist death; we have seen it maintain or instigate the most terrible of local wars as parts of itself; we have seen it set its sights on a new type of enemy, no longer another State, or even another regime, but the "unspecified enemy"... Yet the very conditions that make the State or the World War Machine possible, in other words, constant capital (resources and equipment) and human variable capital, continually recreate unexpected possibilities for counterattack, unforeseen initiatives determining revolutionary, popular, minority, mutant machines...the unassignable material Saboteur or human Deserter assuming the most diverse forms (Deleuze and Guattari 1987: 422).

The second installment of the diptych *Capitalism and Schizophrenia* was originally published in 1980, eight years after the publication of *Anti-Oedipus* and as a result of about ten years of cooperation between the two co-authors. It is, of course, very difficult to reconstruct with any accuracy the historical context of what they then called 'the present situation.' Nonetheless, the policies adopted by a number of Western powers in the late 1970s to counter internal and external threats were the source of the 'discouragement' felt by many activists at that time.

A few, certainly insufficient, reminders do in fact allow us to reconstruct some aspects of the book's present, in a highly interdependent international context: the escalation of the American–Russian conflict in Iran and Afghanistan at the end of Jimmy Carter's presidency in the US;

the brutal repression of socialist regimes in Central and South America throughout the 1970s, largely fomented by the US secret services; the internal repressive tactics adopted by Western countries to quell internal dissent, Italy being a particularly relevant case in point; the protection of Western-backed autocratic rulers in the Muslim world, from Mubarak in Egypt to Suharto in Indonesia; the cynical use of the Arabo–Israeli conflict to maintain a Western, capitalist bastion in the Middle East; the continuing intervention of the former colonial powers in the national politics of the African states. All of the above, of course, was occurring at terrible human costs, easily accepted in the name of the 'peace' that reigned in the hegemonic political and economic centers – no longer easily identifiable as 'states,' since the democratic institutions were already being deprived of their significance by global corporate interests – that could bring 'death' through 'local wars' to populations deemed unworthy of preservation. Whether those populations were dissenting minorities within specific states, or burgeoning democratic republics in certain key areas for global capitalist investment, the result was the same: an unrelenting pounding from the capitalist 'war machine.' The last years of the Cold War, in this respect, were particularly ferocious, and would continue to be so throughout the 1980s. The progressive realization that the so-called 'socialist' republics only reproduced capitalist economic imperatives, transferring them on a bureaucratic state apparatus, contributed to an intense feeling of impotence and pessimism.

I offer these blatantly inadequate historical pointers not so much to reconstruct what would have been the 'unique' context of *Thousand Plateaus*, but rather to underscore how the 'present situation' of capitalist hegemony is *always* 'discouraging' and potentially soul-crushing for its subjects. Indeed, equally dramatic lists could be offered when discussing many other historical 'conjunctures,' including our own, and none would appear much rosier. Still, *A Thousand Plateaus* also registered the specific fatigue felt by many activists after what was called 'the long 1968' in Italy, Germany and France (Félix Guattari being himself a particularly poignant case in point). There is certainly a shift in tone from the expansive, ebullient pages of *Anti-Oedipus*, which was written in the years between 1969 and 1972, when a more revolutionary tone and a certain kind of Marxist critique were still commonly heard in many different variations not only in France but in several Western European countries. By the time the first French edition of *A Thousand Plateaus* went to the presses, the repressive side of the Western 'state apparatuses' was back in full, self-congratulatory swing. When the two volumes of the diptych reached their Anglophone audiences – *Anti-Oedipus* in 1983 and *A Thousand Plateaus* in 1987 – their audiences were fully into the grips of the reactionary capitalist politics of the Thatcher–Reagan era and the last military flashes of the Cold War.

Not surprisingly, the 'present' geopolitical situation was once again quite bad. But even then, new forms of progressive political engagement saw the light of day – think about the environmentalist movements and the LBGT[1] mobilizations: clearly, there is no absolute, unique determination of subjectivity, but an infinitely modulated continuum of sociopsychological investments. While all of them are eventually captured by collective assemblages, the opportunity to orient one's libidinal investments along axes diverging from capital's command is implicit in the deterritorialized forms of existence that capital itself creates. Since the production of affect is intrinsic to any material assemblage, from molecular energy to the emotions of human beings, any structure of power rests on and at the same time is canceled by subjective investments that can move away from it through autonomous social redirections of affective investments, if only for a time. Such redirections were, as we have already seen, the very task of schizoanalysis, since its job is to 'discern, at the level of groups or individuals, the libidinal investments of the social field' (Deleuze and Guattari 2009: 350). The libidinal subject appearing at the crossing of these investments is the schizoanalytic subject that later in this chapter I call the *anthropos*.

It is essential to remember that neither Deleuze nor Guattari thought that any 'present situation,' however dire, was irrevocably and uniquely bound to the deadly consequences of capital's grip on power. On the contrary, it is precisely after this assessment that they remind us that both technology – 'constant capital'– and people – 'human variable capital' – always retain the potential to create minoritarian 'mutant machines' able to 'sabotage' and escape molar and molecular capitalist imperatives. But how can the schizoanalytic process operate such as shift, and go, so to speak, from 'discouragement' to 'counterattack,' from 'terrifying' to potentially 'revolutionary' situations? Is it possible to affirm, socially, psychologically and philosophically, that figures such as saboteurs, deserters, strikers and *occupiers* are indeed possible, even when they appear historically doomed, without resorting to the abstract and factually inadequate principles of liberal democracies, such as human equality and freedom of speech? In the rest of this essay, it will be my contention that yes, there is a way to think the immanent potentialities of the social subject, and that it may be present, more than anywhere else, precisely in the kind of thought that is present in *Capital and Schizophrenia*, and more specifically in the conceptual configuration of the schizoanalytic subject. It is this new 'anthropolitical' figure that I will try to delineate in the remainder of this paper, taking a little pre-emptive detour through the objections that have been raised against it.

One More Effort, If You Want to be Materialist!

After decades of controversies, it is inevitable that before articulating the outlines of what I consider to be the innovative conception of subjectivity that emerges from the combination of Deleuze's brand of materialist thought and the analytic, *practical* anthropology that he elaborated with Félix Guattari, I should address some of the objections that have been raised against its politics, because they are extremely useful to the articulation of the affirmative moments of my argument. I focus on the issue of materialism because the stakes of this appellation are still quite high when one wants to position one's critique within the Marxist legacy of the political critique of capital.

First of all, the highly interdisciplinary and somewhat unruly philosophical lexicon of *Capitalism and Schizophrenia*, with its concomitant revision and expansion of classically Marxist categories and fields of inquiry, certainly contributed to its muted political reception in many leftist academic circles, in France and abroad. Additionally, the unorthodox theoretical credentials of Félix Guattari, joined to what is considered a more 'bourgeois,' classical practice of philosophy on the part of Gilles Deleuze prior to their collaboration, have determined several thinkers to either completely ignore the books the two co-authored during the last twenty years of their lives, or to simply focus on the indictment of the political implications of Gilles Deleuze's own philosophy. Some, in fact, have done both; most notably Alain Badiou, more indirectly Jacques Rancière and more recently Peter Hallward. Since all of these thinkers are involved in revised continuations of the Marxist critical field, with its attendant claim to an immanence-based, material understanding of politics and subjectivity, a brief recapitulation of their positions is an essential first step in articulating the specificity of schizoanalysis, precisely because it has been so blatantly misrepresented by other self-defined leftist and post-Marxist philosophies.

I will not delve into the personal aspects of Badiou's *ressentiment* against Deleuze, that François Dosse details in his excellent double biography of Deleuze and Guattari, and Badiou himself acknowledged in his introduction to *Deleuze: The Clamor of Being* (1997). For the sake of this essay, we should simply remember that Badiou's critique of Deleuze's philosophy rests on two main theoretical objections: Deleuze's ontological grounding of the concept of difference in the Spinozian understanding of the modal, singular but infinite unfolding of substance, and his adherence to a stoic version of materialist metaphysics, which finds in matter itself the principle of its own evental appearance.

Without going into great detail, we can say that Badiou's main argument is that Deleuze is too much of a 'vitalist' to be really revolutionary, since a Stoic understanding of matter does not allow for absolute discontinuities, such as, for instance, political revolutions. As he says in his book, 'it remains impossible to subsume such change under the sign of Life, whether it is renamed Power, *élan* or Immanence. It is necessary to think discontinuity as such' (Badiou 2009: 362). According to Badiou, only a highly formalized understanding of multiplicity, rooted in mathematical representations such as set theory, accompanied by an equally formal representation of a Lacanian subject of absolute discontinuities – historically embodied in a recurring cast of characters, such as Saint Paul, Mallarmé, the Maoist Red Guards or indeed Badiou himself as faithful monument to May 1968 – can prevent us from sliding into an inherently conservative praise of Life as ahistorical, inherently conservative substance.

The most important and not-enough-discussed political consequence of this position is that for the Badiouan subject of truth, neither psychological nor bodily determinations are really necessary, since those pertain to life and not to the discontinuous event: what *somebody* will or will not be, will or will not do in a specific sociohistorical framework doesn't really enter Badiou's original field of argumentation. While in a recent essay he has acknowledged that any truth procedure is dependent on subjective supports that are 'spatial, temporal and anthropological' (Badiou 2010: 2) he does not consider them essential enough to actually talk about their psychosocial materiality. Even in *Logics of Worlds* (2006), when he recognizes that the theories exposed in *Being and Event* (1988) could not distinguish fascist processes of subjectivation from progressive ones, Badiou does not get involved in any analytic, conceptual assessment of specific 'subjects to truth.'[2] To be fair, Badiou does not really enter into issues of materialism as he rejects any critique coming from 'empiricist' positions, and his activist past does not prevent him from saying that 'communist is no longer an adjective qualifying a politics' (Badiou 2010: 3). But how can we not acknowledge that the very essence of the Occupy movements is in fact a 'communist' politics, both in theory and in practice? Clearly, Badiou's reliance on mathematical and monumental representations prevents his political philosophy from accounting for these historical occurrences, since such an account needs to broach issues of political economics and social critique, which are ultimately excluded from Badiou's thought, which in turn is entirely narrated through symbolic abstractions, such as 'Idea,' 'Humanity,' 'History,' the 'State,' and monumental subjects, such as Mao Tse-tung, Robespierre or Saint Paul, even as their lack of reality is constantly reaffirmed. The 'imaginary' nature of political subjectivation is affirmed in distinctly Lacanian terms, as if this were still the only valid model for unconscious mechanisms of subjectivation: this is precisely the crux of Deleuzian/Guattiarian schizo-analytic theory, and is one that Badiou never confronts.

While different in theoretical arguments and presuppositions, it becomes increasingly clear that there exists, in fact, a kind of continuity between Badiou's positions and those elaborated by Jacques Rancière, who, like Badiou, needed to distance himself from an Althusserian past that seemingly condemned the political subject to an eternal entrapment in ideological determinations. Rancière's first book, *Althusser's Lesson*, originally published in 1974, was an early indictment of Althusser's version of 'scientific Marxism,' which seemed to negate the possibility of political awareness for a subjectivity unmediated by a knowledge administered by didactical powers, such as a party or an academic discipline, be it economics or psychoanalysis.

In the following years, Rancière refreshingly demonstrated that, historically, things don't really happen that way, since the people always – although rarely – find a way to break through the ideological chains forced upon them. For Rancière, language does not inevitably push us in the domain of ideology or of the unconscious shackling of the Lacanian field, but is the privileged faculty allowing all antagonistic processes of political subjectivation. While the linguistic contents showered on us by power might seem overwhelming, the linguistic faculty per se remains a beacon of equality for all political subjects, no matter how socially degraded.

Rancière builds a precious archive of examples illustrating this basic principle, from the Roman plebs seceding on the Aventine Hill, to the French students reacting against university policies in the 1990s. Rancière's affirmative, non-apocalyptic version of the people's history is indeed a welcome contrarian voice in the midst of postmodernist political defeatism – one might think about Baudrillard's apocalyptic prophesies, or even Derrida's latest recourse to de- and then re-constructed ethical principles. However, as I have argued elsewhere, it is precisely the indiscriminate applicability of Rancière's principles that also makes them, so to speak, almost politically unusable in their tautological self-presentation. Badiou's recourse to logic and mathematics can be likened to Rancière's almost exclusive reliance on the faculty of language – both largely considered as an ahistorical *a priori* – for the founding of an egalitarian political project. The Aristotelian identification of language as the defining faculty of the human being, along with Aristotle's separate definition of man as 'political animal,' are powerfully bridged by Rancière, who establishes a poignant causal continuity between the two.

It is indeed surprising that two former students of Althusser, the powerful theorist of the *conjointure* as the historicist understanding of what Deleuze might have called a 'state of affairs,' should have spent the best part of their philosophical careers trying to distill the 'pure' principles – in the case of Rancière – or 'logical' presentations – in the case of Badiou – of an eternal figure of political subjectivity. Neither of them, it should be noted, is the least concerned with issues of political economics, political anthropology or social psychology. Even when Badiou talks of the exclusion of the Inuits from Quebec's electoral laws between 1918 and 1950, nothing is said of them, or by them: only logical schemes of 'relations' between them and the state are drawn in a way irrespective of whether they occurred or not (Badiou 2009: 307–24). Understandably wary of falling into the traps of determinism, both Badiou and Rancière stay away from temporal considerations altogether, condemning the bodily incarnations of political subjectivities – what Badiou calls 'incorporations' to an Idea – to theoretical irrelevance, keeping them only as the names attached to a monumental historical archive. It is not surprising, in this context, to hear Rancière ask, in the context of a 2009 colloquium about the rebirth of the 'communist' hypothesis in light of the financial crisis, 'with whom, with what subjective forces, can you imagine building this communism?' (Rancière 2010: 175). The reliance on the verb 'imagine' is very significant in this respect, since if Occupy showed us something it is that communist subjectivities don't need to be imagined externally: rather, they constitute themselves according to variable personal and historical circumstances, retraceable through and by a schizoanalysis of desire and realization.

The fact that Rancière still conceives of 'communism' as a project situated outside of its specific actuation – if only to negate it – tells us that there is a surprising lack of involvement, on his part, in the sociopsychological mechanisms that allow such actuations to occur. What is at stake in political insurrections is not the presupposed equality of all minds, but the workings of the bio-political unconscious, of the bodies struggling for the access to their own potential energies, of the brains polluted by cultural inanities and creating life spaces that eschew some of the most destructive determinations brought upon us by the current stage of cognitive capitalism.

Language is not an empty faculty, free to create any locution at any given time: our lexicon, and therefore our conceptual arsenal, both depend on the conditions of our cognitive experiences. While I praise and share Rancière's invaluable openness to the future of politics and his admirable refusal to assess historical postmodernity along apocalyptic lines, I consider his understanding of language dangerously detached from what Bateson once called 'the ecology of the mind,' that is, the environmental milieu that supports our brain function. Similar objections could be levied against the Italian philosopher Paolo Virno, who, like Rancière, seems to be too dependent on Aristotelian and formal linguistics to engage in a genuinely materialist critique of psychosocial structures and physical determinations.

Both Badiou and Rancière – and more recently Paolo Virno – have found an eager audience in British and North American academia. As a concrete and remarkable case of derivative theory, I will reference here Peter Hallward, a much younger, Canadian political philosopher, who is greatly indebted to both philosophers and shares several of their basic theoretical moves. Hallward, however, maintains a strong Leninist background that leads him to the formulation of a political 'voluntarism' even more radical than the apostolic 'fidelity' requested of the Badiouan 'subject of truth.' And like Badiou, he is staunchly anti-Deleuzian. His 2006 book, tellingly entitled *Out of This World: Deleuze and the Philosophy of Creation*, recasts and radicalizes Badiou's critique of Deleuzian politics, most notably in the methodological exclusion of the volumes co-authored with Félix Guattari and the accusation of Stoic, even aristocratic, detachment linked, once again, to a naturalistic vitalism considered incapable of formulating a political critique of contingent forms of power. Hallward proposes nothing less than a neo-Leninist vanguardist practice for the engaged intellectual, predicated on a strict – one might say ascetic – adherence to certain principles, or truths. This is almost paradoxical, since Hallward had already reproached both Deleuze and Guattari for formulating a 'non-specific' theory of singularity in his earlier text, *Absolutely Post-Colonial* (2001), while at the same time he himself was rejecting the inscription of the political subject in his or her own sociohistorical determinations. The political subject appears as process of relational 'de-specification,' always consciously embraced by a 'responsible' agent (Hallward 2002: 50). It is true that in his work on Haiti, Hallward devotes unrelenting attention to the economic, cultural and social specificities of that particular community; however, his inflexible, transcendental conception of political subjectivity puts him in a difficult double bind when thinking about issues of political agency. This is a difficulty that he shares most clearly with Badiou, but also, I would contend, with the kind of linguistic understanding present in Rancière's conception of equality and democracy.

My critique should not be interpreted as hostile: I do appreciate the fact that all of these thinkers remain steadfast in their opposition to present and past forms of capitalist and bureaucratic domination. However, I think that all of them, and maybe most notably Hallward, who explicitly declares his own inscription in Marxism–Leninism, need to operate an exceedingly difficult intellectual torsion in order to maintain their theoretical presuppositions. They all engage with but ultimately reject materialist empiricism – maybe the most concise definition of Deleuze and Guattari's thought – as viable foundation for political critique in general and for the description of the political subject in particular. To a certain extent, even the ultimate Marxist legacy, which remains the critique of political economy, is tossed to the side. Their 'political unconscious,' to quote Jameson, is entangled in the formal positions attributed to it by psychoanalytic and linguistic representation. Whether such representation is 'true' or 'false' is not, of course, what is at stake here. Rather, what needs to be questioned is the impossibility, for them, of theoretically accounting for the 'here' and 'now' of political constitution. What Deleuze and Guattari allow us to think is the materiality of such constitutions, in their transversal crossing of the striated spaces of social organization. It is in the 'empiricist' – or even Stoic – articulation of materiality and autonomy, of singularity and immanent collective connectivity that the most precious contribution of Deleuze – and Guattari – to political philosophy is to be found, as I will argue in the rest of this chapter. In the articulation of the schizoanalytic subject as anthropolitical agent we can find maybe the most faithful rendition of the occupier, a figure that is as material as it is complex, embedded in the deepest recesses of contemporary forms of subjective formation.

From Anthropological Abjection to Anthropolitical Autonomy

It is not by chance that I evoked Hallward's 2001 book on post-coloniality: in fact, powerful objections to the political content of Deleuze and Guattari's two volumes on capitalism and schizophrenia have also come from scholars deeply engaged in post-colonial studies, although others have readily embraced their understanding of singularity as a powerful antidote to theories of alterity. While Gayatri Spivak famously attacked both Deleuze and Foucault for what she considered their adherence to a non-examined model of Western authoritarian discourse – male, white and European – Chris Miller furthered this critique to denounce Deleuze and Guattari's very use of anthropological sources. For him, it was outrageous to see how these sources were often the work of researchers actively involved in colonial administrations, or at least always structured according to the anthropologist's own hegemonic cultural framework. In her essay, Spivak embraces Derrida's deconstructive project as a radical questioning of Western knowledge, and considers it the only political horizon for the self-aware Western intellectual. Miller, on the other hand, rejects the very possibility of combining archival research – anthropological or other – with any theoretical content, lest we reproduce the discursive domination of the Other in making him or her a simple 'case in point' for an abstracted, de-contextualized concept, such as 'nomadology' or 'the war machine.' Neither Spivak nor Miller considers the theory and practice of schizoanalysis worthy of mention, while I would argue that the white, male and European subject of thought is completely debunked by the transformation it incurs during the schizoanalytic process.

In fact, what is rejected without theoretical examination by these otherwise brilliant scholars is the very possibility that Deleuze and Guattari's conception of 'machinic,' 'desiring' subjects – fully articulated in their material constitutions but not ideologically pre-programmed by an external, univocal power (be it the state or capital) – might indeed be a *truthful* one, to be affirmed not according to an empty, Badiouan 'fidelity,' but as a powerful extension of Marxist political economy and Engel's attempts at a socialist anthropology. In this respect, only an examination of the basic tenets of schizoanalytic theory and practice can truly account for the desirability of Deleuzian-Guattarian political theory.

This is why the use of anthropological materials in *Capitalism and Schizophrenia* is to be understood as an effort to detach the construction of subjectivity from its current, hegemonic forms, all tied to capitalist de- and reterritorializations of subjective productions. Far from indulging in sentimental primitivism, Deleuze and Guattari repeat a typically Marxist gesture; that is, they construct a diversified, historical archive of economic and social subjects, organized around the two axes of space and time. This is in fact the mode that organizes the project of *Capital* as narration. Therefore, when Paul Patton says that Deleuze and Guattari engage in a neo-Marxist 'universal history' (Patton 2000: 88), it is important to introduce an essential modification: while Marx relegates the primitive mode of production to a historical past that conceives the modern capitalist mode of production as the inevitable *telos* of modern forms of progress, Deleuze and Guattari adopt a slightly different 'universal' perspective. For them, capital and the state apparatus are both present and absent in all societies, either as accepted realizations or, more importantly, as rejected virtualities.

In their treatment of primitive and despotic societies in *Anti-Oedipus*, and later in the separate but interconnected chapters of *Thousand Plateaus* devoted to nomadology and the war machine, segmentarity, and apparatuses of capture, they give us a way to conceive different world populations in their respective social inscriptions. What emerges from these pages, densely populated with more or less realistic characters, is a world crisscrossed by innumerable political striations, where nothing is truly impossible or, inversely, absolutely necessary. This is why not only history, but also anthropology, have been essential to the formulation of the political theses of *Capitalism and Schizophrenia*. Far from being 'primitivist,' the recourse to anthropology is essential in trying to assess the psychosocial constitution of today's collective becomings, such as those that prompted a people to occupy public spaces in the Occupy movements.

Of course, one has to be careful: we are not talking here of the structural anthropology of Levi-Strauss, which is still excessively dependent on an unrepresentable center – the incest taboo, for instance – for the subsequent representation of family and social segmentarity emanating from it, but rather an account mediated to Deleuze and Guattari by Pierre Clastres, a friend and contemporary of Félix Guattari and an assiduous participant in Deleuze's seminars at Vincennes in the mid-1970s. Before his premature death in 1978, Clastres had furthered in his fieldwork some of Marshall Sahlins' earlier discoveries: most notably, in *Stone Age Economics* (1972), the Marxist anthropologist had reported that many world populations were not frugal and stateless because of scarcity and political primitivism, but as a consequence of an explicit political decision, notably the unwillingness to engage in labor contracts and political representations. These were 'societies of abundance,' although they appeared destitute to 'bourgeois ethnocentrism' (Sahlins 1974: 3). Sahlin's arguments extended to politics: in these societies, the political sphere is often unrecognizable to us simply because the political function has not been reified by a bureaucratic apparatus, but has been retained by the social body itself.

Clastres pushed Sahlins' argument a step further: it is precisely because the primitive society refuses the alienation of power that it also prevents the accumulation of wealth on the part of one or several of its members. Some primitive societies, therefore, invest their psychosocial affects and productive energies in ways that are not pre- but anti-modern. They are, in sum, fully 'communist,' both economically and politically, even if such a definition can appear Western-centered and anachronistic. Furthermore, Clastres recognizes the very profound political motivation for the immense amount of technical and human effort that primitive societies devote to war. In many respects, war defines the community and, among other things, ensures one of the most common social axiomatics, the one that defines specific gender roles. Additionally, war allows the primitive subject to deal with death and other forms of natural and cultural exteriorities.

Against all odds and maybe counter-intuitively, it is through war that social subjects reaffirm themselves as 'free' and 'autonomous' within the bounds of their collective organization and biological determinations. Such an affirmation does not need to concern itself with the 'reality' of its claims: it just works, insofar as it ensures a certain kind of collective organization. Even more importantly, Clastres shows how the primitive socius was perfectly able to 'modulate' its own apparently rigid dichotomies, such as male/female, warrior/mother, and so on. In certain cases, he observed that some male subjects refused the ultra-masculine association with 'warrior societies,' adopting a more domestic, village-bound existence. Same-sex physical relations were also widely present, and were accommodated in different manners, allowing for 'men' to actually dress as women and share in their occupations.

In other words, far from being rigid, blind, limited, anti-statist, and anti-capitalist, communities were even able to decode their own segmentarity, and to allow some of the deterritorialized affective 'flows' traditionally associated with capitalist monetization. Their struggles against capitalist imperialism within the different national incarnation of the Western colonial project should not prevent us from recognizing that, as a self-declared Deleuzian Brazilian anthropologist recently said, 'the molecular dissemination of "subjective" agency throughout the universe, in testifying to the inexistence of a transcendent cosmological point of view, obviously correlates with the inexistence of a unifying political point of view' (Viveiros 2010: 48). In fact, already in the 1990s, the French anthropologist Marc Augé thought that anthropology could be reborn around the project of substituting multiplicity for otherness, starting to see how different subjective singularities could aggregate in different collective assemblages, producing 'an effective, lived contemporaneity' (Augé 1999: 53). This is why I believe that the anthropological subjects that allowed Deleuze and Guattari to formulate their theory of schizoanalysis were not simply a 'bad faith' version of the Western, capitalist *matrix*. The *anthropos* – neither man nor woman, rich nor poor, powerful nor subjugated – that constitutes this kind of collective organization is – at least as far as I can see – one of the most powerful practico-theoretical figures for our understanding of the emergence of the Occupy groups.

We should not romanticize what I call here *anthropolitical* thought: there is no individual freedom or desire, since if anthropology and social psychology tell us anything, it is that libidinal investments are always attributed to and captured by a 'body without organs,' the socius. The utopia of desire is not present in *Capitalism and Schizophrenia*, nor anywhere else in schizoanalytic thought: such a utopia is capital's ruse, which makes us believe that its own deterritorialized monetary flows are in fact synonymous with subjective 'freedom.' Deleuze's thoroughly Spinozist attentiveness to issues of rationality, knowledge and power, as well as his stoic sobriety, prevent him from ever landing into utopian territory. Guattari's awareness of the micro-politics of psychological and political collective investments also keeps him within an expanded Marxist framework of local and contingent struggles, to be fought in the affective re-directions of otherwise deadly global imperatives.

Occupy as Anthropolitical War Machine

The Italian autonomist activist and sociologist Franco 'Bifo' Berardi powerfully commented on the success that *Anti-Oedipus* had in the political organizations flourishing in Italy – and in other European countries, one might add – in the 1970s. This interest was reciprocal, and when Bifo escaped to Paris in 1977, chased by an arrest mandate, Deleuze and Guattari told him that they were very interested in the Autonomia movements, where '*Anti-Oedipus* had made an impact' (Berardi 2008: 145). It is well-known that practices such as the unauthorized occupation of public spaces, and other minor legal infractions such as squatting and even limited self-supportive theft – then called 'proletarian expropriation' – or the payment of a lower fee for a certain service – then called 'self-price reductions,'[3] were widely used in the Autonomia version of anti-capitalist politics.

Remarkably, the various movements tied to this kind of activism were also heavily invested in the establishment of deterritorialized modes of communication and affective networking: Bifo himself established the now famous Radio Alice on the newly liberalized radio frequencies, where one could hear both political discussions and children's fairy tales. Feminist groups, students, squatters and other subjects could use the radio facilities. The temporary nature of these non-institutional arrangements did not prevent them from playing a fundamental role in the nurturing and perpetuation of anti-capitalist thought and practice during otherwise very difficult years.

It is undeniable that Guattari's understanding of 'transversality,' as a practice able to cut through macro-political forms of social organization, and the consequent politicization of the schizoanalytic understanding of the unconscious, were possible within the context of an intense, international web of concrete political engagements. These groups are indeed re-enactments of the anthropologically excavated 'war machine,' as a subject of political and social struggle for autonomy and self-definition. It would be wrong, of course, to attribute to the war machine intrinsic terroristic, military or fascist determinations. The collective assemblages autonomously organized by the *anthropos* as psychosocial subject can be directed away from deadly forms of capture, and instead flourish as alternative life forms, against and in spite of bureaucratic and capitalist command.

Even during the 'dark years' of global capitalist triumph – mostly the 1980s and the 1990s – the dissident political subjectivities that had started their political engagements within the framework of autonomist redirections of Marxist anti-capitalist critique kept to their guns, theorizing, among other things, the advent of cognitive capital and 'immaterial' forms of command and the necessity of rethinking anthropological categories such as gender and even humanity. In other words, even as the military-bureaucratic state apparatus commanded by globalized capitalist organization extended its grip on present forms of life, it also brought with itself new morphologies of political engagement.

There is no doubt that we are the utterly embedded subjects of global capital. However, there is always the possibility for an affective and political redirection of our subjective investments. Today's *anthropos*, understood as the body carrying the constantly mutating unconscious, machinic investments theorized by schizoanalysis, can break through the capitalist axiomatic, and challenge, at least for a while, its political arrangements. Anthropological and sociopsychological considerations – the very stuff of schizoanalytic critique – are necessary if we want indeed to constitute collective environments that make such redirections possible. An understanding of political subjectivity fully engaged in the materiality of the minds and bodies actually living in a certain social milieu is necessary if we want to extract ourselves from formalist and ultimately extremely abstract definitions of the political subject.

Even more importantly, we have to understand that language, and the equality that it presupposes, is not independent from the brains that conceive it, each time anew. We are engaged in a struggle for concepts, for bodies: will we promote the global space of capital's domination, or will we 'occupy' it, exposing its exploitation and living against it? What the Occupy movements demonstrate, is that these occupational practices do indeed occur, and they do so because the affective investments of the *anthropos* are never fully exhausted by the powers encroaching on them. In fact, the anthropolitical thought of Deleuze and Guattari might, indeed, help us to keep cultivating the falsely 'primitive' reflex that refuses the instauration of inequality and exploitation that is the main form of the capitalist relation to the *anthropos* and to the earth. This is what Occupy was and is about, and in this respect, if *Capitalism and Schizophrenia* can indeed teach us anything, I deem it to be a good lesson.

Works Cited

Augé, Marc. 1999. *An Anthropology for Contemporaneous Worlds*. Stanford: Stanford University Press.

Badiou, Alain. 2009. *Logics of Worlds*. London: Continuum.

Badiou, Alain. 2010. 'The Idea of Communism'. In *The Idea of Communism*. Ed. Costas Douzinas and Slavoj Žižek. London: Verso: 1–14.

Berardi, Franco 'Bifo'. 2008. 'Interview with Giuseppina Mecchia, July 11 2005'. In *Félix Guattari: Thought, Friendship and Visionary Cartography*. London: Palgrave 2008: 141–68.

Clastres, Pierre. 1989. *Society Against the State: Essays in Political Anthropology*. Brooklyn: Zone Books.

Clastres, Pierre. 2010. *Archeology of Violence*. New York: Semiotext(e).

Deleuze Gilles and Guattari, Félix. 1987. *A Thousand Plateaus: Capitalism and Schizophrenia*. Minneapolis and London: University of Minnesota Press.

Deleuze Gilles and Guattari, Félix. 2009. *Anti-Oedipus: Capitalism and Schizophrenia*. London: Penguin Books.

Hallward, Peter. 2002. *Absolutely Post-Colonial: Writing Between the Singular and the Specific*. Manchester: Manchester University Press.

Hallward, Peter. 2006. *Out this World: Deleuze and the Philosophy of Creation*. London: Verso.Miller, Christopher L. 1993. 'The Post-Identitarian Predicament in the Footnotes of *A Thousand Plateaus*: Nomadology, Anthropology and Authority'. *Diacritics* 23 (3): 6–35.

Patton, Paul. 2000. *Deleuze and the Political*. London: Routledge.

Rancière, Jacques. 2010. 'Communists Without Communism?'. In *The Idea of Communism*. Ed. Costas Douzinas and Slavoj Žižek. London: Verso: 167–77.

Sahlins, Marshall. 1972. *Stone Age Economics*. Chicago: Aldine-Altherton.

Spivak, Gayatri. 1988. 'Can the Subaltern Speak?'. In *Marxism and the Interpretation of Culture*. Ed. Lawrence Grossberg and Cary Nelson. Urbana and Chicago: University of Illinois Press: 271–313.

Viveiros de Castro, Eduardo. 2010. 'The Untimely, Again'. Introduction to *Archeology of Violence*. Pierre Clastres. New York: Semiotext(e).

Virno, Paolo. 2002. *Quando il verbo si fa carne: Linguaggio e natura umana*. Torino: Bollati Boringhieri.

Notes

1. The acronym for Lesbian, Bisexual, Gay and Transgendered people did not exist at the time. However, it is in the late 1970s and in the 1980s – thanks in part to another crisis, the AIDS health emergency – that these groups entered the sociopolitical scene on the footsteps of the receding feminist wave.

2. Badiou seeks to follow a 'materialist dialectic' understood as 'the deployment of a critique of every critique' (Badiou 2009: 8). Even in this restricted sense, he says that the complexity of subjective operations 'was not even broached in the purely ontological treatment of *Being and Event*' (Badiou 2009: 8).

3. Respectively, *espropri proletari* and *autoriduzioni* in the original Italian.

Chapter 2

Semantic, Pragmatic, and Affective Enactment at OWS

JOHN PROTEVI

Housecleaning

The Occupy movement shows us how the semantic, pragmatic, and affective – meaning, action, and feeling – are intertwined in all collective practices. The intertwining of the semantic and the pragmatic – what we say and what we accomplish in that saying – has been a topic of interest in the humanities and the critical social sciences for almost 50 years, since its thematization by Austin and its codification in speech act theory; widespread interest in affect has been more recent, but the interplay of its twin roots in Tompkins and Deleuze – producing a sort of evo-neuro-Spinozism – has been usefully explored in *The Affect Theory Reader* (Gregg and Seigworth 2010). It's now time to bring speech act theory and affect theory together in understanding the role of political affect (Protevi 2009) in the Occupy movement.

To do that, we'll need some housecleaning. The first thing that needs to go is the concept of ideology. Deleuze and Guattari say in *A Thousand Plateaus*: 'Ideology is a most execrable concept concealing all of the effectively operating social machines' (Deleuze and Guattari 1987: 68). I take that to mean that we have to thematize political affect to understand 'effectively operating social machines.' From this perspective, the real 'German ideology' is that ideas are where it's at, rather than affect. It's political affect that 'makes men fight for their servitude as stubbornly as though it were their salvation.'

Why won't 'ideology' cut it? It doesn't work because it conceives of the problem in terms of 'false consciousness,' where that means 'wrong ideas,' and where 'ideas' are individual and personal mental states whose semantic content has an existential posit as its core, with emotional content founded on that core, so that the same object could receive different emotional content if you were in a different mood.[1]

Thus to take up the great OWS poster, 'Shit is fucked up and bullshit,' the core act posits the existence of shit, and then we express our emotional state by predicating 'fucked up and bullshit' of it, whereas we could have predicated 'great and wonderful' if we were in a different mood.

But that is 'execrable' for Deleuze and Guattari, because it's far too cognitivist and subjectivist.

It's too cognitivist because it founds emotion on a core existence-positing act, and too subjectivist by taking emotion to be an 'expression,' something individual that is pushed outward, something centrifugal. For them, emotion is centripetal rather than centrifugal, or even better, emotion is for them the subjectivation, the crystallization, of affect. Now Deleuze and Guattari do have a corporeal/Spinozist notion of affect involved with the encounter of bodies, but they also have what we could call a 'milieu,' or 'environmental' sense of affect. Here affect is 'in the air,' something like the mood of a party, which is not the mere aggregate of the subjective states of the party-goers. In this sense, affect is not emergent from pre-existing subjectivities; emotional subjectivities are crystallizations or residues of a collective affect.[2]

Enacting the Political

Having done away with 'ideology' as an analytical concept, we can turn to a simple, powerful talk by Judith Butler at OWS (Butler 2011a), which calls upon the classic 'very well then, we demand the impossible' trope, and ends with the wonderful line, 'we're standing here together, making democracy, enacting the phrase, "We the People".'

A longer talk by Butler in Venice (Butler 2011b) discusses constituting political space while acknowledging the material precarity of bodies, developed alongside a critical analysis of Arendt's notion of a political 'space of appearance.' The overall aim is set forth here, where Butler states, 'a different social ontology would have to start from the presumption that there is a shared condition of precarity that situates our political lives.'

A brief excerpt from the beginning of Butler's Venice talk sets out some of the main lines of thought that would go toward this 'different social ontology':

> assembly and speech reconfigure the materiality of public space, and produce, or reproduce, the public character of that material environment. And when crowds move outside the square, to the side street or the back alley, to the neighborhoods where streets are not yet paved, then something more happens. At such a moment, politics is no longer defined as the exclusive business of public sphere distinct from a private one, but it crosses that line again and again, bringing attention to the way that politics is already in the home, or on the street, or in the neighborhood, or indeed in those virtual spaces that are unbound by the architecture of the public square. (Butler 2011b)

But in the case of public assemblies, we see quite clearly not only that there is a struggle over what will be public space, but a struggle as well over those basic ways in which we are, as bodies, supported in the world – a struggle against disenfranchisement, effacement, and abandonment.

The role of the body in social ontology need not be limited to shared precarity, however, as important as that is to emphasize in order to break down notions of individuals as disembodied bundles of rights. We can also think the positive affective contribution of public assemblies. In this case, the city government of New York unwittingly helped OWS tap into the affective potential of collective 'bodies politic.' I'm talking here about the human microphone, which works, quite literally, to amplify the constitution of political space by assembled bodies.

The human microphone thus offers an entry into examining political affect in the enacting of the phrase 'We the People' at OWS. It shows us how direct democracy is enacted by producing an intermodal resonance among the semantic, pragmatic, and affective dimensions of collective action. It also shows how the production of contemporary neoliberal subjects (*homo economicus* as self-entrepreneur, as individual rational utility maximizer) is so successful and so pervasive as to be invisible. The city thought they were hurting OWS by banning bullhorns when in fact they helped them immensely by allowing the affect produced by entrained voices, a collective potential they could not grasp.[3]

Entrainment

For some time now I've been fascinated by William McNeill's *Keeping Together in Time: Dance and Drill in Human History* (1995). McNeill studies the political affect dimension of entrainment (the falling into the same rhythm) by collective bodily movement as in communal dance and military drill. The neuroscientist Scott Kelso has studied all sorts of small-scale examples of entrainment (toe-tapping and so on) by using dynamic systems modelling (Kelso 1995). A famous macro example of spontaneous entrainment is the Millennium Bridge episode in which the unconscious synchronization of walkers produced a resonance effect on the bridge that caused a dangerous lateral sway (Newland, no date). The developmental psychologist Colwyn Trevarthen has studied mother–infant inter-corporeal rhythms in terms of 'primary intersubjectivity' (Trevarthen 1979).

The upshot of this research is that humans fall into collective rhythms easily and that such collective rhythms produce an affective experience, a feeling of being together, an *eros* or *ecstasis* if you want to use classical terms, the characteristic joy of being together felt in collective action.[4]

So I wonder if the human microphone (Ristic 2011), an invention of the OWS assembly when NYC banned electric bullhorns, doesn't contribute a little to the joyful collective affect of OWS. (Needless to say, the prospect that the human microphone might aid in the production of such collective joy frightens the right-wing commenters (Dyer 2011)). It's not quite a choir, but it's a chorus, and so the bodies of the chanters (their chests, guts, throats, eardrums) would be vibrating at something close to the same frequency, something close to being in phase.

Now I'm not a reductionist; the semantic cannot be reduced to the corporeal; the message isn't dissolved into the medium. What interests me is how in the human microphone the message (enacting the phrase 'We the People') is resonant with and amplified by the medium (collective rhythm). In her Venice talk Butler analyzes the Tahrir Square chant translated as 'peacefully, peacefully' in these terms:

> Secondly, when up against violent attack or extreme threats, many people chanted the word 'silmiyya' which comes from the root verb (salima) which means to be safe and sound, unharmed, unimpaired, intact, safe, and secure; but also, to be unobjectionable, blameless, faultless; and yet also, to be certain, established, clearly proven. The term comes from the noun 'silm' which means 'peace' but also, interchangeably and significantly, 'the religion of Islam.' One variant of the term is 'Hubb as-silm' which is Arabic for 'pacifism.' Most usually, the chanting of 'Silmiyya' comes across as a gentle exhortation: 'peaceful, peaceful.' Although the revolution was for the most part non-violent, it was not necessarily led by a principled opposition to violence. Rather, the collective chant was a way of encouraging people to resist the mimetic pull of military aggression – and the aggression of the gangs – by keeping in mind the larger goal – radical democratic change. To be swept into a violent exchange of the moment was to lose the patience needed to realize the revolution. What interests me here is the chant, the way in which language worked not to incite an action, but to restrain one. A restraint in the name of an emerging community of equals whose primary way of doing politics would not be violence. (Butler 2011b)

This is an insightful, eloquent analysis of the pragmatics and semantics of the chant. So it's not to undercut it that I call attention to the material dimension of the resonating bodies that accompany the semantic content and pragmatic implications of this chant. It's to point to the way in which an analysis of material rhythms reveals the political affect of joyous collectivity, and the intermodal (semantic, pragmatic, affective) resonance such chanting produces.

Shame and Joy

Joy in entrained collective action is by no means a simple normative standard. There is fascist jy; the affect surging through the Nuremberg rallies, building upon and provoking even more feeling, was joyous. If there is to be any normativity in political affect it will have to be active joy rather than passive joy; active joy I understand as 'empowerment,' the ability to re-enact the joyous encounter in novel situations, or to put it in semi-California-speak, the ability to turn other people on to their ability to turn still others on to their ability to enact active joyous collective action, on and on in a horizontally radiating network, or, to use Deleuze and Guattari's term, a 'rhizome.'

Now political affect doesn't occur in a vacuum. It's not a matter of implanting a new feeling in any empty body; it's a matter of modulating an ongoing affective flow. So the joy of OWS has to convert a mood of shame.

What counts in the 'effectively operating social machine' demonizing welfare in the USA is the shame attached to receiving public aid without contributing to society with your tax dollars. It's shameful to have lost your job or your home; you're stupid, a loser to have been in a position to lose it, and you're a lazy, stupid loser if you haven't found another one, or if you never had one in the first place. You don't arrive at this American shame by aggregating individualized, subjectivized, packets of shame; you get shamed subjects as the crystallization of the collective affect of shame in the American air.

And so you don't combat this shame by trying to change individual people's ideas, one by one, with information about unemployment trends; you combat it by showing your face, by embodying your lack of shame, by putting a face on unemployment or homelessness. You counteract the existing collective affect by creating a positive affect of joyful solidarity. Shame isolates (you hide your face); joyful solidarity comes from people coming together. Its joy is released from the bondage of shame, to follow up on the Spinozist references.

What's especially heartbreaking, then, about the wearethe99percent.tumblr site, is that so many people still have some shame, as they only peek out from behind their messages. Hence the importance of the

Occupy meetings; shared physical presence, showing your whole face: these create the positive affect, the shamelessly joyful solidarity needed to fully overcome shame.

Fighting the residual shame, the half-faces of private pictures sent to a website: that's what makes the collective occupation of space so important: bodies together, faces revealed, joyously.[5]

So I'm going to propose that a full enactment of direct democracy means producing a body politic whose semantic ('we are the people, we are equal, free, and deserving of respect in our precarity and solidarity'), pragmatic (the act of respecting and supporting each other the assembly performs), and affective (the joy felt in collective action) registers resonate in spiralling, intermodal feedback.[6]

Works Cited

Butler, Judith. 2011a.'Judith Butler at Occupy Wall Street'. YouTube video. Accessed November 5, 2011 from: http://www.youtube.com/watch?v=JVpoOdz1AKQ

Butler, Judith. 2011b. 'Bodies in Alliance and the Politics of the Street'. European Institute for Progressive Cultural Policies. Accessed November, 5 2011 from: http://www.eipcp.net/transversal/1011/butler/en

Deleuze, Gilles and Guattari, Félix. 1987. *A Thousand Plateaus: Capitalism and Schizophrenia*. Trans. Brian Massumi. Minneapolis: University of Minnesota Press,.

Dyer, Jennifer, E. 2011. 'The Human Microphone Tactic: Scary or Just Moronic?'. *Theoptimisticconservative's Blog*. Accessed April 26, 2015: http://theoptimisticconservative.wordpress.com/2011/10/09/%E2%80%9Chuman-microphone%E2%80%9D-tactic-scary-or-just-moronic/

Gregg, Melissa and Gregory Seigworth (Eds.). 2010. *The Affect Theory Reader*. Durham: Duke University Press.

Kelso, JA Scott. 1995. *Dynamic Patterns: The Self-Organization of Brain and Behavior*. Cambridge: MIT Press.

McNeill, William. 1995. *Keeping Together in Time: Dance and Drill in Human History*. Cambridge: Harvard University Press.

Newland, David. No date. 'Vibration of the London Millennium Footbridge'. Accessed April 26, 2015 from: http://www2.eng.cam.ac.uk/~den/ICSV9_06.htm

Ostrom, Elinor. 2005. 'Policies that Crowd out Reciprocity and Collective Action'. In *Moral Sentiments and Material Interests: The Foundations of Cooperation in Economic Life*. Ed. Herbert Gintis, Samuel Bowles, Robert Boyd, and Ernst Fehr. Cambridge: MIT Press: 253–75.

Protevi, John. 2009. *Political Affect: Connecting the Social and the Somatic*. Minneapolis: University of Minnesota Press.

Protevi, John. 2010. 'Adding Deleuze to the Mix'. *Phenomenology and the Cognitive Sciences* 9 (3): 417–36.

Ristic, Igor. 2011. 'The Human Microphone #OccupiesWallStreet'. *Communicationblog.net*. Accessed November 5, 2011 from: http://igorristic.wordpress.com/2011/10/11/the-human-microphone-occupieswallstreet/

Trevarthen, Colwyn. 1979. 'Communication and Cooperation in Infancy: A Description of Primary Intersubjectivity'. In *Before Speech: The Beginning of Interpersonal Communication*. Ed. Margaret Bullows. Cambridge: Cambridge University Press.

Notes

1. There are many ways of relating cognition and emotion, without even bringing in the relations of this 'analytic' vocabulary with that of the Husserlian *noesis/noema* scheme. Still, I hope this will suffice just to get some traction on the problem.

2. When I was unemployed, some 15 years ago, for six months, I was often overcome with shame, no matter how often I reminded myself of the objective factors, the nonsensical nature of the affect, etc. But where did I pick up this shame? I can't see how it was transmitted to me by another actual instance of shame. You could say I had been socialized so that I carried a latent disposition to shame that became occurent in the right circumstances. But that's hardly less 'metaphysical' than an account of virtual or environmental collective affective with shamed selves crystallized out of that. I don't think we'll escape metaphysics that easily; there's a lot of potential versus actual metaphysics to be worked out there in the latent versus occurent disposition scheme, as I try to do in Protevi 2010.

3. Another topic for analysis would be the bike generators being set up at OWS. In another possible blunder, recalling that of the banning of bullhorns, the city confiscated gasoline generators prior to the late October snowstorm. The brilliant OWS response was to acquire bicycle generators. Will there be an analogous affective supplement from taking turns on the bikes to generate electricity?

4. We touch the question of emergence here, which is notoriously difficult, as it intersects methodological individualism. But that is not just a method of the social sciences. It's all too often the source of policy prescriptions, so that methodological individualism tends to slide into ontological individualism; as the quip goes, "methodology becomes metaphysics" (Ostrom 2005).

5. Faces are an extremely important factor in political affect. In analyzing OWS we'd have to consider the use of the Guy Fawkes/*V is for Vendetta* masks; 'faceless corporations'; and the 'faciality machine' in Deleuze and Guattari 1987.

6. Many thanks to *The New APPS Blog*, authors and commenters alike, for help with this essay.

Chapter 3

Pack of Leaders: Thinking Organization and Spontaneity with Deleuze and Guattari

Rodrigo Nunes

The issue of leadership is one of several overlaps that have been spotted between the thought of Deleuze and Guattari and the movements that arose in 2011 – a heady year that began in late 2010 with the English student movement, saw the emergence of the Arab Spring, Spain's 15M, the English riots, Occupy Wall Street, and continued into 2012 with Mexico's Yo Soy 132 movement, among others. Whether it is because of a debt to anarchism (Graeber 2011), because networking and web 2.0 are like second nature to most participants, or because their acute awareness of the crisis of representative politics spills over into distrust of any form of representation, these movements have tended to eschew leaders, spokespeople and fixed structures beyond open assemblies and working groups. In doing so, they have been widely perceived as subscribing to a logic that Deleuze and Guattari describe as *rhizomatic* (open, mutable, horizontal, spontaneously organized) as opposed to *arborescent* (closed, fixed, vertical, structured).

In what follows, I argue that this is not the whole picture. As much as a closer reading of Deleuze and Guattari makes any simple opposition between rhizomatic and arborescent more complex, a more attentive examination of these movements shows that they are not entirely free from phenomena of leadership and representation. This does not mean that they are at fault in any way, failing to meet some standard of openness and horizontality, or are somehow disingenuous. On the contrary, it is the idea of such a standard, or the notion that 'organization' and 'organizational form' necessarily denote hierarchies and vertical structures, that Deleuze and Guattari can help us put into question. Rather than disproving the overlap between their philosophy and these movements, then, we can actually discover a deeper, more complex connection that helps shed light on how these movements work and some ways in which they could transform their practice.

This essay's first two parts are dedicated to showing how phenomena of leadership, vanguard and representation manifest themselves in contemporary movements, arguing that these are not just 'residues' of a representative politics to be overcome, but an unavoidable aspect of politics itself. In particular, I will draw on Deleuze and Guattari's distinction between the *crowd* and the *pack* to argue that these movements, rather than leaderless, display what could be called *distributed leadership*. In the third, I will develop some consequences of this by showing how the relation between spontaneity and organization must be rendered complex, and how distributed leadership calls for thinking organization in terms of *complementarity*. In the last section, I argue that Deleuze and Guattari's concept of *becoming-imperceptible* offers a key with which to think the organizational and strategic tasks facing these movements today.

I. Synecdoche Wall Street

One of the reasons why movements like the Arab Spring, 15M and Occupy are seen as bypassing representation and leadership lies in their relation to mass organizations. For much of the nineteenth and twentieth centuries, mass organizations were a pillar of radical or progressive politics. Forming, maintaining and perfecting them were indispensable steps towards social transformation; their development was both a condition for, and the material substrate of, the historical movement of social transformation itself. Mass organizations were burgeoning class consciousness in externalized, materialized form; what gave that consciousness a visible face and a cadre that could spread it. Mass organizations were something like a collective memory device, whose very body registered its development: the tactics that worked, the mistakes that cost dearly, the victorious 'lines,' the individuals who had acquired greater experience and prestige. As such, they were indispensable to a collective learning process that proceeded towards ever greater unification: organization by trade leading to organizations uniting workers across trades, and then to a party through which the class could represent itself politically, in parliament and outside it.

By contrast, most important mass movements since the late 1990s have gone without – or even against – mass organizations, or involved them in minor roles. This is partly because of the historical crisis of left-wing parties and trade unions, and the broader crisis of representative politics. While the emancipatory movements of 'really existing socialism' became exploitative and oppressive regimes, parties and trade unions in countries where socialism did not 'win' not only manifested the same problems to variable degrees (authoritarianism, lack of accountability, bureaucratization), they often effectively worked to stymie social mobilization and radical demands. This process, already visible in the post-war welfare state and national liberation struggles, became more acute with the neoliberal restructuring from the late 1970s onwards.

This is where the crisis of representation in the left opens onto the crisis of representative politics in general, in response to which protesters around the world have risen in recent years. Most 'mature' democracies have effectively become two-party systems where both parties represent essentially the same interests, so that the key political antagonism today is between the *over*represented ('the 1%' with disproportionate economic and political clout) and the *under-* or *un*represented (everyone else, 'the 99%'). Whereas from the 1940s to the 1970s the welfare state was, in the global North at least, the gravitational center of politics, and the political system offered a more or less accurate representation of the two key opposing forces – capital and (stable, Fordist, industrial, unionized) labor – neoliberalism functions less as a point of equilibrium than as a naturalized, almost invisible background. As a result, the options on the table tend to be only slight variations on the same formula, tailored to cater for the small interest groups which, in a context of indifference generated by the lack of real options, decide whether an election goes this or that way. While no doubt far from the extremes of Egypt or Tunisia, even the 'best' Western democracies are mired in cronyism and elite rule. This is what has been dramatically laid bare by the crisis begun in 2008. It is hardly surprising that contemporary movements should bypass, even avoid mass organizations, when the parties and unions that historically represented the working class are equally implicated in the crises's causes and results, helping usher the 'bailouts' and 'austerity measures' with which governments have made populations pay the ransom exacted by finance.

This subjective rejection is, however, not a sufficient cause for how they have developed. We must add to it an objective condition, the widespread access to means of production and diffusion of information, of which the material substrate is above all the internet. It may be true that 'drums, fires, incendiary tracts, running down the backstreets, word-of-mouth, ringing bells' (Badiou 2011: 39) were 'for centuries' what mobilized masses of people; but just hurriedly dismissing 'Facebook and other such nonsense of alleged technical innovation' (Badiou 2011: 39) we risk missing the quantitative and qualitative differences that our technological conditions represent.

Quantitatively, they vastly increase both the potential reach of calls to action and the information on which they are based, as well as the speed of their spread across networks; not only do they generate more instant connections among a greater number of people, they create connections among people and groups that are distant from each other, to some extent transcending the requirement of physical proximity. Qualitatively, they create a continuous background of exchange of information, participation and collaboration beyond the limits of physical proximity (neighborhoods, workplaces, countries) and belonging (to a political organization, a movement, an ethnicity). Under certain special conditions, this can scale up in unpredictably big and fast ways, and move from the virtual environment into the 'real' world.[1] For that same reason, social technologies also provide a sort of continuous 'schooling' in networked organization, so that it appears as the 'natural' organizing logic for most people living in the landscape created by these technological transformations. Consequently, less open and flexible, less collaborative and participatory logics will tend to be seen with suspicion.

If we abstract too quickly from specifics in search of universal, transhistorical 'constants' we end up treating material media as indifferent and interchangeable, as if the internet and drums were just instruments to do the same thing, and our materialism becomes impoverished. However, we can find a first approach to questions of leadership in one of the eternal constants of uprisings identified by Badiou. As he puts it, 'however large a manifestation' or revolt, 'it is always hyper-minoritarian [*archi-minoritaire*],' (Badiou 2011: 90) composed of an 'acting and thinking minority' (Badiou 2011: 134) whose irruption makes a previously hidden social antagonism visible. In these conditions, 'the "deep country"[2] disappears and the spotlight is put on what could be called a *mass minority*' (Badiou 2011: 134; italics in the original). Badiou calls this phenomenon 'contraction': 'the situation is contracted into a sort of representation of itself, a metonymy of the overall situation' (Badiou 2011: 104). It is, in fact, a specific case of metonymy called *synecdoche*, the figure of speech in which a part stands for the whole.

Is *any* politics thinkable without synecdoche? Even in the direct democracy of a General Assembly is there not a split between those who speak and those who stay silent? Does not even the most immediate form of mass politics, the multitudinous expressiveness of street protest, create a cleavage between those who are there and those *in whose name* they are there? While concepts like 'emancipation' and 'revolution' obviously suggest ideas of people getting rid of representatives, taking charge etc., the only political process in which a part ('the most active,' 'the most conscious,' 'the most enraged', 'the most experienced') would not, at least temporarily, stand in for the whole ('the workers,' 'the poor,' 'the oppressed') would be one in which all concerned became equally active, conscious, enraged, experienced at the same time.[3] This, whether we like or it not, is at best improbable; despite the large numbers that have become mobilized across the world in recent years, it is certainly not the case with the movements we see now. As Jodi Dean (2011: 229; italics in the original) pointedly remarked, 'Occupy Wall Street is not *actually* the movement of the 99 percent of the population of the United States (or the world) against the top 1 percent. It is a movement mobilizing itself around an occupied Wall Street in the name of the 99 percent'. Inevitably, even non-representative politics involves a moment of representation. The difference is rather between a representation that strives towards its own overcoming (in non-representative) and towards its own stabilization (in representative politics).

There is, of course, nothing wrong with this: it is a necessary feature of political processes, whether in the slow work by which some organizers catalyze a collectivity's dissatisfaction into political action, or in the mass upheavals that divide and energize whole countries. Apparently, the absence of mass organizations, rather than eliminate this, multiplies it. Until not long ago, mass mobilization tended to be the preserve of mass organizations; initiative came from them, their backing was crucial for success. As the heyday of mass organizations receded, their numbers dwindled and their mobilizing capacity shrunk, we have seen more and more relatively small groups of people – lone individuals at the limit – take initiatives which, amplified by technological interconnectedness, may strike the right affective tone to connect with widely shared feelings, and offer relatively clear and feasible action points that masses of people can engage in, producing effects that far exceeded their original conditions. If it is possible to speak of a 'twilight of vanguardism' (Graeber 2004), it seems to be an ironic consequence of the proliferation, rather than the end, of vanguards – the dawn of *diffuse vanguards*.

II. The Crowd, the Pack, the Vanguard-Function

'Vanguard' was, particularly in the Marxist tradition, the name given to this synecdoche; a metaphor borrowed from military language, it indicated 'the most advanced detachment' in the struggle of the proletariat. In *The Communist Manifesto* (1848), Marx and Engels (2000: 255–6) presented communists as 'the most advanced and resolute section of the working-class parties of every country, that section which pushes forward all others,' while also having 'over the great mass of the proletariat the advantage of clearly understanding the line of march, the conditions, and ultimate general results of the proletarian movement.' We can see how this fits in the narrative about class-consciousness and mass organizations laid out above. Even if it is the capitalistic development of productive forces that creates a politically conscious proletariat (by creating consciousness of material conditions), the process does not take place all at once and in uniform manner; it is driven by a fraction of the proletariat that becomes increasingly purposive, active and experienced, and whose job it is to share that purposiveness, activity and experience with others. 'Vanguard' thus refers to *two* synecdoches, one contained in the other. Internally to a movement or political process, there is one part ('communists') that shows others the way ('other working-class parties'); yet this movement or process, taken as a whole, expands by attracting those around it ('the great mass of the proletariat' and fractions of other classes).

While retaining these two different moments, 'vanguard' is used here in a way that differs from the orthodox Marxist idea in a crucial aspect. So as to get to this difference, let us first go through Deleuze and Guattari's analysis of two different logics of group function – identified, following Elias Canetti, as the *crowd* and the *pack*.[4]

The crowd is characterized by 'large quantity, the divisibility and equality of number, concentration … unitary hierarchical direction, the organisation of territoriality or territorialisation'; the pack, in turn, by 'small or restricted numbers, dispersion … qualitative metamorphoses, inequalities as remainders or thresholds, the impossibility of a fixed totalisation or hierarchisation, the Brownian variation of directions, the lines of deterritorialisation' (Deleuze and Guattari 2004: 46).[5] The distinction between the two is projected directly onto that between the arborescent and the rhizomatic – and, as with the latter,

> '[t]he point is not to oppose the two types of multiplicities (…) according to a dualism that would not be worth more than that of One and multiple. There are only multiplicities of multiplicities that constitute a single *assemblage*, that operate in the same *assemblage*: packs in crowds, and vice-versa. Trees have rhizomatic lines, but the rhizome has points of arborescence.' (Deleuze and Guattari 2004: 47; italics in the original).

In other words, these are oppositions *in thought* that *in reality* only ever occur in a mixed state (Deleuze and Guattari 2004: 593). They indicate two *tendencies* present in every assemblage, and two *frames of reference* according which to analyse them, depending on whether we look at them from the point of view of already given differences (and identities) or 'understand [them] in intensity' (Deleuze and Guattari 2004: 44). And while Deleuze and Guattari (2004: 31) oppose the arborescent and the rhizomatic 'not as two models,' but as something 'acting as a model … even if it produces its own flights,' and something 'acting as an immanent process that upsets the model … even if it produces its own hierarchies,' it is better to stress the processual nature of both. The model is not imposed from the outside without being immanently produced: the pack can become a crowd the moment it starts holding up a model of itself and defining itself according to a group identity, a bivalent logic of belonging/not belonging, identification with a leader etc. Still, it remains affected by what pulls it in different directions and partially upsets arborescence with new rhizomatic processes. However fixed a territory, it is 'inseparable from vectors of deterritorialisation that work it from the inside,' (Deleuze and Guattari 2004: 635) and so it is always possible that arborescence be reverted and what is (mostly) crowd develop back into (mostly) pack.

The question of how leadership functions in the pack and the crowd helps us clarify how the word 'vanguard' can apply to phenomena like Occupy and the Arab Spring. Confounding schematic oppositions between hierarchy and non-hierarchy, vertical and horizontal structures, Deleuze and Guattari speak of 'equality' in relation to the crowd and 'inequalities' in relation to the pack, and of leaders in relation to both. There is equality in the crowd in the sense that all places are assigned, and everyone (apart from leaders) is the same before the group; there is inequality in the pack to the extent that there are no fixed roles or places, rather constant movement as the pack itself changes direction in Brownian (that is, random) motion.

In this sense, even if the pack and the crowd 'at times oppose each other and at times interpenetrate,' (Deleuze and Guattari 2004: 46) it can also be said that the pack is the truth behind the crowd, or the ground zero of group behavior. Not because it is an 'elementary anarchism' repressed by social organization, or a primordial formlessness behind form, or an originary evolutionary state, but because social organization and institutionalization is what selects and stabilizes *some* ways of organizing, *some* forms, which the pack instead is constantly producing and destabilizing. At the limit, the whole of society, to the extent that it is open to deterritorialization, is virtually a pack, however much it may be actually segmentarized as a crowd.

This allows us to draw a distinction between the objective, teleological understanding of a vanguard whose sway over the Marxist tradition helped engender the pathology of vanguardism, and what can be called the vanguard-*function*. The latter is what Deleuze and Guattari (2004:

298) call the 'cutting edge of deterritorialisation' of a situation or grouping – that part which, having started to function in a different way, opens a new direction that, after it has communicated to others, can become something to follow, divert, resist (or 'imitate', 'oppose' and 'adapt', as per Gabriel Tarde's three social laws).[6] The vanguard-function is objective in the sense that, once the change it introduces has propagated, it can be identified as the anomalous cause behind a growing number of effects. Yet it is not objective in the traditional Marxist sense of a deterministic or transitive relation between an objectively defined position (class, class sector etc.) and the occurrence of a subjective political breakthrough (event), itself underpinned by a conception of history as following necessary laws. Where a process starts, which direction it takes, who 'steers' or 'diverts' it, what is its course – these can be determined retrospectively, but never in advance. While it is no doubt possible to hazard more or less educated guesses (depending on how well one can read the symptoms announcing potential events), there are no laws behind this. It is only in this objective but non-transitive sense that the Arab Spring, 15M, Occupy etc. can be called 'vanguards.'

We can now extend this concept beyond the synecdoche between these movements and the rest of society to its second moment, the vanguard (or vanguards) *within* the vanguard. What changes the pack's course is an animal pulling the group in one direction and the rest suddenly following it, changing the group's shape and structure as they do. It is not the case that the pack is leaderless, then, but the opposite: every member is a potential leader. And this, rather than an ideal of horizontality that would amount to no less than absolute equality, is what best defines the way in which the movements of the last few years organize. *Distributed leadership*, not assemblies or horizontality, is their defining trait.[7] If the pack is the degree zero of collectivity, and distributed leadership is the kind of organization proper to it, we can conclude that distributed leadership is the degree zero of organization. That would no doubt be true; at the same time, it is important that we appreciate the extent to which contemporary communication technology expands the potential for it.

When crowd and pack are contrasted according to large and small numbers, as Deleuze and Guattari do, this should be understood less in terms of an actual numerical limit (the pack is non-denumerable and defined by intensive relations, and, as we know from recent experience, can be very large indeed) than as referring to a problem of *scalability*: the greater the number, the harder it is for the pack not to become a mass. The consequence here is the same as that of stressing the interpenetration and processual nature of crowd and pack: notions like 'verticality' and 'horizontality' cease to be substantialized, or treated as properties that necessarily adhere to certain substances or organizational forms ('the party', 'the multitude'), and are instead regarded as vectors, virtual tendencies that it may be necessary to foster or check in a given situation. Now, the problem of scalability applies to direct democracy much more stringently than it does to distributed leadership, especially in the present conditions: there is a limit to how far an assembly can be scaled up without either ceasing to be functional or ceasing to be an assembly. From before they hit the streets until now, the movements of the last few years have effectively moved like packs, with small groups (even individuals) starting initiatives that would snowball into much larger effects. Therefore, not only can they be collectively described as parts functioning as vanguards in relation to the whole of society, their very development is characterized by different groups, occasionally even individuals, occupying vanguard-functions at different points, breaking through inertia and impasses on how to move forward. This is why the twilight of vanguardism is not the same as the end of vanguards but, on the contrary, a result of their proliferation: the more there are potential occupiers of the vanguard-function, the harder it becomes for a single vanguard to become stabilized.

The point about the pack being the ground zero of social organization can be taken further still. If the way group formations move *at the most elementary level*, even when under control 'from above,'[8] is through distributed leadership, it follows that *absolute* horizontality – a completely level playing field, a strictly leaderless situation – is impossible: 'There is no going back, there is no anarchism' (Guattari 2006: 196). There is no situation in which phenomena of distributed leadership do not occur, essentially because there is no situation in which deterritorialization does not occur, and pack leaders or vanguard-functions are no more than vectors of deterritorialization. Does this then mean that the demand for 'real democracy' can never be realized? Certainly not in the sense of a fully stable final state of perfection. 'Real democracy' is ultimately no more than the endless work of unmaking and bypassing the stratifications that create imperfection, as much as allowing other, more useful stratifications to develop (while trying to keep some of their dangerous tendencies in check). There is only *less* or *more* democracy, not *full* democracy (or equality, or horizontality), and embracing imperfection as *necessary* – which need not, but can no doubt also work as an excuse for defeatist pragmatism – is at the same time a pre-requisite for clarity regarding the goals of struggle, and a realistic appraisal of existing practice.

At the same time, while distributed leadership is no definitive guarantee against arborescence, it is not undemocratic either (unless, that is, democracy is understood in absolute terms). Its very principle is that 'vanguards' can in principle emerge from anywhere, and the more connected and mobilized a movement is, the more likely this is to happen. It is true, of course, that the more connections or prestige a group or individual have, the more likely they are to be noticed. However, to speak of a vanguard-function is to say that something *leads* to the extent that it is *followed*: it 'works' when it 'works,' and does not work when it does not, in ways that may even damage its power to 'work' in the future. As Deleuze and Guattari (2004: 46) put it: 'The leader of the pack or the gang plays move by move, must wager everything in every hand, whereas the group or crowd leader consolidates or capitalizes on past gains.' Therefore, while it precludes the possibility of a perfectly level playing field, distributed leadership leaves the field open to difference, making the rise and wane of different 'vanguards' possible.

III. Becoming, Spontaneous and Organized

What an examination of the pack suggests is a complication of the usual opposition between leadership and spontaneity: the pack's 'spontaneous' movement results from its following one or more individuals that come temporarily to occupy a vanguard-function.[9] Besides, this function both occupies a singular point and progressively propagates across the whole, so that 'vanguard' can be said of an action's originator, but also of the first to follow it, those who join in subsequently, and so on. At the same time, the occasional 'leader of the pack' is said to be a vector of deterritorialization, itself following a movement that was already present at least in potential, a 'creator' or 'originator' only in being the first to grasp it. In order to better understand this, it is worth taking the time to unpack what Deleuze and Guattari mean by 'events,' the generic term that they ascribe to such 'spontaneous' changes in direction.

Events have a complicated structure. The same event happens on different levels and, in a way, more than once; it is at once a discontinuity concentrated on a point and a continuous process, an 'eventing' that happens over time. To begin with, for any event there will be several layers of causality at play; these will be, for example, a series of long-held grievances, a history of collective frustrations and personal humiliations, etc. At this point, however, those under the effect of these causes will still be operating within a pre-defined space of possibilities that constrains what reactions are imaginable: the situation itself cannot be overcome, although there may be individual routes of negotiating it (small acts of transgression, escapist compensation, episodes of 'acting out,' opportunistic collaboration, etc.). Something boils under the surface, but there is no way it could emerge; acting on it does not even appear as a possibility yet. Then, however, a new cause may act as a catalyst, focusing the existing layers of causality on a point, and a virtual threshold is crossed – new dispositions and potentials emerge, accompanied by a transformation in sensibility: the situation is now perceived as intolerable. In a sense, the event has already happened; the field of possibilities expands, and even rational calculations change – just yesterday you were wondering how long you could extend a cigarette break, now you are asking yourself how to organize a walk out.

The event is a rupture, firstly, because it is an excess over its causes, a break with linearity, 'a bifurcation, a deviation in regard to laws, an unstable state' (Deleuze and Guattari 2003: 215). It is unpredictable in advance and only appears as possible after the fact: 'as much as one can and must assign in the causal series the objective factors that made such a rupture possible … only what belongs to the order of desire and its irruption can account for the reality that [this rupture of causality] acquires at that moment, in that place' (Deleuze and Guattari 2005: 453). Secondly, it creates new possibilities, which in a sense makes it a necessary given for what comes afterwards: 'an event can be countered, repressed, recuperated, betrayed, it nonetheless ... cannot be surpassed: it is an opening of possibles' (Deleuze and Guattari 2005: 453).

This is the event as 'pure becoming,' a virtual transformation abstracted or subtracted from actual states; but the event is not just a pure becoming, it is also a becoming *something else*. A 'virtual mutation' must be followed by an 'actualising mutation' (Zourabichvli 2000: 344), which is the means through which a shift in sensibility is given a form: new words, acts, behaviors, the actual and perceptible inscription of a virtual and sensible change in bodies and assemblages. It is through them that the event *actually* takes place, transforming the world around it, and is *communicated*. It may be that only a few have crossed the threshold, but once they change, that change can be shared.

This is how the event, which has already happened once in a virtual mutation and twice in the creation of new individuations, can happen many more times as it spreads. But this means that 'spontaneity' is not, as is often thought, the absence of any form; on the contrary, the event's actualizing side is precisely the passage from *formlessness* to (new) *form*. Gilbert Simondon (2005: 549), whose philosophy of individuation profoundly influenced Deleuze, draws an explicit comparison between a metastable state of 'supersaturation,' in which 'an event is ready to take place, or a structure ready to emerge,' and a 'pre-revolutionary' one: 'all it takes is for a structural germ [*germe structural*] to appear.' An actualizing mutation (a perceptible change in behavior, practices, relations) is such a 'structural germ': a new form that spreads across a field that is ripe for the event – even if, while the event is still 'eventing,' not exhausted in its potential, this new form is far from fixed, and rather than being a model to be consciously imitated or rejected, it is communicated and propagates through changes in sensibility.[10] Here we see the correlation between event and subject: it is 'when history tips over into meaninglessness,' literally 'breaks the norm' and creates something new, 'that the subject comes onto the scene, bringing everything into doubt and producing a new utterance, an operation of the signifier as expression of a meaning, a possible split in a given order, a breach, a revolution, a cry for radical reorientation' (Guattari 1984: 175). Yet this subject is not an autonomous, sovereign agent, but the way in which the event expresses itself. It exists to the extent that it affirms the event, as much as the event exists only because it expresses itself in this subject. '[T]he event creates a new existence, it produces a new subjectivity' (Deleuze and Guattari 2003: 216), but not as a cause external to its effects; it is *in producing such transformations* that the event 'events.' The subject is therefore what constitutes itself around the feeling that a rupture has taken place ('it cannot go on like before'), and must respond to the event by 'forming new collective assemblages that correspond to the new subjectivity' (Deleuze and Guattari 2003: 216).

Thus, if we still speak of spontaneity – a discontinuity, an excess over causes, a break with existing constraints and the previously mapped space of possibilities – it is neither as a free creation nor as an absence of form. The event expresses an expansion of freedom and contingency, not an elimination of all constraints, and is inseparable from the 'structural germs' that, in giving it viable forms, actualize it.[11] We can therefore see why there is no contradiction in speaking of spontaneity and distributed leadership. In fact, we can easily track the emergence of recent movements by observing how a few spontaneously created forms, in propagating across networks, brought those very movements into existence: the protests in Sidi Bouzid around Mohamed Bouazizi's suicide mushrooming into protests across Tunisia, as the first cries of 'Step down, Ben Ali' were heard; the camps that spread from Tahrir Square to the Maghreb and Mashreq, then to Spain, Israel, the US and around the world; the original Adbusters 'Occupy Wall Street' meme, 'taken seriously' by activists who started organizing around the idea, until its replication across the US.

What these examples also show is that, even if there is a sense in which the event is a rupture 'out of the blue, … in its becoming, it escapes history' (Deleuze and Negri 2007: 231), there is nothing magical or ethereal about it. On the contrary, it demands work; to say that propagation happens at a virtual or sensible level does not make its conditions any less material. The examples above make it evident that the various 'vanguards' (several of them for each movement) had to spend a fair amount of time honing their messages, building alliances, creating the necessary channels and platforms (face-to-face meetings, Facebook pages, websites, Twitter and Youtube accounts etc.), organizing protests, producing and circulating videos, images, texts, memes.[12] There is a much more complex interplay between 'spontaneity' and 'organization' than a simple opposition between the two would allow. On the one hand, the tactics that succeeded in producing large-scale outbursts generally did so because they were sufficiently open-ended, inclusive and adaptable to allow people to become involved in their own terms and through progressive steps, rather than having to conform to a predefined activist style and identity overnight. Some have described this as 'open code activism' in comparison to open code software.[13] On the other hand, if it were not for a backbone of committed activists working from the early days, many of which had years of political experience behind them and belonged to pre-existing groups and networks, these movements would not have turned out the way they did. The fantasy of thousands of entirely unconnected individuals magically turning up at the same place at the same time is simply a myth; the reality is closer to a continuous 'eventing' in which small 'vanguards' slowly built up (and others no doubt withered), until the event irrupted in full force on the streets. A series of small, ever growing synecdoches, leading to that sudden, exponentially larger synecdoche that Badiou calls 'contraction'.

If we understand spontaneity as formlessness, it is easy to slip into imagining organization as its total opposite – the fixation of a rigid form, the party. It is certainly common that unreconstructed Leninists 'pay lip service to a certain right to spontaneity in a first moment' (Deleuze 2004: 278), but only as 'a transitional manifestation that must be left behind for a "superior" phase, marked by the setting-up of centralist organisations' (Guattari 1984c: 66). But the problem also works the other way round: a paranoid fear of organization, too sharp a distinction between the 'good', 'spontaneous' moment (which 'belonged to everyone') and the 'bad', 'transcendent' one (in which 'some people tried to take control') can block the way to necessary new creations. Understanding spontaneity as the creation and propagation of new form, on the other hand, poses a different set of problems than any binary choice between *either* spontaneity or organization: what forms to propose, what forms to select, which forms to connect to.

There are, of course, many steps between selecting some incipient forms that manifest themselves in actions, conducts, discourses etc., and developing organizational consistency (more clearly defined responsibilities, structures and criteria of membership, more permanent participation etc.). But the point is, first, that 'organization' should be understood as a continuum that stretches between those two things and, second, that it will always be a matter of choosing how to manage tendencies towards openness or horizontality, closure or verticalization.[14] The 'formlessness *or* party' option not only posits organization as synonymous with a radical discontinuity, it assumes organizational unification as a self-evident value, or the *telos* towards which organization should tend. Thinking in terms of distributed leadership, on the other hand, suggests that a movement choosing a course of action (which is necessary) does not entail choosing a *single* course of action (which is not). If different initiatives spring up that are not defined by mutually exclusive group identities, but coalesce around complementary strategic and organizing wagers (fighting foreclosures, debt, austerity measures etc.), divisions appear as the means to better pursue different but convergent goals, rather than as splitting a presumed common goal several ways.[15] A political process is then more like an ecosystem than an army, even if ideally it should also be capable of functioning as an army when necessary. It is possible to advance without advancing as a single column, as long as the forms created adequately respond to real tendencies or potentials, possess the organizational consistency required by the tasks they pose themselves, and remain open and responsive to their, continuously recalibrating strategy and tactics, and avoiding bad forms of stratification.

IV. Becoming-Anonymous, Becoming-Imperceptible

As we have seen, an event 'events' if it is actualized into something new; 'without history, experimentation would remain indeterminate, unconditioned' (Deleuze and Negri 2007: 229). If nothing is done to actualize existing potentials into new forms, they could simply be incorporated into the existing situation (opportunism, identitarianism), or be displaced into much worse forms (what Deleuze and Guattari call 'black holes': fascism, terrorism, suicide, etc.). To avoid decisions, and the divisions they bring, in the name of an indefinite potential or diversity to be preserved at all costs, is therefore not an option. In fact, remaining steadfastly against any actuality often belies an implicit reliance on teleology

– something we should be all the warier of if we abandon the orthodox Marxist's *explicit* reliance on the notion of a historical development governed by necessary laws. The notion that strategic initiatives or new forms should be rejected because 'the process,' left to its own devices, will produce the right solutions is not only paradoxical – 'the process' is treated as something separate from the individuals that constitute it, and having the power to arrive at solutions without any of its participants actually proposing any – but also premised on some kind of teleological necessity.[16] As Deleuze and Guattari remind us, it is necessary to create 'collective assemblages' that can give a body to the event, and we shirk that challenge at our own peril. The wager that defines their political thought, perfectly summarized by Guattari in 1973, is that we can hope for nothing else than a continuous effort to keep in balance the two fundamental – and fundamentally contradictory – demands of revolutionary struggle.

> 'These two struggles *need not be mutually exclusive*:
> The class struggle, the revolutionary struggle for liberation, involves the existence of war machines capable of standing up to the forces of oppression, which means *operating with a degree of centralism*, with *at least a minimum of coordination*.
> The struggle in relation to desire requires collective agencies to produce a continually ongoing analysis, and *the subversion of every form of power*, at every level.' (Guattari 1984: 62; my italics)

Against the usual misconception that sees them as unwavering partisans of openness against closure, diversity over unity, spontaneity over purposive organization, rhizome over arborescence, deterritorialization over reterritorialization, the point for Deleuze and Guattari is rather that, even if the poles in each pair *tend* to be conceived as mutually exclusive, this *need not* and *should not* be the case.[17] Rather than simply invert the choice historically made by Marxism–Leninism (for closure, unity, purposive organization, arborescence, reterritorialization), the challenge is to invent forms capable of maintaining the two poles in *maximal tension*: the most openness with the most closure, the greatest unity with the greatest diversity, and so on.[18] 'The good form,' as Simondon (2005: 543;

italics in the original) describes it, '*approaches paradox without becoming a paradox, contradiction without becoming a contradiction.*' It is not stable (cancelling out potentials), but metastable (capable of retaining the most tension). It is therefore not a matter of finding a stable 'golden mean' – as a recipe that could be transposed to any set of conditions – but of a constant readjustment under every new situation so as to prevent either pole from taking over. 'As long as we see ourselves as having to choose between *either* the impotent spontaneism of the masses *or* the bureaucratic and hierarchical encoding of a party organization,' says Guattari (1984: 230–1; italics in the original), 'all "liberation movements" of desire will find themselves taken over, or encircled and marginalized.'[19] Or, as Deleuze (2004: 279) summarizes it: 'It is evident that a revolutionary machine cannot be satisfied with local and punctual struggles: hyper-desiring and hyper-centralised, it must be all of it at once.'

Instead of fighting or ruing organization and its risks as something that comes from outside, that 'others' impose on 'us,' the real test lies in *becoming* those 'others,' that is, in taking responsibility both for the creation of collective assemblages and for their risks – for developing collective capacity to act *and* mechanisms to analyse and subvert 'every form of power' that endangers the continuity of a process, including one's own.[20] To be truly anti-Oedipal is to be self-subversive.[21] This is why Guattari (1984: 41) says that 'the fundamental problem of institutional analysis' (the field in which he started out) is: '[C]an the group face the problem of its own death? Can a group with a historic mission envisage the end of that mission … ? Can revolutionary parties envisage the end of their so-called mission to lead the masses?'[22] Starting with the Zapatista Army of National Liberation's (EZLN) Subcomandante Marcos, facelessness and anonymity have been a recurring trait among movements of the last decades. Both a weapon against the targeting of leaders and a way of demonstrating the struggle's openness to all comers, this has been a key element in creating an 'open-code activism.' Besides, when distrust of representation is rife, calls for action that are not 'authored' by established organizations have a better chance of catching on.[23] It is fitting that one of the most important groups to appear in recent years – if it can even be called that – is called Anonymous, and that their visible 'face' is the Guy Fawkes mask worn by Alan Moore's V, a sort of fictional forerunner of Marcos.

At the same time, it is clear that one cannot be 'anonymous' forever. Even if we do not know Marcos' face, he is still identifiable as an EZLN leader, and while the individuals in Anonymous may remain anonymous, the collectivity called 'Anonymous' itself cannot. If the vanguard-function leads, it inevitably becomes recognizable, even if only as something like a Twitter alias. Besides, there is an important difference between the localized kind of intervention that acts as a catalyst for a protest and the more continuous, long-term work of a campaign or group. In the latter case, becoming identifiable is unavoidable, and it is more likely that, however informal an organizational format might be, internal structures and leadership figures will emerge.

Another of Deleuze and Guattari's concepts may help us think beyond the limits of invisibility and anonymity: 'becoming-imperceptible.'[24] At first, the three may seem synonymous, or becoming-imperceptible can sound like the opposite of acting or leading. I would like to suggest, however, that it offers ways of thinking how to act and lead *better*, rather than not at all. The first thing to stress about the concept is that it refers to a kind of *action*. Although initially defined as becoming 'like everyone/the whole world [*tout le monde*]' (Deleuze and Guattari 2004: 342), it is poorly understood if treated as mere inaction or 'going with the flow.' To begin with, one *actively* strives to become imperceptible, choosing to suppress 'everything that prevented us from slipping between things' (Deleuze and Guattari 2004: 344); one *takes a step* back from a constituted position (*my* group, *my* beliefs, *myself*) facing other constituted positions so as to become attuned to their common background: their virtual or unconscious conditions and the potentials present in the situation. It is a *striving* to place oneself in the position of the 'anomalous' element that is a pack's vector of deterritorialization, of which Deleuze and Guattari (2004: 299) say that it is 'neither an individual nor a species' and has 'neither familiar nor subjectified feelings, nor specific or significant characteristics,' but 'only affects.'

This means neither an elimination of the self nor the attainment of an 'objective,' God's-eye perspective on the whole. It is true that Deleuze and Guattari (2004: 348) speak of a 'plane of consistency or immanence' that, in the process of becoming-imperceptible, is 'perceived in its own right.' But it is so 'in the course of its construction,' that is, through experimentation, and hence partially, rather than as if through external contemplation. If 'the unconscious must be constructed, not rediscovered' (Deleuze and Guattari 2004:), it is because it is never given as such, as in some sort of fusional mystical experience, but only ever through a conditioned, perspectival effort. *Constructing* means acting, selecting, connecting to some elements and not others, and in that process producing a new set of orientations for actual behavior. To have 'only affects' is to enhance one's sensibility to the conditions of the environment and, as a consequence, to be better prepared to detect the latency of events and to intervene so as to bring them about.

This can be thought in relation to the distinction between *actualizing* and *realizing* that François Zourabichvili (2000) correctly highlights as central to Deleuze and Guattari's politics. To 'realize a project' is to depart from an already existing image or goal, and attempt to shape the actual according to it; to actualize is to experiment with or construct actualizations for a situation's potentials, creating something qualitatively different not only from what came before, but from what could previously be imagined as possible. The conception of action that corresponds to the first is that of a form that exists as a mental image being imposed on inert matter. In the second, an image cannot exist in advance – it is at best a hunch – because the matter acted upon is not inert: it has potentials of its own, with an agency of their own, responding to action, resisting it, diverting it or accelerating it, so that the final result is truly unpredictable. 'To realise a project produces nothing new' if all it does is add existence to an idea that was already given as a possibility; 'those who intend to transform the real according to their previously conceived idea do not take transformation itself into account' (Zourabichvili 2000: 337).

Furthermore, if the matter on which the agent intervenes is not merely passive, it is because this matter is the very environment in which the agent moves – which therefore acts back on her, even to the point of transforming what she might desire or imagine. Instead of expecting to control that environment or wishing to fully determine its future states, the goal of actualization is more modest: to propose or induce a change, to introduce positive and negative feedbacks that indicate a direction without predetermining it (which would be impossible). To see oneself as an element that is both passive and active in a milieu that is also both things, instead of a separate agent seeking to mold inert matter according to a preconceived image, weakens the egoic, heroic investment in oneself as 'the vanguard,' 'the radicals,' 'the revolutionaries' is undermined. One's actions and identity cease to be the be-all and end-all condition for change, and are placed in a broader picture in which agents can be relativized to the point of 'facing their own *death*' – that is, the partiality and limits of their intervention and even, as the case may be, the need for its overcoming or disappearance if it becomes superfluous or counterproductive. It is not just that this conception is less prone to authoritarian drifts, or more open-ended; it also involves greater attention to the conditions of action, and thus tends to be more flexible both in 'meeting people where they are' and in anticipating and negotiating changes in the environment. Ethereal as it may sound, 'becoming-imperceptible' should therefore be understood as becoming *more realistic* about oneself and the real potentials and limitations of a process.

This relativization of the agent in favour of the environment and a situation's conditions might suggest that becoming-imperceptible involves an unconditional commitment to seeking compromises or maintaining broad consensus at any cost; but one thing does not follow from the other. First of all, becoming-imperceptible is *precisely not* about negotiating differences understood as given or striking balances among fixed positions identifying each actor or part of a process. While *constituted* difference is what stops agents from 'slipping between things', becoming imperceptible means looking for the *constituent* differences that underlie them, and acting on those. Differences *as they exist* are not absolute values in themselves, although they are part of the material that one must act upon, and must be taken into account as such. From the point of view of becoming imperceptible, it matters more that one is sensitive to differences that *can exist* – that already exist in potential – and to construct the transversal connections that can provide them with a plane of consistency, without those necessary leading back to the agent herself. To turn one's gaze away from discontinuities (constituted difference) and towards continuity (the potentials that traverse a situation and can constitute new differences) does not entail that the goal should always be that of maintaining continuity, let alone assuming or producing homogeneity. Divisions exist – between 'the 1%' and 'the 99%', the over- and the under-represented, white and non-white, majorities and minoritarian becomings etc. –, and overcoming them will more often than not require asserting their existence and creating new ones.

To the extent that events are ruptures, and that one seeks potentials in order to elicit and propagate events, becoming imperceptible is part of intervening so as to create ruptures; it is a moment in the hard work of 'eventing'. The question is *what* ruptures to produce, and *how* – where to draw the lines, in which direction to move, how to retain enough openness, where to be divisive and where inclusive, when to go with the flow and when to interrupt it. Sometimes, attempting to push things beyond the vaguest agreement will result in a process' implosion or one's own isolation; if new ruptures are to be created, one will have to wait, to be flexible, to 'read the mood'. In other cases, a 'spontaneous' action that initially garnered little consensus can produce a widely shared qualitative change – for example, the way in which the storming of Conservative party headquarters in London galvanised the UK student movement of 2011 (cf. The Free Association 2011).

This shows that neither 'maintaining continuity' or 'asserting division' can be turned into categorical imperatives for political action. Whether continuity or division is preferable is a badly posed problem. Properly political (that is, practical) problems are always a matter of what continuity, what division, when, how, how much. The experimental character of becoming-imperceptible, its reference to a specific process or situation, highlights this. By the same token, it indicates that the point of an intervention is not itself, but what it does: one intervenes not in order to assert oneself or the correctness of one's position, but in order to produce effects. There is no advantage to respecting differences if that only means that existing differences will remain the same; nothing is gained from asserting division if all it does is divide us from everyone else. It is key to the idea of an 'open code activism' that revolutions should be 'come as you are' affairs; but they will not have been revolutions if they do not result in 'leaving as you were not'. The whole point of political practice is what happens in the middle, and how to make it happen.

Works Cited

Badiou, Alain. 2011. *Le Réveil de l'Histoire*. Paris: Lignes.

Brighenti, Andrea Mubi. 2010. 'Tarde, Canetti, and Deleuze on Crowds and Packs'. *Journal of Classical Sociology* 10: 292–315.

Canetti, Elias. 1981. *Crowds and Power*. Trans. Carol Stewart. New York: Continuum.

Comité Invisible. *À Nos Amis*. Paris: La Fabrique.

Dean, Jodi. 2012. *The Communist Horizon*. London: Verso.

Deleuze, Gilles. 2004. 'Trois problèmes de groupe'. In *L'Ile déserte. Textes et entretiens 1952–1974*. Paris: Minuit: 270–284.

Deleuze, Gilles and Félix Guattari. 2003. 'Mai 68 n'a pas eu lieu'. In *Deux régimes de fous. Textes et entretiens 1975–1995*. Paris: Minuit: 215–20.

Deleuze, Gilles and Félix Guattari. 2004. *Mille Plateaux*. Paris: Minuit.

Deleuze, Gilles and Félix Guattari. 2005. *L'Anti-Oedipe*. Paris: Minuit.

Deleuze, Gilles and Tony Negri. 2007. 'T Contrôle et devenir'. In *Pourparlers*. Paris: Minuit 2007: 229–39.

Deleuze, Gilles and Claire Parnet. 2004. '"G" comme gauche'. In *Abécedaire*. Paris: Montparnasse.

The Free Association. 2011. 'On Fairy-dust and Rupture'. Accessed May 2, 2015 from: http://freelyassociating.org/on-fairy-dust-and-rupture/

Graeber, David. 2004. 'The Twilight of Vanguardism'. In *World Social Forum: Challenging Empires*. Ed. Jai Sen and Peter Waterman. New Delhi: Viveka Foundation: 329–35.

Graeber, David. 2011. 'Occupy Wall Street's Anarchist Roots'. *Al Jazeera*. Accessed May 3, 2015 from: http://www.aljazeera.com/indepth/opinion/2011/11/2011112872835904508.html

Guattari, Félix. 1984. *Molecular Revolution: Psychiatry and Politics*. Trans. David Cooper and Rosemary Sheed. Harmondsworth: Penguin.

Guattari, Félix. 2006. *The Anti-Oedipus Papers*. Ed. Stéphane Nadaud. Trans. Kélina Gotman. Los Angeles/New York: Semiotext(e).

Guattari, Félix. 2009a. 'Institutional Intervention.' In *Soft Subversions: Texts and Interviews 1977–1985*. Ed. Sylvère Lotringer. Trans. Emily Wittmam. Cambridge: Semiotext(e)/MIT Press: 33–63.

Guattari, Félix. 2009b. 'The Unconscious is Turned Towards the Future'. In *Soft Subversions: Texts and Interviews 1977–1985*. Ed. Sylvère Lotringer. Trans. Arthur Evans and John Johnston. Cambridge: Semiotext(e)/MIT Press: 177–83.

Leibniz, Gottfried Wilhelm. The Principles of Philosophy, or the Monadology, In *Philosophical Essays*. Ed. and trans. Roger Ariew and Daniel Garber. Indianapolis: Hackett: 213-25.

Malo, Marta. 2011. 'Sol, o Cuando lo Imposible Se Vuelve Imparable'. *Madrilonia*. Accessed May 3, 2015 from: http://madrilonia.org/2011/05/sol-o-cuando-lo-imposible-se-vuelve-imparable/

Marx, Karl and Friedrich Engels. 2001. 'The Communist Manifesto'. In *Karl Marx: Selected Writings*. Ed. David MacLellan. Oxford: Oxford University Press: 245–72.

Nunes, Rodrigo. 2013. 'Notes Towards a Rethinking of the Militant'. In *Communism in the Twenty-First Century*, vol. 3. Ed. Shannon Brincat. Santa Barbara: Praeger.

Nunes, Rodrigo. 2014. *Organisation of the Organisationless. Collective Action after Networks*. London: Mute/PML Books.

Nunes, Rodrigo. Forthcoming 2016. 'The Network Prince: Leadership between Clastres and Machiavelli'. *International Journal of Communication* 10.

Simondon, Gilbert. 2005. 'Forme, Information, Potentiels'. In *L'individuation à la lumière des notions de forme et d'information*. Grenoble: Jerôme Millon: 531–51.

Tarde, Gabriel. 2002. *Les Lois Sociales*. Paris: Institut Synthélabo,

Thoburn, Nick. 2010. 'Weatherman, the Militant Diagram, and the Problem of Political Passion'. *New Formations* 68: 123–40.

Toret, Javier. 2013. 'No es la revolución Facebook o Twitter, es una nueva capacidad tecnopolítica'. *Madrilonia*. Accessed May 3, 2015 from: http://madrilonia.org/2013/04/no-es-la-revolucion-facebook-o-twitter-es-una-nueva-capacidad-tecnopolitica-entrevistamos-a-toret/

Viveiros de Castro, Eduardo. 2009. *Métaphysiques cannibales*. Paris: PUF.

Žižek, Slavoj. 2009. *The Parallax View*. Cambridge: MIT Press.

Zourabichvili, François. 2000. 'Deleuze e o possível (sobre o involuntarismo na política)'. In *Gilles Deleuze: uma vida filosófica*. Ed. Eric Alliez. São Paulo: Editora 34: 333–55.

Notes

1. Javier Toret (2013) notes that, while 'the nodes more connected to the explosion' of the movement became weaker, 'a remarkable flow of interaction and daily work has remained,' being occasionally reactivated by 'the connection with circles that are less internal to the process' through 'new (even if smaller) events that make social malaises transversal with network processes,' and thus are 're-actualisations of the 15M DNA.' This leads him to distinguish four moments of the 15M process: 'gestation,' 'explosion and birth of the network-system,' 'globalisation' (including Occupy and the October 15, 2011 day of action) and 'evolution, development and mutation.'

2. *Pays profond*, in the sense that one speaks, for example of the United States' 'deep south.'

3. This helps explain the appeal that activists of a radical libertarian and egalitarian bent sometimes find in a certain millenarianism: thinking a radical change that happens 'at once' (brought about, for example, by ecological collapse) allows us to bypass all the dangers (the formation of leaders and hierarchies, compromise) and the daunting work of a transformation taking place over time.

4. I follow the standard English translation of the German *Masse* (*masse*, in French) as 'crowd'; cf. Canetti (1981). Brighenti (2010: 297) compares Canetti, Gabriel Tarde and Deleuze and Guattari as proponents of a concept of multiplicity eschewing classical dichotomies between individualism and holism, agency and structure, micro- and macro-sociology by making the individual into 'something that exists only within ... a range located between two other regions,' the infra- and the interindividual (which we could, following Gilbert Simondon, name 'pre-' and 'trans-individual'). It is curious, then, that he fails to note how Deleuze and Guattari misread Canetti, opposing 'pack' and 'crowd' as intensive and extensive multiplicities, when Canetti sees both in intensive terms. For him, the pack is defined primarily by its coming together around a specific goal and possessing only two of the characteristics (equality, direction) of the crowd (which also include density and the tendency to grow). Because of the latter trait (lack of growth), the size opposition between 'crowd' (larger) and 'pack' (small) has an importance for him that, as I will argue, it does not to Deleuze and Guattari – whose 'pack' and 'crowd' are arguably closer to Canetti's 'open' and 'closed' crowds.

5. Throughout the following pages I will be working from the opposition as it is set out by Deleuze and Guattari, rather than Canetti's actual definitions. If anything, Deleuze and Guattari develop in the crowd and the pack the opposition (itself drawn from Jean Paul Sartre) developed by Guattari (1984) between subjected and subject groups, which is taken up in *Anti-Oedipus*, where it appears as opposing groups that are revolutionary at the level of pre-conscious investments to those that are revolutionary at the level of desire

(Deleuze and Guattari 2005: 470 et seq.). Later in his life, Guattari (2009a: 48) would claim: 'I no longer have much faith in the specificity of the group, and I would even say that I believe less and less in the existence of the group as an entity ... I would like to start from a much more inclusive, perhaps more vague, notion of assemblage'. Cf. also Guattari (2009b: 179): 'I've changed my mind: there are no subject-groups, but arrangements of enunciation, of subjectivization, pragmatic arrangements that do not coincide with circumscribed groups.'

6. Cf. Tarde (2002).

7. This point is developed at greater length in Nunes (2014).

8. Again, this does not mean that people are always 'really free' under control, but that the constraints put on their actions (which elicit and modulate as much as repress and prohibit them) never fully determine their content. It is to the extent that their actions are underdetermined that they are 'free,' not only to operate under those constraints but also, under certain conditions, to change the constraints themselves.

9. While I am staying close to the animal metaphor here, it should be clear that this need not be an individual; the cutting edge of deterritorialization could be a group, a new material relation, a human/non-human assemblage etc.

10. Cf. Simondon (2005: 544): 'There can be no taking of form [*prise de forme*] without two conditions coming together: a tension of information, contributed by a structural germ, and the energy imprisoned by the milieu that begins to take form; the milieu ... must be in a metastable, tense state, like a solution in supersaturation or superfusion, so as to pass into a stable state by liberating the imprisoned energy' through the structuring work of the structural germ.

11. Guattari (1984: 17–23) introduces the concept of 'coefficient of transversality' to speak of the degree of freedom and contingency, or openness and indeterminacy – and the capacity to become aware of and manage them – in a group or institutional situation.

12. This point is further developed in Nunes (forthcoming).

13. I have heard the expression on three separate occasions from friends involved in the Spanish 15M movement.

14. On organization thought as a continuum, cf. Nunes (forthcoming).

15. That initiatives should be based on political wagers means that they should arise from strategic appraisals of the situation rather than mere personal preference. Cf. Dean (2012: 228): 'fearful of excluding potential opportunities, Occupy tried early on to avoid confronting fundamental divisions within the movement. (...) The effect, though, was to reduce

division to forking (in other words, to sublimate it). People pursued their own projects, perpetually splitting according to their prior interests and expertise.'

16. Other forms of implicitly teleological discourses that exist in the orbit of contemporary movements include a certain historical and technological optimism that places contemporary movements in a struggle between the old (representative democracy, rigid structures, hierarchy, monopoly, 'proprietary code') and the new ('real' democracy, networks, decentralization, participation, 'open code'), in which the victory of the new over the old would be assured by the arrow of time, rather than seen as the very object of the struggle; and an appeal to a 'generic humanity' seen not as the outcome of a struggle to overcome social antagonisms, as in the Marxist account, but as an underlying reality 'veiled' by divisions, ideologies, antagonisms etc., and therefore the object of a spontaneous self-reflexive awakening. Once the veils are lifted, the idea goes, it is inevitable that we see ourselves as essentially equal, and so inevitably bound to agree on the basics of how society is to be run. I develop the critique of positing a transcendence of the process over agents in Nunes (2013).

17. The problem of organization appears then as profoundly Leibnizian: 'obtaining as much variety as possible, but with the greatest order possible' (Leibniz, 1989, § 58).

18. Deleuze and Guattari never had any illusions, however, that this tension can be indefinitely sustained – stasis always wins in the end, as it is inevitable events exhaust themselves in their 'eventing,' eventually consuming their potentials or being captured by strata. This does not mean that they return us to the same place, which would make them mere blips in a constant underlying order, but that there is no final, perfect state, and at one point new potentials will have to be harnessed to go beyond the forms created by previous events – in that sense, movement always wins in the end. This is what leads Deleuze (with Parnet 2004) to jest – 'but who did ever believe that revolution turn out well? ... All revolutions fail. Everyone knows it... That revolutions fail, that revolutions turn out bad, that has never stopped people from becoming revolutionary ... What people have to do in a situation of oppression or tyranny is effectively to become revolutionary, for there is nothing else to do.'

19. At around the same time, Guattari (1984: 65) comments on May 1968: 'it is true that problems are now seen differently, but, equally, there has been no real break. This is undoubtedly because there is no large-scale machine for revolutionary war. We have to recognize that certain dominant images are still perpetrating their destructive effects even within revolutionary groups themselves.'

20. An example of the incapacity (or fear) of abandoning the position in which the vicissitudes of political experience can always be blamed on 'others' would

be the Invisible Committee's (2014: 75) critique of the notions 'constituent power', 'democracy' and 'government' – which sounds woefully inadequate in its suggestion that the defeat of uprisings such as the one in Egypt would have resulted from failure to 'deprive power of its legitimacy, make it acknowledge is arbitrariness,' when they were actually interrupted by the arbitrariness of sheer force.

21. I borrow this explanatory short-circuit from Viveiros de Castro (2009: 239).

22. Interestingly, Guattari (1984: 202) comments that 'one should still be a Leninist, at least in the specific sense of believing that we cannot really look to the spontaneity and creativity of the masses to establish analytical groups in any lasting way – though "Leninist" is perhaps an odd word to use when one remembers that the object at this moment is to foster not a highly centralized party, but some means whereby the masses can gain control of their own lives.'

23. Treating *pásalo* (the 'pass it on' tag tacked to the end of emails and text messages calling for actions) as the 'unpredictable actor' behind the movement of the indignados in Spain, Marta Malo (2011) observes that, as 'the son of decades of political disaffiliation,' '"pásalo" is wary, especially of organised groups'; when the latter attempt to use the same mechanism of viral spread, their initiatives fall flat.

24. Nicholas Thoburn (2010: 137) emphasizes Deleuze and Guattari's 'affirmation of "becoming imperceptible ... as a political figure,' aptly characterizing it as 'not a sublime end-point of spiritual inaction, but the immanent kernel of a militant political composition,' and departing from 'a clear disarticulation of political practice from the construction of coherent collective subjectivities,' 'but in a fashion that bypasses the anti-group position with an orientation toward the discontinuous and multilayered arrangements that traverse and compose social – or, indeed, planetary – life.'

Chapter 4

Resistance to Occupy

CLAIRE COLEBROOK

I

The title of my chapter indicates two senses of the concept of resistance, and two senses of the concept of occupation. The two contrary tendencies of the concept of resistance take us to the heart of Deleuze and Guattari's political philosophy. There is no authentic proletariat to whom one might appeal in political protests. Rather than think of a populace's resistance *to* power or the state, in terms of opposition, one needs to think of political resistance at the molecular level: how might some forces – forces that compose us and what we take to be our interests – produce new formations that are not those of the standard political identities that make up political analysis? We might think of standard (molar) political resistance as – to use Foucault's terms – too bound up with sovereign conceptions of power, as a repressive 'power over,' or as a 'top-down' power, against which life and liberty would be set. By contrast, Deleuze and Guattari theorize a sense of multiple and genuinely *political* resistance: it is not a question of life *resisting* power, but of thinking – within each body – of resisting forces. In his book on Leibniz Deleuze describes the play of forces that would generate a relatively unified body. On such an account, for a body to resist would *not* be to appeal to natural desire or interests, but to have a feeling for the multiple tendencies that would then yield an *inflection*:

> I hesitate between staying home and working or going out to a nightclub: these are not two separable "objects," but two

orientations, each of which carries a sum of possible or even hallucinatory perceptions (not only of drinking, but the noise and smoke of the bar; not only of working, but the hum of the word processor and the surrounding silence …). And if we return to motives in order to study them for a second time, they have not stayed the same. Like the weight on a scale, they have gone up or down. The scale has changed according to the amplitude of the pendulum. The voluntary act is free because the free act is what expressed the entire soul at a given moment of its duration. That act is what expresses the self. Does Adam sin freely? In other words, at that instant his soul has taken an amplitude that is found to be easily filled by the aroma and taste of the apple, and by Eve's solicitations. Another amplitude – one having retained God's defense – is possible. The whole question turns on "laziness." (Deleuze 1993: 70).

Adam chooses because he is taken over by the smell of the apple and the sounds of Eve's voice, even though at another instant he might have been swayed by a contrary feeling for God. Put more concretely, we might say that political resistance would not lie in *opposing* power, but in having a sense or feeling for the inflections of power: why, if a body is tending one way towards refusing work (because of hunger and the fatigue from working multiple jobs) does another tendency take over, such as a feeling of obligation or fear? Deleuze seems at once to suggest that the question is less one of opposition than *amplitude*: if all I can feel, perceive and *be* is the immediacy of hunger and cold then that will be what prompts me to act (and so I may go to work, yet again, for just enough to survive). If however I could feel and perceive just a little more – if on the way to work another hungry, fatigued body described some other possible way of feeling – then I might choose to sit down, not work, occupy a city space and think of a different world: 'The whole questions turns on "laziness"' (Deleuze 70). This 'laziness' is that of amplitude, of how much we are able to feel, perceive and think. In his book on Leibniz, Deleuze suggests that rather than follow Descartes's notion of clear and distinct ideas – such that we know certain truths indubitably – we should understand that everything perceives the infinite, but with its own degree of confusion or clarity. Rather than base politics on the subject's own certainty

– each individual deciding for herself because only she can determine her own good – a collective politics might generate alternating relations of clarity and distinction. While Occupy may have been characterized by indistinction – never clear just who or what the movement represented, coming into being prior to any formation of an end or aim – its force and presence were clear (clear but indistinct), and as the movement grew in size it became capable of different and varying amplitudes. The political nature of Occupy cannot be understood by way of the subject, whose finite knowledge would determine a range of expertise, but does make sense according to Deleuze and Guattari's sense of perception as a form of occupation and resistance: one perceives and knows according to where one is, and what impedes or enhances one's range. This is not just to say that Occupy managed to generate a broad, indistinct but clear perception of its own force by gradually gaining self-perception by way of social media, but also that within each Occupy site there were moments of relative distinction where divergent demands of racial, ethnic, sexual and gendered justice came into relative conflict. It was occupation, or the assembling together of bodies, that generated multiple lines of resistance – both resistance to Occupy's outside – the 1% – and within Occupy.

The use of relative quantities to name relations of resistance is closer to a Deleuzian politics of the monad rather than the subject: rather than a self who perceives its outside, political resistance is achieved by shifting and constantly redistributed relations of force. There are not subjects who occupy and then resist; rather, there is an assembling of force, the formation of a territory, and then the self-perception of that force by way of its relative range of clarity and confusion. From the stable monad, a being defined by it locus and force of perception, Deleuze and Guattari argue for the nomad: a range of perception and force that is constantly shifting (Deleuze and Guattari 1987: 573–4).

Deleuze and Guattari's work therefore manages to weave together two contrary senses of resistance. The *political* concept of resistance is oppositional – as in the 'French resistance' – and is a resistance *to* an occupying power. Deleuze and Guattari's micro-politics intertwines oppositional resistance, especially in *Anti-Oedipus,* with the psychoanalytic concept of resistance: what stops a body, force or desire from doing what it wants to do? If one wants to resist politically, and oppose a power, then one needs to ask about the powers within every body and every perception that impede or enhance its amplitude. Let us say that the political concept of resistance, captured in the historical moment of the French resistance (but also more broadly in anti-colonization movements), was that of opposing an occupying power, and that such a concept of oppositional resistance has been increasingly problematized by another notion of resistance articulated by psychoanalysis: how is it that desire resists itself? It was this sense of immanent (rather than oppositional resistance) that Paul de Man deployed in the notion of resistance to theory: rather than imagine theory as something that could be easily achieved, such that we might step back from a field of forces and relations and grasp its higher logic, de Man argued that theory or the gaze of wise distance was not something that could ever be fully achieved. Resistance – or a certain immanent impossibility of fulfillment – is constitutive of any event of reading, or any attempt to grasp the sense of what one encounters. Blindness is constitutively coupled with insight, just as – for Deleuze and Guattari – all perceptions are distinct *and* confused, clear *and* indistinct. A body occupies a field and encounters its resistances with counter-resistance. The theoretical desire is at once necessary to break with relations as already constituted, but always remains as a desire, never a final object (de Man 1982).

When Deleuze and Guattari write about micro-facisms, they focus the question of resistance and opposition at the level of desire (Deleuze and Guattari 1987: 31). If there is fascism, or the *social*-political organization of all force towards a single transcendent end – *the* state, *the* people, *the* party – this is not because there is something that simply opposes desire; rather, desire itself has a tendency towards becoming resistant to its own tendencies:

> You may make a rupture, draw a line of flight, yet there is still a danger that you will reencounter organizations that restratify everything, formations that restore power to a signifier, attributions that reconstitute a subject – anything you like, from Oedipal resurgences to fascist concretions. Groups and individuals contain microfascisms just waiting to crystallize ... Good and bad are only the products of an active and

temporary selection, which must be renewed. (Deleuze and Guattari 1987: 9–10)

All those tendencies that might have once been so liberating when set against earlier modes of corporate capital, such as a stress on individual freedom, creativity, goals, and unity in opposition to a quantifying and reductive capital, might now need to be abandoned. Notions of individual freedom, creativity, personal fulfillment and work-life balance now service capital, while concepts of disorganization and lack of clear ends might be genuinely resistant. Such a shift of focus, away from a simple oppositional resistance towards internal resistance, is particularly relevant today, looking back upon the potentiality of the Occupy movement.

In *Anti-Oedipus* Deleuze and Guattari reverse the usual notion that a politics of resistance would require strongly formed identities (in the mode of resistance to power by the populace). On the contrary, resistance occurs through what has not yet taken on the form of 'interests' and certainly not of organization: 'In order to resist organ-machines, the body without organs presents its smooth, slippery, opaque, taut surface as a barrier. In order to resist linked, connected, and interrupted flows, it sets up a counterflow of amorphous, undifferentiated fluid' (Deleuze and Guattari 2004: 10). Like Foucault who also argued against the notion that power represses desire, Deleuze and Guattari do not accept that there is a good desire lying in wait for political liberation; politics, or the polity, begins precisely with the formation of objects or interests and does so by repelling a desire that is not yet organized. Disorganized desire is revolutionary; or, desire *is* disorganized and therefore *is resistance* and revolution, not because it opposes power, but because what we take to be power – the power of distinct terms – emerges by way of repelling or organizing desire. This is why Deleuze and Guattari specifically use the term desire rather than power (and this is where they mark their difference from Foucault). While accepting, following Foucault, that power is positive, they nevertheless seek to mobilize *desire* rather than power, for while power constitutes relations and points of stability, it is desire that exceeds any of the terms through which it flows, and is therefore not bound by the relations or organizations that generate the socius – desire exceeds resistance as opposition:

> Our only points of disagreement with Foucault are the following: (1) to us the assemblages seem fundamentally to be assemblages not of power but of desire (desire is always assembled), and power seems to be a stratified dimension of the assemblage; (2) the diagram and abstract machine have lines of flight that are primary, which are not phenomena of resistance or counterattack in an assemblage, but cutting edges of creation and deterritorialization. (Deleuze and Guattari 1987: 531)

Placing their work in context one might say that the French resistance, and then the political milieu prior to May 1968, relied on a dichotomous notion of occupation and resistance: in the Nazi occupation of France, an outside had invaded the inside or the territory, and this outside must be resisted. But Deleuze and Guattari's political theory, well before the Occupy movement, precluded any simple sense of an inside/outside of political territories. It is not the case that there is something like 'a' territory – a marked out and defined space – that is then occupied: this is the myth of nations, or the notion that space and place have some intrinsic proper being. Rather, it is by way of occupation, or by filling a zone or moving across a field, that something like 'a' space or territory is formed. This primary nomadism always occurs in relation (and by way of contestation). In the beginning is the potential for occupying a space, and the mapping out of a territory; but the territory is therefore the outcome of deterritorialization: forces of desire enter into relation, producing a certain quality or space. Property is occupation, or the taking up of a space and of marking or 'signing' it as one's own. There is something like a quality that is desired; there is 'a' desiring, and it is from this tendency to take up a quality that a territory is formed:

> The expressive is primary in relation to the possessive; expressive qualities, or matters of expression, are necessarily appropriative and constitute a having more profound than being ... No sooner do I like a color that I make it my standard or placard. One puts one's signature on something just as one plants one's flag on a piece of land. A high school supervisor stamped all the leaves strewn about the school yard and then put them

> back in their places. He had signed. Territorial marks are readymades. And what is called *art brut* is not at all pathological or primitive; it is merely this constitution, this freeing, of matters of expression, in the movement of territoriality: the base or ground of art. (Deleuze and Guattari 1987: 316)

Here, Deleuze and Guattari articulate a politics of occupation and resistance that is *improper*; in the beginning is the chance taking up of what is not one's own as one's own. It would follow from this theory of original occupation that it is not the case that there is a proper space of one's own, that might then be taken over or occupied, and that this occupation must be resisted by some proper or innocent 'outside' of power. Rather, desire encounters resistance, and in so doing generates a space of ownness or an occupation. Occupation is the outcome of resistance, which in turn is dependent upon a desire that has no proper home or being. I would argue that there is something 'necessarily appropriative' about the mode of Deleuze and Guattari's political theory: not only do they see the notion of the proper and property as dependent upon the seizing of a quality, their very style of thinking about politics transforms how we think about political theory. Rather than politics following on from an idea, rationale or decision – a commitment to freedom, the market, the individual or even justice – they commence with aesthetics in the strictest sense: a quality is seized. The notion that this quality is then a sign *of* one's own identity or territory or property is a consequence of a certain reversal. In this respect their own theory is not only an overturning of Platonism (by placing ideas as effects of sensations) but also an overturning of a certain conception of resistance that would focus on a politics of good ideas: rather than demystifying or informing the masses of what they ought to desire, and rather than focusing on a politics of good thinking, they stress the event of occupation. Take up a space; write a placard, and sign it as your own. Philosophically, we might say that Deleuze and Guattari insist on *internal relations*: there are not qualities that enter into relation, but there are powers that have tendencies to establish certain styles of relation. This is to say that rather than a matter that is neutral and that is then differentiated from outside, there are tendencies to establish relations by way of matter's inflections. Matter is not blank quantity without quality. Along with the commitment to internal relations, Deleuze and Guattari *also* insist that *relations are external to terms*; to be weaker or stronger, master or slave, owner or thief, is not something one simply is, but occurs as the outcome of a field of contestation, resistance and occupation:

> What does matter *do* as a matter of expression? It is first of all a poster or placard, but that is not all it is. It merely takes that route. The signature becomes style. In effect, expressive qualities or matters of expression enter shifting relations with one another that 'express' the relation of the territory they draw to the interior milieu of impulses and exterior milieu of circumstances. To express is not to depend upon; there is an autonomy of expression. On the one hand, expressive qualities entertain internal relations with one another that constitute *territorial motifs*; sometimes these motifs loom above the internal impulses, sometimes they are superimposed upon them, sometimes they ground one impulse in another, sometimes they pass and cause a passage from one impulse to another, sometimes they insert themselves between them – but they are not themselves "pulsed." ... On the other hand, expressive qualities also entertain other internal relations that produce *territorial counterpoints*: this refers to the manner in which they constitute points in the territory that place the circumstances of the external milieu in counterpoint. (Deleuze and Guattari 1987: 317)

The upshot of this ontology of internal relations, even though relations are external to terms is that resistance and occupation are 'originary.' Force or desire is not some bland undifferentiated generic void that requires relations to produce difference; desire differs and has a tendency to 'pulse' in distinct ways (internal relations, or a potentiality to express in a certain manner). By the same token desire does not determine in advance the terms that will be effected from encounters; whatever tendencies or 'pulses,' a desire might express there are also relations that are irreducible to the relatively stable points generated:

> we should say that there are *two* politics involved ... a macropolitics and a micropolitics that do not envision classes, sexes, people, or feelings in at all the same way. Or again,

> there are two very different types of relations: intrinsic relations of couples involving well-determined aggregates or elements (social classes, men and women, this or that particular person), and less localizable relations that are always external to themselves and instead concern flows and particles eluding those classes, sexes and persons. (Deleuze and Guattari 1987: 196)

I would suggest that the first wave of French post-structuralism, or the first uptake of French post-structuralism, stressed external relations: a system of differences (such as *langue*) was the condition for some point of stability or sameness. It would follow, then, that politics might depend on solicitation or disturbance of a system from within, given that there would be nothing (or no thing) outside the constitutive differences that enable points of seeming identity. By contrast, Deleuze and Guattari combine internal relations (a force's desire or tendency) with external relations, or the constituted differences that generate stable points.

We might think, then, of the genealogy of French post-structuralism as an initial phase focused on the resistance *to* occupation. Nazi occupation of France was, ostensibly, the intrusion or installation of a foreign and pernicious body into a democratic polity; the French resistance directed against occupation relied upon the rebellion and refusal by a polity that could conceive itself as other than the invading forces. Deconstruction's ongoing response to this notion of occupation as intrusion or contamination by an external evil has increasingly been one of a politics of auto-immunity: there is no innocent body politic that is accidentally or tragically overtaken by forces of violence, terror and totalizing power, for in order to constitute *any* 'we' or body proper there must have been some violent and homogenizing event of recognition that established the purity of the border and the putative innocence of the 'we.' Put in an overly simple way we might say that in an age of self-satisfied democracy and good feeling – where violence and terror appear to be located *elsewhere* – it would be theoretically requisite to point out that 'our' supposedly democratic and inclusive body politic was always already contaminated by violence, terror and exclusion. From Derrida's early work on Levinas (where he argues that *some* domestication of the other is necessary to avoid a worse violence of absolute exclusion) to the vogue for Agamben's notion of sovereignty as necessarily premised on violent abandonment, I want to suggest that a politics of pointing out law's non-purity or 'our' complicity was appropriate for an epoch of seeming democracy. Derrida frequently situated his work in opposition to the seeming triumph of liberalism; *Specters of Marx* (1994) was at least in part a criticism of Fukuyama's theory of the late twentieth-century's freedom from imposed ideologies (Derrida 1994a: 70–1). Lest we be too smug about *our* freedoms and the sanctity of law and the polity, or lest we feel that we can enjoy the good conscience of being open to the otherness of the other, deconstruction was always there to remind 'us' that the condition for hospitality and recognition was always, necessarily and essentially, a 'lesser violence' (Derrida 1978). I would suggest, though, that the twenty-first century requires a shift in the modalities of political critique: rather than insisting that the claims for liberal freedom are alibis for market freedom, it is more appropriate to consider why late capitalism seems to have abandoned even the ideal of liberalism.

One of the figures of the Occupy movement designates a shift in proportions; the '99%' motif is part of a broader and highly complex narration of changes of distribution (the way in which income differentials have broadened, the increase of wealth in the hands of a few, the difference in wages rises for the top few as compared to the bottom few, and the very figure of 1% indicating contraction rather than the quality or structure of power per se). Let us say that deconstruction was concerned with a post-Marxist politics of contamination and complicity; there is no pure nature, no spirit, no woman, and no original use value outside the logics of technology and exchange. Any claim to good conscience or to being purely democratic, in a space outside the rationalization of modernity, would need to be demystified, such that deconstruction could not posit any actual or grounding justice, but only a justice or democracy to come (Derrida 1994a). But, as the Occupy narratives make clear, things have changed, and it is perhaps *not* the ideological lie of capitalist freedom, democracy and individualism that needs to be an object of critique; the problem is *not* liberal capitalism. In the heyday of critiques of bourgeois liberalism what had presented itself as capitalism (freedom of the market, choice, opportunity, autonomy and equality) was actually an ideological lure to cover a logic of market ruthlessness; it would make sense, in an era of individualism, to demystify the supposedly free subject, and point out that the free individual has always been determined as free to buy, sell and choose – once market conditions are accepted. And it would then make sense to think deconstructively about the forces of exchange, signification and relation that preclude any simple self of reflection or deliberative reason.

But what if even that minimal alibi of capitalist liberal theory is over and we are now in the grips of a flagrant neo-feudalism that does not even pay lip service to liberal ideology? In such a case, theory that deconstructed autonomy, self-presence and liberal self-determination – theory that pointed out contamination – might be less pertinent than a theory that aimed to think points of resistance within a general economy. Perhaps we can put it this way: against notions of presence, deconstruction was always a strategy of complicating and de-purifying sites of supposed origin (such as nature, the individual, consciousness or reason), and it would follow from this deconstructive force that liberalism would always have to be held to account if it tried to appeal to 'the' individual as some sovereign point upon which a polity of fairness might be based. Theoretically, such a mode of critique is all sound and pertinent, and it would always serve as a lever against notions of political purity and integrity, and would also – as Derrida's critiques of occupation and the French resistance proceeded to do – be necessary to point out that the supposedly evil, external and occupying power against which one poses resistance is never quite as *other* as one might like to believe. Deconstruction tirelessly resists any notion of a simply accidental and evil other against which one might posit one's self as a beautiful soul.

But here we need to think about *another* or supplementary theoretical logic focused less on pointing out the absence of purity or the impossibility of a locus outside systems of difference and exchange, and more on the point at which subtle differences of degree reach singular points and then create differences in kind. Rather than insist that there is nothing outside the text, we might want to examine the ways in which text – or forces of difference that are better thought of as *desire* – generate relations. We might need to do this because today we are experiencing *not* the liberal lie that a deliberating subject precedes and tempers capitalist exchange, but a full-blown abandonment of any notion of force or resistance.

I would suggest that May 1968 is a date that marks a demystification of the innocence and purity of labor as a simple outside of capitalism and ideology: there is no authentic human materiality that one might appeal to as a lever of resistance beyond capital. It would become the task of post-68-theory – as deconstruction evidenced – to problematize the relations among political bodies. If 1968 marks a threshold beyond which labor could no longer act as a foundation, there is a futher disturbance once liberal capitalism becomes subject to new forms of restriction in the name of security. I would suggest that 9/11 operates as a counter-date that allowed for the suspension of liberal illusions and that various crises – from the war on terror to the global financial crisis – enabled exceptional and executive interventions that abandoned all attempts at illusions of freedom and individualism. If corporations are now individuals then it is perhaps *not* the figure of the individual that needs to be deconstructed, and instead one needs to generate some resistance from *within* the system, *techne,* and difference that does not come from the purity of an outside. That is, rather than democracy or 'justice to come' (which would rely on us being critical of any sense that 'we' have achieved a position of legal good conscience), we need to think of *occupation*. What is sought is not some outside or beyond of capital but a rendering radical of capital *from within*. The problem with the 2008 global financial crisis was not that it was a victory of liberal capitalism, or even neoliberalism, but that it was the hijacking of the means of capital – exchange – while allowing some points to be exempted from the general terrain of difference and relations. The banks that were too big to fail emerged from what Deleuze and Guattari refer to as archaisms: feudal strongholds that remain rigid despite shifting into the openness of money, credit, speculation and futures. Not everything was subjected to the axiomatic of capital, and not everything was deemed to be no more significant than the flows that passed through it. If banks were too big to fail this was not because liberal ideology had triumphed, but because something that had always been radical in liberalism was reterritorialized: the very capacity for money to create flows and exchanges was impeded by the unit and mechanisms of money itself (banking, finance, traders).

The enemy, in short, is no longer bourgeois ideology and the putative benevolence of the market, but archaisms and rigidities that were never fully eliminated in the illusory heyday of post-war liberalism. What the concept of occupation offers is not an outside, but a way of calculating capitalism's rigidities and points of surplus. By occupying Wall Street the protestors re-mapped the notion of an open, decentered and 'global' crisis: the resistance to the 1% was not some Manichean appeal to the purity of the people but a form of minor politics in which the point of resistance had no identity other than that of its situation within an already distributed terrain. The 99% do not share a common ground, for the number labels a mass not an identity. The objections to the 1% were not directed to a 'who' or some essential enemy, but to the terrain or territory that by differences of degree created new thresholds and points of survival. To take an analogy from gender politics: if we think of 'woman' as some redemptive outside to patriarchy, then we remain in a logic of good and evil. To free oneself from this moralism it would be necessary to deconstruct sexual difference and abandon the figure of some great feminist beyond. There is no woman, only something like 'woman to come.' But in a post-feminist (or supposedly post-racial) America where it is vulgar to talk in essentialist terms about gender (or race or class), what happens when one no longer has an outside or resistant counter-identity? When Deleuze and Guattari theorized 'becoming-woman' they did so in the context of minor politics, and in a way that is pertinent for Occupy in the twenty-first century: there is no 'man' and we cannot try and save ourselves by way of the values of humanity or mankind, *but* we can think of the formation – by way of occupation – of local movements that disturb and decenter a system (such as Wall Street) that does not circulate widely and freely but constantly exempts itself and saves itself. Just as 'becoming-woman' created a line that was not that of self-constituting man, so 'occupy' generates a different line of becoming that is not that of capital growth and renewal.

II

Chronologically deconstruction does not precede Deleuzism, just as Jacques Derrida is hardly of an earlier generation than Gilles Deleuze. Today, though, there does seem to be some sort of sequence whereby one begins logically with the notion that it is difference or external relations that constitute relatively stable terms, and that one cannot step outside difference (deconstruction); then one takes the next step and starts to think about just what force, life or matter it is that generates difference (Deleuzism). Even in terms of literary history there is the high postmodernism of quotation, linguistic and textual self-reflexivity, and then a shift to local and multiple narratives focused on perception, feeling and the body. One can think here of Don Delillo's classically postmodern *White Noise* (1985) with its reference to simulacra, media, spectacle and cliché, and then the same writer's later *Body Artist* (2001) or *Point Omega* (2010) concerned far more with the visible and the sensible. Similarly, feminism seemed to be dominated by constructivist or linguistic conceptions of gender, subsequently displaced by a turn to the body; more often than not the same texts were involved but were read differently. Historically or critically (at least for the English-speaking world) the high era of deconstruction was in the 1980s and 1990s, and was then followed by a series of 'turns' away from a perceived textualism or overly literary post-structuralism towards a more vital, material and engaged Deleuzism.

This sequence coincides, I would suggest, with different political problems. For deconstruction one needed to problematize liberal anti-foundationalism; it is not sufficient to say that in the absence of any determined law one must decide for oneself, for one is always already complicit, determined and within the domain of difference that enables one to think and speak. There is no pure outside, and no site of good conscience. The liberal individual simply substitutes rather than displaces the onto-theology of the West, and needs to be deconstructed by insisting on one's inescapable location within difference. Deleuzism, from a similar genealogy, is less about demystifying origins and instead *remystifying*: how do some figures seem to rigidify or reterriorialize, despite our cynicism? Or, why is it that despite capitalism and cynicism desire is still enslaved to Oedipal, familial and personal rigidities? How did capital manage to escape difference and allow one axiom to overcode all others? More specifically, how – in this era of late capitalism and the supposed liberation of all exchange from moral conceptions of justice and fairness – were some entities (banks, money, and economic wisdom) deemed to be too important to be exposed to the contingency of force and survival? The problem is no longer the ideology of capitalist individualism and its dream of free exchange that needs to be tempered by an insistence on the constitutive differences that open the field of the market and the polity. Rather, one needs to ask, as Deleuze and Guattari do, about the ways in which figures like the family, the self, the economy, and even one's own desire impede desire's own tendencies.

These different political problems – deconstruction's war on the tyranny of pure presence and Deleuze's attempt to think, within difference, of a difference that makes a difference – present two modes of occupation. For deconstruction, one is always already occupied from without; when 'I' speak I do so by way of anarchical and archival forces of inscription that will always open any text or anything I say to an unpredictable future. For Deleuze and Guattari concepts of minor politics and 'becoming-woman' are less about the futural force of an utterance and more about the creation of minimal, barely discernible, not quite identifiable forces that occupy a field, taking on the same voice and then stuttering and reproducing different relations and combinations: resistance is not a question of borders or futures but is immanent. Consider what Derrida, in *Specters of Marx*, does with Marxist utopianism: there is no proper spirit that has been alienated by capital, but one can think, from within capital and technology, of that which haunts, repeats and solicits capital. Such a force is anarchic and cannot be held to account. It is radically futural, promissory and quasi-Messianic. It follows, for deconstruction, that literature is allied to justice because literature liberates a text from any grounding voice or context, allowing it to say anything whatever. By contrast, Deleuze and Guattari's politics is less that of a virtual future and less aligned with a mode of writing that is sent like a missive into an unimagined series of contexts. Rather, minor politics and minor literature occur as positive deflections and new forces that open in the here and now. For Deleuze and Guattari, Kafka generates minor literature, not because he imagined a Law beyond actual laws, but because he wrote of burrowing animals, corridors, castles, and endless machinations that were *so cramped* that they offered no outside and certainly no conception of man or 'the people.' Deconstruction tirelessly opened texts to a transcendence or promissory power they could not contain: 'justice to come,' 'absolute forgiveness' or 'infinite hospitality,' and was no doubt a great rejoinder to the smug post–Cold War ethics of the end of history. But by theorizing minor politics, nomadism and becoming-woman, Deleuze and Guattari offer a counter-foil not so much to liberal dreams of the end of history, but to today's neo-feudalisms that have reinstalled centralized power by way of notions of either financial emergency or post-political market freedom. That is, whereas capitalism was once moralized as a natural outcome of individual freedom, and was therefore haunted – as Derrida argued – by a necessary alienation that resided in any linguistic or economic system, twenty-first century capitalism has emptied the concept of personhood and markets of all moral sense. Corporations are people, and markets are not the means through which individuals exercise freedom; the market as such takes on its own godly being. Rather than the grand ideas of justice, democracy, hospitality and forgiveness that marked deconstruction, Deleuze and Guattari look at local, multiple and rogue incursions: rather than focus on the radical promise that resides in philosophy's never vanquished promise, their minor politics emphasizes the ways in which the introduction of the smallest distances and differences enables a new relation to the whole.

Don't rewrite Plato or Heidegger from within, re-read the metaphysics of the West; reconfigure all the voices, desires and potentials that already compose the assemblage of the world. Occupy a site; think locally, and destroy the globalizing tendencies that generate notions of *'the market,' 'the people.'* As John Protevi has argued, the attention to politics at the level of ideas is itself an ideology; rather than see the polity as effected from our systems of language and thought, we might think more various layers of forces that are material, virtual, linguistic, textual, local, geological and so on (Protevi 2013).

This distinction and sequence of deconstruction preceding Deleuzism (as it plays out in the history of Anglo-American theory) is partly an effect of the order of translation, and partly to do with intellectual and institutional history: phenomenology rather than Bergsonism was dominant in US and UK continental philosophy departments. Perhaps, also, the fact that 'theory' took place in literature departments rather than philosophy departments meant that a tendency towards textualism would win out over theories (such as Bergson's) that were based on intuition rather than language. I want to make another suggestion about the way we think of these two broad theoretical dominants, which are sometimes seen as opposites (the linguistic focus of deconstruction versus Deleuze's materialism and vitalism), and sometimes seen as a sequence, with Deleuze taking the problem of difference further, beyond language and humans. Sometimes this is how Deleuze and Guattari present themselves in relation to deconstruction, and how Deleuze thinks about his own relationship to writers like Foucault (Deleuze 2006: 62). One way to read Deleuze today is to see him as having picked up on a Spinozist tradition of politics and Marxism that has been overshadowed by French Hegelianism and that is being rethought today. But to state the relation and sequence this way is to think at the level of the history of ideas, and to think that ideas have a semi-autonomous history (which is itself a Marxist–Hegelian notion). But what if ideas are expressive, and what if the Deleuzian-Spinozist-materialist 'turn' were an unfolding of new potentialities and forces of life? I want to suggest that this is indeed the case and that the vogue for a Deleuzian mode of politics is enabled by a positive sense of occupation and a mode of politics that is less attuned to resistance; by the same token I want to suggest that deconstruction was broadly focused on the positivity of resistance in opposition to occupation.

Thinking about the shifting sense of occupation is not merely an observation in the use of a word – or what it means to occupy – so much as a different mode and style of political force. If occupation once figured the imposition of illegitimate power in an otherwise democratic polity, then it would make sense to question – as Derrida does – the supposed purity and integrity of the putatively innocent democratic state. If, as is increasingly the case, it is no longer a question of a state presenting itself as democratic by excluding and abandoning a few, then one needs to reconsider how concepts such as democracy have increasingly less force. This is what I mean by referring to a new feudalism: rather than promoting the free and open market that accidentally leaves a few at the bottom, it is now widely accepted that the few at the top will do all they can to maintain wider and wider difference; the very concept of banks that are 'too big to fail' reinstalls a power that exists by fiat rather than right. A few – the 1%, who now flagrantly name and mark themselves as exceptional by means of bonuses and stately architecture (such as Manhattan's Trump Tower) – have abandoned any pretension of the good polity. How does political critique proceed when bourgeois liberalism is no longer an ideology that sanctifies *laissez faire* capitalism, and when capitalism is no longer a general egalitarianism but operates as an all-inclusive, global and crisis-ridden system that requires autocratic intervention and various states of emergency in order to save the few who are too big to fail? I would suggest that we need to shift from a deconstruction of presence, consciousness, autonomy and integrity (which would be required in order to resist the lures of liberal individualism, or to resist the figure of the integrated and bound political body), and move towards a positive sense of occupation. How might one take up some point of disturbance within an already disturbed, distributed and decentered political field that is now flagrantly open to appropriation by an opportunistic and contingently autocratic 1%?

III

Deconstruction can be seen as bound up with the type of politics required by the French resistance: a politics in which something like occupation occurs – a hegemonic power installs itself and produces an internal outside such that one's state and language are no longer one's own. (And this problematic resistance continues with post-68 theorizations of how one might be politically mobilized without appealing to some innocent or natural outside, such as 'the worker,' or 'the other.' It also continues in post-colonial theories of mimicry, irony or parody: disturb the system of differences from within.) The politics of resistance in this sense is at once oriented against imposed power from without, while being critical of any posited innocence or freedom that would naturally resist occupation.

The Nazi occupation of France had a particularly profound effect on intellectual life, but Jacques Derrida's experience of occupation was even more tortured. The problem of one's own identity and displacement within one's own country and language were intensified by the fact that Derrida lost his French citizenship as a youth under the Vichy regime. From his own account this meant that Derrida was alienated from the simple resistance to occupation. Those who considered themselves to be 'purely' French could regard the intrusion of Nazism as an external evil, robbing them of the proper. For Derrida, there was an 'occupation without occupation': the supposed interiority of one's own language and identity was already an intrusion of an outside. There is never anything natural about citizenship for Derrida, but the experience of one's identity as precarious occurs not only in events of explicit political occupation (where one is overtaken by an other), but in modes where no occupation is required, for the very regime in which one lives and is a citizen may suspend belonging, producing one as a foreigner in the same place where one was once at home. The passage in which Derrida describes 'occupation without occupation' is worth quoting at length for its marking of three points: the way in which a 'mass' becomes stateless; the way in which this displacement occurs without one knowing, and without one being spatially displaced; and the curious relationship this bears to occupation, for it is the valiant notion of the French *resistance against occupation* (or that a certain evil was deemed to be external) that Derrida challenges. Displacement, non-identity and foreignness are internal, and become forces for a life-long mourning:

> As we know, citizenship does not define a cultural, linguistic, or, in general, historical participation. It does not cover all these modes of belonging. But it is not some superficial or superstructural predicate floating on the surface of experience.
>
> Especially not when this citizenship is, through and through, *precarious, recent, threatened,* and more artificial than ever. That is "my case"; the at once typical and uncommon situation of which I would like to speak. Especially not when one has obtained this citizenship in the course of one's life, which has perhaps happened to several Americans present at this colloqium, but also, and above all, not when one has lost it *in the course of one's life,* which has certainly not happened to almost any American. And if one day some individual or other has seen their citizenship *itself* withdrawn (which is more than a passport, a "green card," an eligibility or right to vote), has that ever happened to a *group* as such? I am of course not referring to some ethnic group seceding, liberating itself one day, from another nation-state, or giving up one citizenship in order to give itself another one in a newly instituted state. There are too many examples of this mutation.

> No, I am speaking of a "community" group (a "mass" assembling together tens or hundreds of thousands of persons, a supposedly "ethnic" or "religious" group that finds itself one day deprived, as a group, of its citizenship by a state that, with the brutality of a unilateral decision, withdraws it without asking for their opinion, and *without the said group gaining back any other citizenship. No other.*
>
> Now I have experienced that. Along with others, I lost and then gained back French citizenship. I lost it for years without having another. You see, not a single one. I did not ask for anything. I hardly knew, at the time, that it had been taken away from me, not, at any rate, in the legal and objective form of knowledge in which I am explaining it here (for, alas, I got to know it in another way). And then, one "fine day," without, once again, my asking for anything, and still too young to know it in a properly political way, I found the aforementioned citizenship again. The state, to which I never spoke, had given it back to me. (Derrida 1998: 15–16)

'Resistance,' for Derrida, names a certain French nationalist myth of noble opposition to occupation; what needs to be thought, against this innocence, is an occupation without occupation, or the way in which *without any physical or actual intrusion of an other* there might nevertheless be an expropriation of citizenship, and one that occurs without the grandeur of an event. Deconstruction therefore refuses the sense of resistance that defines itself *against occupation,* and instead poses another resistance, one that is internal and complicit, without innocence or purity. Rather than resistance being a force that a body exerts on an intruding outside, deconstruction worked with a constitutive and *positively negative* resistance. That is, rather than see the self as occupied from without by repressive forces, it is from the experience of resistance or opposition that one imagines that there must have been a pure and present subject; it is after the intrusion of otherness that one imagines an original subject. It follows that we might think of deconstructive politics as a war against the myth of occupation as an oppression that comes from without; we are constituted through resistance, but this resistance is against the impossible truth that there is nothing outside the text. It is a resistance to theory.

Derrida will insist on a politics that does not yearn for some space outside the limits of law, but that uses the logic of law to think a justice that will always remain 'to come.' Resistance, thought in terms of psychoanalysis, names the subject's own stifling of the truth: their symptom is not an affliction from without but something taken on such that they can imagine themselves suffering from an outside. If we accept constitutive resistance then justice will not be what the other destroys by way of occupying my proper terrain of citizenship, for there is no proper, no justice and no terrain of one's own. Resistance is first and foremost a resistance to the very forces of non-presence, negativity and non-identity; these differential forces, though precluding pure presence are nevertheless capable of generating justice, *if there is such a thing*. Writing on Foucault's attempt to (as Derrida sees it) find a historical space *outside* the rationalization and incarcerating logic of modernity, Derrida responds with a 'perpetual threat' that will always destroy the logic of opposition:

> For, in principle, all these determinations are, for the historian, either presences or absences; as such, they thus exclude haunting; they allow themselves to be located by means of signs, one would almost say on a table of absences and presences; they come out of the logic of opposition, in this case, the logic of inclusion *or* exclusion, of the alternative between the inside and the outside, and so on. The perpetual threat, that is, the shadow of haunting (and haunting is, like the phantom or fiction of an Evil Genius, neither present nor absent, neither positive nor negative, neither inside nor outside) does not challenge only one thing and another, the very logic of exclusion or foreclosure, as well as the history that is founded upon this logic and its alternatives. What is excluded is, of course, never simply excluded, not by the cogito nor by anything else, without this eventually returning – and this is what a certain psychoanalysis will have also helped us to understand. (Derrida 1994b: 242)

For Derrida, then, psychoanalysis is both about internal resistance, or a self that cannot confront its internal occupation, its own non-presence to itself. For Paul de Man, certainly not speaking in psychoanalytic terms, resistance to theory is *not* about refusing to believe this or that claim or argument; it is not like resistance to climate change or resistance to other inconvenient truths. It is resistance to the *untruth of truth*: one imagines that one's beliefs, attitudes, memories and narratives are faithful doubles of the real world. Theory, for de Man, is the cold and ruthless stare one directs at the inscriptions that compose one's world and one's innocence – the truth being elsewhere but never assimilable, certainly not in some graspable 'outside' (de Man 1982). Theory is at once necessary and impossible: the task of reading and thinking lies *not* in finding the proper foundation or ground of politics, but in a blank ungrounding. Theory strives to see the world without the joys of meaning and ownness, even if theory necessarily falls back into yet one more narrative of the proper. I would suggest that de Man's concept of resistance to theory – that there is not some simple lapse that precludes us from confronting the misprision between the inscriptions we take to be ours as opposed to the world that we take to be natural and there for representation – allows us to grasp deconstruction's conception of politics at its most rigorous. If there is no seamless or natural relation to the real, then political theory has as its task a form of anti-foundationalism that emphasizes the impossibility of finding a space outside the contested field of differences; this impossibility and undecidability is what we resist, and what we resist most notably in myths that would posit evil as some external occupying power.

That is, far from the emphasis on resistance (or our necessary captivation by inscriptive systems) generating a political *laissez faire* and acquiescence to late capitalist abandonment of truth, it is our necessary resistance to truth (or the untruth of truth – the truth that there is no truth) that provides one way of thinking politics outside the mode of occupation. We should reverse the anti-theory notion that French thought destroyed truth and left us with a world of amoral nihilism and relativism. Quite the contrary: today there is no shortage of truth. Fox News, tabloids, MSNBC, the Tea Party, what's left of the left: all declare quite shrilly that a certain path must be followed. And as Bruno Latour (2014) has pointed out, we seem to have abandoned scientific doubt when it comes to economists who tell us that we must bail the banks out *now*, and not wait for further evidence. At the same time we seem so committed to the idea of truth and verification that we do not act on evidence for climate change, because we are waiting for all the acts to come in. We suffer – today – not from doubt and relativism, but from a literalist notion that there is a truth and that there is one system that grants us access to the world: the new positivism of finance. So when Deleuze insists in his books on cinema that we have stopped believing in the world, and when (with Guattari) he describes capitalism as a dominance of cynicism, this needs to be understood alongside the theory of the despotism of the signifier: it is as though there is at one and the same time an abandonment of the distance between sign and world, *and* a simple acceptance of the single system of signs that compose the shrill certainty of the world as it is, capitalism as we know it in its flagrant 'just so.' The value of de Man's insistence on theory and Deleuze and Guattari's insistence on minor politics is that rather than aim to disturb language from within, one accepts the non-coincidence of linguistic systems with other strata, *and* refuses the privilege accorded to any single system that would present itself as the code of all codes, the narrative of all narratives. This is not simply another form of liberalism whereby the absence of ultimate truth places us in a position of deliberation and ongoing communicative reflection: for there will always be some sort of appropriation of one strata by another, and a laziness that resists the complex multiplicities that go beyond any single polity. Resistance is constitutive; there will always be some refusal of the blank stare of theory that abandons hope of grasping some innocent 'outside' (de Man), always a resistance to immanence as such that is not immanent *to* any transcendence (Deleuze). But there are two ways of thinking radical immanence or non-transcendence. What the absence of any privileged outside meant for the time of deconstruction in the 1980s and 1990s was that capitalism should not be opposed in any simple way. There has always been *techne* and alienation. It is not the case that we might step outside ideology and find the truth for the very notion of an original truth that some sign system might grasp is ideology. Resistance to the necessary distance of signs and the banality of inscription *is ideology*; that resistance is neither avoidable nor capable of being reformed. Instead, all we have is a tireless war on all the modes of transcendence that might present themselves as good or benevolent outsides.

In response to this we might want to ask: was not the 2008 global financial crisis precipitated precisely by just this abandonment of reference? But things are not so simple, for while it is the case that futures, derivatives, hedge funds and the selling on of toxic assets enabled an ungrounded and uncontrolled system that went into free fall, the problem was neither unbridled exchange nor the absence of real value, but some ongoing notion that exchange was grounded in assets and that there would ultimately be a way of translating numbers back into material wealth (if there is such a thing). There is nothing at all valid in the notion that post-structuralism's critique of representation plays a role in nihilism, relativism and capitalist cynicism. On the contrary, it is still the case that incontrovertible truths are asserted without any sense of the impossibility of determination; we are now referring to corporations as individuals, assuming that these entities are real, bounded and agential. Indeed, the 2008 crisis was possible precisely because some myth of reference precluded examination of an essentially virtual network: supposedly, at the base of it all, there were commodities, homes attached to mortgages, speculation about buyers and sellers – all real and material things. The problem lay in the notion that financial circulation was ultimately grounded on things, or that financial speculation wasn't the entirely fictional enterprise that it was. The very idea that banks operated as some necessary structure that was so significant as to be too big to fail did *not* come from a postmodern notion that reality is untethered, quite the contrary.

What is required, then, is not some naïve reaction that turns us *back* to reality, and that expels deconstruction as a 'sign of the times' of late capital. Rather, the next question or problem *after* we accept anti-foundationalism, is how deterritorialized, groundless, unnatural, and open exchange gets reterritorialized into some manufactured or hallucinated center? How is that in all this free-floating speculation *some* bodies came to be foundational, and eventually too big to fail? How did certain bodies, faces and persons maintain the prestige that enabled them, after the 2008 US election, to suspend social policies for emergency bail-outs, as though crisis rendered certain forms of expertise more powerful? The problem is not nihilism, decentering and lack of foundations and values; it is the failure to render nihilism active, for it was the experience of crisis and ungrounding that allowed for a seizing of autocratic authority and an ongoing practice of disaster ethics: in an age of volatility and precarious life – we are told – we cannot afford to be too relativist, and need to turn back to management and expertise. Should we really be thinking that in a time of crisis we need to buoy up some sites of concentrated capital in order to keep the rest of the field in play? Or, would it not be a question – without any illusion of stepping outside of capitalism – of exposing points of *theft*? When Deleuze and Guattari insist that the social field begins with *theft* not exchange, they do not so much oppose capitalism as they create an idea of powerfully destructive excessive capital. If life were simply free exchange then there would be no basic stability, but if force is 'originally' stored, taken, harbored and then squandered, one site in the field appears as powerful and even structural. It is not from scarcity that political assemblages are formed, but from excess and theft: a body seizes and stores force, and from that pooling of force an organized or deterritorialized reference point is constituted. Political life occurs as the repression of exchange, not because exchange is foundational but because radically unimpeded flows of exchange would destroy the relatively stable points achieved by marking out quantities or properties as one's own: desire begins not from a stable point that one might then establish as a site of exchange, but from a seizing of force that establishes a stability (territorialization), and that enables a system of exchange that – in turn – is never fully free but always referred to a locus (deterritorialization). One steals therefore one becomes. It is only by impeding an absolutely deterritorialized flow that anything like a territory is assembled:

> It is theft that prevents the gift and the countergift from entering into an exchangist relation. Desire knows nothing of exchange, *it knows only of theft and gift* ...
>
> Will it be said that, if desire knows nothing of exchange, it is because exchange is desire's unconscious? Will this be explained by the exigencies of generalized exchange? But what entitles one to declare that shares of debt are secondary compared with a totality that is "more real"? Yet exchange is known, well known in the primitive socius-but as that which must be exorcised, encasted, severely restricted, so that no corresponding value can develop as an exchange value that would introduce the nightmare of a commodity economy. The primitive market operates through bargaining rather

> than by fixing an equivalent that would lead to a decoding of flows and a collapse of the mode of inscription on the socius. We are brought back to our point of departure: the fact that exchange is inhibited and exorcised by no means attests to its primary reality, but demonstrates on the contrary that the essential process is not exchanging, but inscribing or marking. (Deleuze and Guattari 1983: 186)

We can think of the way plants store energy by way of photosynthesis, with the whole human strata being possible because of the appropriation of that energy. In the beginning is metabolism or the enhancement of one body by the appropriation of energy of another. Bodies are distributed according to the extent to which they can appropriate (and then squander) to the point of elevating themselves above the threshold of need. If we accept *this* account of politics, concerned less with beliefs, consciousness, identity and rights and more with pure quantities (or intensities that create quantities, for it is storing and harboring that enables the calculation and exchange mechanisms of money), then we might think less of finding some outside of capital and instead think of the way in which theft produces authority.

Is this not what the Occupy movement succeeded in part in achieving? Rather than the identity of friend and enemy, good and evil, or inside and outside, it was a question of distribution and hoarding to the point where shifts in quantity produced kinds – we are now dealing with percentages, not individuals. We need to reverse the notion that late capitalism is calculative without morality, and instead say that exchange and genuine calculation – who has taken what – is impeded by morality, by wars on welfare and various other supposed threats to life and family. Again it is sanctimonious truth – the truth of capitalism in its current form as the only way – that needs to be destroyed by a sense of simulation, inscription and a mode of theory that refuses such smug certainty. Power has always been achieved by impeding exchange and establishing a moral center, but the new feudalism that marks the present is closer to a primal horde of flagrant appropriation and imposition of necessity than it is to a falsely universalizing bourgeois township of self-interested traders.

In this respect, we need to think beyond deconstruction's sense of necessary occupation and resistance, but not because what we need is a good old-fashioned dose of truth and reality. Think of how futures and hedging 'worked,' or the ways in which speculation enabled persons who were nothing more than agents of exchange (day traders, brokers); this system of exchange was made possible only by way of the lure that there was some ultimate reality or substance to what was being exchanged. Ostensibly, hedge funds bet on future outcomes, just as mortgages are originally debts attached to property, but are subsequently circulated and repackaged. Money markets also function on the lure of substitution, or that money is the sign of value. There is, in the world of unbridled finance no shortage of realist fictions. The crisis was enabled precisely by what de Man referred to far more broadly as aesthetic ideology: the notion that the figures that captivate our attention are signs of an underlying and amenable reality. One needs to criticize speculation *not* because it takes its gaze off reality and starts to bet wildly on what has no substance, but because it deploys a language (or tropology) of substance and reality. What is really occurring is the creation of power by way of the illusion of substance in the hands of a few who are stealing the practice of exchange. On the surface the numbers being circulated in the years leading up to the crisis were signs of people's savings, houses and futures; but as pyramid and Ponzi schemes disclosed, there was no pyramid, no base that was big enough to support the heights of financial fantasy.

IV

What does this mean for thinking about theory and politics today? First, I would suggest that what Deleuzian or Deleuzo-Guattarian modes of politics offer is an intensification, rather than reversal, of the positive sense of resistance and occupation. Their use of the term 'desire' is the very opposite of the 'desires' of consumers for products; desire is revolutionary – directly – because it is without anchor in identities or investments (Deleuze and Guattari 1983: 113). What is resisted and repressed is desire, and desire is not a quality so much as a quantity without quality:

> Capitalism institutes or restores all sorts of residual and artificial, imaginary, or symbolic territorialities, thereby attempting, as best it can, to recode, to rechannel persons who have been defined in terms of abstract quantities. Everything

> returns or recurs: States, nations, families. That is what makes the ideology of capitalism "a motley painting of everything that has ever been believed." The real is not impossible; it is simply more and more artificial. Marx termed the twofold movement of the tendency to a falling rate of profit, and the increase in the absolute quantity of surplus value, the law of the counteracted tendency. As a corollary of this law, there is the twofold movement of decoding or deterritorializing flows on the one hand, and their violent and artificial reterritorialization on the other. (Deleuze and Guattari 1983: 34)

To take up a space – to occupy – and then to do so in the name of a differential – 1% versus 99% – is to begin to destroy the field of political identities, interests and realities, and to do so by way of thinking intensities: at what point does a differential produce an intolerable relation? Second, this shift in inflection opens up a different way of thinking about capitalism: deconstruction would, strictly, not be able to posit some historical outside to the system of capital. The notion of a proper relation to work, the earth, nature or production, that would then be overtaken by some external evil needs to be countered by thinking of internal occupation: to speak, write, think, work, dream, desire and demand justice is already to speak in a language that comes from elsewhere, that is other. For deconstruction this means that rather than trying to think of some point before or outside capital, and rather than resist capital, one needs to think justice, democracy, hope and the future as that which disturbs all the forces of resistance and occupation that preclude any pure outside.

By contrast with this critical and negative mode of deconstruction, Deleuze and Guattari think quite positively about what it is to be occupied by the voice of an other, what it is to be invaded, overtaken, by a voice not one's own. It is in their book on Kafka that they take the same starting point of deconstruction – signs are *not* signs of the world but are positive creations of territories – but generate a different line of departure. Rather than accept the mournful distance of the destruction of the dream of reference, they theorize a minor politics. Kafka, a Jew, wrote in German and in doing so was a foreigner in his own tongue; far from seeing this in terms of being internally occupied (having an identity disorder), language becomes a force liberated from expression, identity and reference. A minor literature frees signification from the ideology of the aesthetic: this is not the great voice or art that is expressive of 'the people.' In Kafka, it is *both* as though language appears as already oddly inhuman, not one's own, *and* as not aligned with any tradition expressive of mankind. The people are missing and the words and signs proliferate less as claims or promises of an imagined future than as disturbances of meaning. If minor literature breaks from the coherence of the canon and is written not as the expression of 'a people' but more as the marking out of inscriptions that stake out differences that do not yet have sense or reference, then minor politics – we might say – could be something like a scream, noise, mark or disturbance that is not yet expressive of a people, nor even of a hoped for reality:

> A minor literature doesn't come from a minor language; it is rather that which a minority constructs within a major language. But the first characteristic of minor literature in any case is that in it language is affected with a high coefficient of deterritorialization. In this sense, Kafka marks the impasse that bars access to writing for the Jews of Prague and turns their literature into something impossible – the impossibility of not writing, the impossibility of writing in German, the impossibility of writing otherwise. The impossibility of not writing because national consciousness, uncertain or oppressed, necessarily exists by means of literature ("The literary struggle has its real justification at the highest possible levels"). The impossibility of writing other than in German is for the Prague Jews the feeling of an irreducible distance from their primitive Czech territoriality. And the impossibility of writing in German is the deterritoralization of the German population itself, an oppressive minority that speaks a language cut off from the masses, like a "paper language" or an artificial language; this is all the more true for the Jews who are simultaneously a part of this minority and excluded from it, like "gypsies who have stolen a German child from its crib." In short, Prague German is a deterritorialized language, appropriate for strange and minor uses. (This can be

> compared in another context to what blacks in America today are able to do with the English language.)
>
> The second characteristic of minor literatures is that everything in them is political. In major literatures, in contrast, the individual concern (familial, marital, and so on) joins with other no less individual concerns, the social milieu serving as a mere environment or a background; this is so much the case that none of these Oedipal intrigues are specifically indispensable or absolutely necessary but all become as one in a large space. Minor literature is completely different; its cramped space forces each individual intrigue to connect immediately to politics. The individual concern thus becomes all the more necessary, indispensable, magnified, because a whole other story is vibrating within it. (Deleuze and Guattari 1986: 16–17)

Thinking of minor politics and minor literature in this way might help us enhance a new sense of resistance and of occupation that was the hallmark of the Occupy movement. First, if we accept that deconstruction has put paid to any notion of innocence or purity outside capital (precisely because to speak is already to be operating within some already constituted system of exchange and differences), then we can take one step further by beginning with minor literature. Rather than accept that one is always already alienated from one's own language, one writes in the manner of an alien and alienates language from itself. Think of the slogan of the 99%: part of the effectiveness of this rhetorical gesture was that on the one hand it had no real referent (for the accuracy of the number did not answer to any constituted group at all, but was something like a bet, as though simply declaring 'we are the 99%' might gesture to a 'people to come'); on the other hand the grouping also performed a certain event of non-identity – not workers, not women, and certainly not those who claimed to possess a grander demystifying knowledge that would be other than the calculus of Wall Street. The group who occupied Wall Street were in no way 'representative' of any 99%, but they were installing themselves precisely in the pseudo-actual or quasi-actual site of the illusion of capitalist reference. One of the main criticisms of the movement was lack of direction, lack of coherence and a certain youthful opportunism, as though there had been a joyful decision just to make some noise and situate oneself somewhere, with rationale and politics being an afterthought.

And it is here that we have to take quite seriously what the concept of minor politics offers, and how it helps us think of a new mode of resistance that emerged in the Occupy movements. How does one resist a power without positing oneself as some more enlightened or more authentic body whose very exclusion from power grants one a right and capacity to speak critically? A certain Marxist conception of the worker (whose labor will always grant them a genuine sense of the struggle of existence and resistance of the real) is easily more authentic than the Wall Street banker whose life consists only of numbers. Similarly a certain conception of feminism, ranging from eco-feminism's insistence on women's proximity or association with nature to corporeal feminism's critique of an abstract and quantifying modernity would seem to offer us levers against the ravages of capital; but such motifs do so by way of a fantasy that resistance comes from outside.

Occupy was not a workers' movement, nor a women's movement; it was – by contrast – a movement that can be thought of by way of a Deleuzian conception of sexual difference, which follows on from the conception of minor politics. As Deleuze and Guattari note in *A Thousand Plateaus* one might accept, now and again, the force of majoritarian claims – such as those that conceive women as a group who have been deprived of a voice and who now wish to speak. But a minor politics is one that begins with *becoming-woman*: what if there is no space outside that might enable one to form a new identity? What if the term 'woman' were composed from the terrain one wishes to destabilize? What if one were always already occupied by the forces from the outside such that it would be more forceful to focus less on identity than anonymity, *not* being of one's own kind, such that becoming-woman would be minor in refusing authenticity, identity and propriety? One does not mourn, but intensifies, identity disorder: mark one's political movement by installing oneself in a space, making noise, then giving oneself a number (99%). This war of becoming is a war of differentials, not peace opposed to war, but a war on the rigidification of the field.

In the beginning of the Occupy movement there was no body, not even a mass, but simply a disturbance *and* a sense of occupation that was spatial and virtual. The movement was in part performative: occupying Wall Street did not occur because of the fulfillment of a task, but instead generated a series of tasks. Install oneself somewhere and then that will constitute *who one is,* 'we are the people who occupy,' rather than 'we occupy because we are the people.' And it is this rhetoric of a non-identity achieved by taking up a space and a number that I would argue is one of sexual difference: for an encounter is sexual when forces enter into relation and composition and then generate rogue and unpredictable (and certainly not productive, but often creative) outcomes. The sense of occupation may once have been marked by a notion that who 'I' am is always already other; I am always already occupied, and this foreignness to oneself is precisely what one most resists. But today there is another sense of what it means to occupy: one does not resist or overthrow external or imposed power from some inside. To occupy is to produce a territory: not a territory *of* bodies who share a common ground. By occupying common ground the multiple bodies of the Occupy movement rendered that ground open, virtual, viral and creative. The spread of Occupy was less by way of identity, belief or program and more by way of replication, such that others started to Occupy in cities as far afield as Melbourne and London, and then produced resistance *not* to some alien and external evil but rather to a distribution and calculus that might be thought otherwise, though not in any moment of purity, nor from some innocent outside.

Works Cited

Deleuze, Gilles. 1993. *The Fold: Leibniz and the Baroque.* Trans. Tom Conley. Minneapolis: University of Minnesota Press.

Deleuze, Gilles. 2006. *Foucault.* Trans. Sean Hand. London: Continuum.

Deleuze, Gilles and Félix Guattari. 1983. *Anti-Oedipus: Capitalism and Schizophrenia.* Trans. Robert Hurley, Mark Seem and Helen R Lane. Minneapolis: University of Minnesota Press.

Deleuze, Gilles and Félix Guattari. 1986. *Kafka: Toward a Minor Literature.* Trans. Dana Polan. Minneapolis: University of Minnesota Press.

Deleuze, Gilles and Félix Guattari. 1987. *A Thousand Plateaus: Capitalism and Schizophrenia.* Trans. Brian Massumi. Minneapolis: University of Minnesota Press.

Deleuze, Gilles and Félix Guattari. 2004. *Anti-Oedipus: Capitalism and Schizophrenia.* Trans. Robert Hurley, Mark Seem, and Helen R Lane. London: Continuum.

de Man, Paul. 1982. 'The Resistance to Theory'. *Yale French Studies* 63: 3–20.

Derrida, Jacques. 1978. *Writing and Difference.* Trans. Alan Bass. London: Routledge.

Derrida, Jacques. 1994a. *Specters of Marx.* Trans. Peggy Kamuf. London: Routledge.

Derrida, Jacques. 1994b. 'To Do Justice to Freud'. Trans. Pascale-Anne Brault and Michael Naas. *Critical Inquiry* 20 (2): 227–66.

Derrida, Jacques. 1998. *Monolingualism of the Other; or, The Prosthesis of Origin.* Trans. Patrick Mensah. Stanford: Stanford University Press.

Latour, Bruno. 2014. 'Beyond Belief: On the Forms of Knowledge Proper to Religious Beings'. *'Religion and Plurality of Knowledge'* (May 12). Groningen. Accessed May 4, 2015 from: http://sggroningen.nl/en/evenement/beyond-belief

Protevi, John. 2013. *Life, War, Earth: Deleuze and the Sciences.* Minneapolis: University of Minnesota Press.

Chapter 5

Preoccupations

VERENA ANDERMATT CONLEY

In the introduction to his translation of Gilles Deleuze and Félix Guattari's *A Thousand Plateaus*, a breathtaking study of capitalism and schizophrenia in the shape of a mosaic, Brian Massumi declares that the philosophers urge those who contest current modes of governance to occupy the street rather than to hold the fort. Taking to the street, the history of civil disobedience tells us over and again, is risky business. Yet of late people have taken to the street in many of the world's urban centers.

Much has been said and written since 2011 about what now is often simply called Occupy, from its possible origin in the Arab Spring (2010) and the Indignants Movement in Spain (2011) to its visibility today as an adventitious worldwide movement. Not only in the media but also in unlikely places such as the academy, discussions have focused on Occupy in the context of social injustices and economic inequality for which banks and financial centers have become symbolic icons. In the United States, 'Wall Street,' a place name (as it had been in the sub-title of Melville's 'Bartleby the Scrivener,' a tale anticipating much of what Occupy happens to be), functions as a synecdoche of an implacable barrier, the great white wall of capital. The occupation of Wall Street (or rather, of the contiguous Zuccotti Park) represented the 99% of the underprivileged and the unemployed in their fight and resistance against the 1% holding the fort, and its outcroppings in and around the stock exchange.

Can it be asked if Occupy was a social and a political movement, bearing comparison with not a full-fledged revolution such as that of 1789 or 1917, but at the very least with a rebellion or a revolt in the manner of 1968, where the Sorbonne was occupied for days and nights on end, the revolt having for a first time united students and workers? If so, and if it has political mettle, what is its future? Or is it simply a ritual celebration that – as Roland Barthes stated long before the fact in *Mythologies* (1957), a collection of studies of popular culture – depoliticizes itself in the pleasure of its performance? Slavoj Žižek, a sympathetic critic, warned the participants of Occupy of the risks of turning their movement into a narcissistic festival in place of a manifestation of *dissensus*. He asked participants not to become enamored with themselves:

> The danger [is] that [the protesters] will fall in love with themselves, with the nice time they are having in the 'occupied' places. Carnivals come cheap – the true test of their worth is what remains the day after, how our normal daily life will be changed. We spend a pleasant moment together here. But remember, carnivals are cheap. Of importance is the day after, when people go on with their everyday lives. That's the moment to ask whether anything has changed? (Žižek 2012)

Other philosophers and cultural theorists have been less critical. Judith Butler argues that Occupy is a bodily outcry and a demand for a physical and mental space in which to live:

> When bodies gather as they do to express their indignation and to enact their plural existence in public space, they are also making broader demands. They are demanding to be recognized and to be valued; they are exercising a right to appear and to exercise freedom; they are calling for a livable life. These values are presupposed by particular demands, but they also demand a more fundamental restructuring of our socio-economic and political order. (Butler 2011)

Michael Hardt and Antonio Negri, in turn, in a pamphlet entitled 'Declaration' write that as a movement of revolt Occupy is symptomatic of 'dominant forms of subjectivity produced in the context of the current social and political crisis. [They] engage four primary subjective figures – the indebted, the mediatized, the securitized, and the represented – all of which are impoverished and their powers for social action are masked or mystified' (Hardt and Negri 2012). When Žižek cautions against slogans and Butler calls for a life worth living; or when Hardt and Negri urge humans who are immobilized and infantilized by the media to go beyond a threshold of revolt, we can read in filigree many of the Gilles Deleuze and Félix Guattari's reflections on resistance. Often in similar terms, on the heels of 1968, denouncing the state of the world under capitalism in a phase of rampant and destructive expansion, they urged students, readers and listeners to pry open spaces within its sphere that might enable the beginnings of a greater reinvention and recomposition.

What are the links between the philosophers' preoccupations and those both of Occupy Wall Street and of Occupy in general? It is well known that the two philosophers consider concepts to be both intellectual and political instruments carried in a 'toolbox.' What can be drawn from their 'toolbox,' Deleuze's metaphor for the arsenal that can be put to the use of rearranging inherited configurations of life? In addition to practical concepts, what is the dynamism and force of conviction that we can lift from their writings to help Occupy thrive? While Žižek, Butler and especially Hardt and Negri (the most 'Deleuzian' of the chosen list) try to address today's problems, I propose first to go back to the philosophers' pronouncements and then to see if and how they can be articulated with Occupy today.

The call to occupying the street rather than holding the fort runs through Deleuze and Guattari both literally and metaphorically. The philosophers emphasize change through movement and flow, be it of people, desire, affects or thought. Advocating an ever-unfinished, non-dialectical, and non-hierarchical model of constructive dissent, they do away with the Marxian notion of class structure to consider social conflict in terms of mobile micro- and macro-cosms, ever-shifting lines, rhythms and harmonics. Already in 1975, in the French version of their first co-authored book, *Kafka, Toward a Minor Literature*, Deleuze and Guattari emphasize the need to put a dominant idiom into a condition of variation. Never stable, a dominant language, a common and unquestioned *lingua franca* that generally controls subjectivity, is modulated where popular use of dialects, vernaculars, verbal aberrations and multilingualism alters its unilateral (and clearly monolingual) character. When used tactically, minor languages instill into dominant rhythms cadences of stunning variety (Deleuze and Guattari 1987: 100–110). In 1976, in *Rhizome:*

Introduction (translated as *On the Line* (1983)), the philosophers write about how the line, *la ligne* – rather than the point or period that tends to 'stop' a harmonic flow – can be drawn to chart new mappings for the ends of mental and physical de- and reterritorialization. When they are drawing lines, diagrams or making maps, individual subjects or groups seek to invent other ways of moving about and through an otherwise highly regimented world. *On the Line* serves as the introduction to *A Thousand Plateaus*, as I suggested, a mosaic, motley, or variegated work that addresses the question of how to occupy a space through what Deleuze and Guattari call rhizomatic or adventitious and multilateral thinking. If *Anti-Oedipus*, the first volume of *Capitalism and Schizophrenia*, had focused on exposing and abolishing a system that blocks all roads to change, the second volume, *A Thousand Plateaus*, of ostensibly more pragmatic virtue, shows how rhizomatic thinking makes transformations both imaginable and possible.

In this very spirit Deleuze and Guattari look to another literary example in an idiom other than their own. Henry James's 'In the Cage' (roughly dated 1884), an aptly titled novella in which the protagonist, engaged to a dull and rigid clerk finds how a simple variation in the order of things happens to change her life (Deleuze and Guattari 1987: 95–100).[1] At the beginning of the story, living within the narrow confines of a routine, she moves on a 'molar, rigid line of segmentarity' (Deleuze and Guattari 1987: 195). An event takes place when a couple enters the shop at which the clerk works to send enigmatic telegrams that put the young clerk, almost unbeknownst to herself, on a 'molecular, supple line of segmentation' (196). She becomes *preoccupied* with what she has heard and witnessed. The heroine eventually reaches a kind of abstract line that ultimately she refuses either to draw or to follow. When she goes back to her fiancé she is no longer on the same line. Her life has been altered. She has traced a line of flight that within her milieu takes her elsewhere or, as it were, that deterritorializes. A seemingly banal, everyday event affects her and makes her occupy space differently. By extension, what and how she becomes can be linked to Occupy whose members, by virtue of a seemingly unimportant event, have a suddenly different purchase on their surroundings. In their reading of 'In the Cage' Deleuze and Guattari distinguish three intermingling sorts of lines: a line of 'rigid segmentarity,' another of 'molecular segmentarity' and an abstract line, a line 'of flight.' The first line, they write, is one of words and interminable conversations and the second of silences and allusions. However, when the line of flight flashes the heroine jumps upon and rides with it. She (and for the sympathetic reader, the ideal personage she would become) can finally speak literally of anything without respect to a given position or place. Implied from the philosophers' reading is that, in a creatively intransitive sense, cage or no cage, she truly *occupies*.

Elsewhere in *A Thousand Plateaus* ways of detaching oneself from a territory by drawing a line or tracing a diagram (which is tantamount to occupying) are discussed in a series of chapters or what, varying on the idiolect of Gregory Bateson, they call 'plateaus.' The latter are territories held together by affective intensities made possible at a specific moment in history from which, in the 'present' (for the authors the aftermath of 1968), they think and write. Next to chapters on variations in language and the tracing of lines and diagrams, the philosophers introduce a set of plateaus that deal specifically with space. A gridded – or striated – city or state space, they claim, is always riddled by another movement that continually 'smoothes' it, that introduces play, that creates openings through which one can move and think otherwise. They advocate the privileging of *nomos* or open spaces over the closure of *logos* and/or reasoned discourse. In short, they urge people to occupy the street mentally or physically rather than hold the fort against an overarching order from outside or above. From an event that took place in 1227, when what they call the 'war machine' appeared on the Asian Steppes, Deleuze and Guattari endeavor to inflect the heavily organizational spaces of their own time with others that they see marked by creative compositions and uncommon rhythms (Deleuze and Guattari 1987: 363). One hundred pages later, they return to the same place, to the steppes, where they note: to write is to resist and to think is to voyage 'in place' (Deleuze and Guattari 1987: 482). To think and to write mean to leave the habitual, repetitious, rigid line of segmentarity while staying in place:

> To think is to voyage … what distinguishes the two kinds of voyages is neither a measurable quantity of movement, nor something that would be only in the mind, but the mode of spatialization, *the manner of being in space, of being for space*

(*emphasis added*). Voyage smoothly or in striation, and think the same way... But there are always passages from one to the other, transformations of one within the other, reversals ... Voyaging smoothly is a becoming, and a difficult, uncertain becoming at that. It is not a question of returning to preastronomical navigation, nor to the ancient nomads. The confrontation between the smooth and the striated, the passages, alternations and superpositions, are under way today, running in the most varied directions. (Deleuze and Guattari 1987: 482)

Elsewhere, they link such transformation and opening of passages to what they call the continual intermingling of affect, percept and concept, or as Deleuze put it in a letter to Réda Bensmaia, new ways of feeling, new ways of seeing and new ways of conceiving.[2] Again, the three modes are simultaneously circulating through one another.

Writing at a time of social and political turmoil arising simultaneously all over the world, from Algeria to Vietnam, from Cuba, Central and Latin America to the civil rights movement in the United States, the philosophers briefly sense a generalized 'becoming-minoritarian' that – they are adamant – has much to do with ways of distributing and occupying space, with putting into variation, or with deterritorializing through drawing lines and crafting diagrams. Now, years later, it can be asked if and how their philosophical pronouncements, which are never celebratory but, based as they are on the irruption of a sudden 'preoccupation,' resonate with Occupy. Has Occupy also put a dominant discourse into variation? Has it led to the creation of new diagrams, the deterritorializing our sensibilities, and conceiving different and varied modes of occupying space?

A response to the question can be broached through the events that meshed with the writing of *A Thousand Plateaus*. The very real though brief euphoria that Deleuze and Guattari felt around May 1968 and that later inspired its sequel did not last (Dosse 2007: 208–21; 297–308). Soon, what Guattari called the 'Winter Years' came with a keenly felt influx of rampant corporatism and economic globalization (Guattarri 1986). In strong contrast Paul Virilio looked upon 1968 dismissively, calling it a simple rehearsal, a piece of play-acting, a kind of pseudo-event.

Sympathetic and possibly in accord with Virilio, notably after the fall of the Iron Curtain, Deleuze and Guattari did not join the chorus of those praising the event as the triumph of liberalism. Without nostalgia or despair, each in turn – Guattari in 1989 and Deleuze 1990 – denounced the new state of the world (Dosse 2007: 458–9). Deleuze's outlook became bleak. At the end of *Negotiations* (1990), first in an interview with Negri titled 'Control and Becoming' and then in a short addendum, entitled 'Postscript on Control Societies,' he notes without nostalgia that we have lost the world (Deleuze 1995: 167–82). It has been taken from us. No real resistance is possible when money, not affect, neither variation nor pulsation, is the currency of life. Because it wafts in the flow of capital, he speculates, even art, that had once produced singularities and made possible invention and creativity, can no longer be countenanced. Perhaps the only thing left is the opening of small vacuoles from and within which to think otherwise. At the time of his suicide in 1995 Deleuze was rumored to have said that mentally and physically he was finished.

In *The Three Ecologies* (1989), Guattari for his part decried the loss of the subject and of human relations in an age that is in the grip of infantilizing media in collusion with omnipotent corporate control of the state. In the post-Fordist era, consumerism, he argued, transforms humans into market samples and collectivities into molar aggregates. He called for a reconstruction of the subject on his terms: by emphasizing singularities, in the making of rhizomatic connections, and by advocating a collective solidarity. Building on an existential vocabulary, Guattari notes the 'fragility' of the subject as a for-itself – opposed to the in-itself, immobilized by debt and lobotomized by the media – and its capacity to change. Crucial for our purposes is that Guattari asserts on the one hand that changes can occur *autopoietically*, unbeknownst to the subject, before she or he even opens onto the environing world. In either case, something suddenly affects the subject that leads to a 'preoccupation' of sorts, an event which produces a change in the individual or in the social body. Even among large aggregates of given populations spontaneous change and types of recomposition are possible. Singularities or groups move about and across striated spaces under the impetus of a different affect, without colliding head-on with the group or territory they are leaving. Guattari speaks of a gradual slippage and of 'soft subversions' (Guattari 2009). On the other hand, in a world reduced to systems of economic, juridical, scientific signs, those who are in a position to affect subjectivities – educators, architects, urban planners, artists, media people, but also those in music, fashion or food – need to show a sense of responsibility in order to induce change in others. They drive a wedge into a given state of things that will cleave and then lead to other mental and social preoccupations from where, eventually, transformations can be addressed. Preoccupations occur spontaneously at the same time that those in a position to affect subjectivities are aware of their responsibility of initiating change.

For Deleuze and Guattari, *revolutions* fail wherever they are anchored in history. What is needed is a becoming-revolutionary of the people, that is, a constant turning away from history and toward the future in anticipation of other events. They privilege art (provided that its relation with the world is not in collusion with capital and marketing), singularity (which is plural insofar as it does not belong to individuals) and invention (which is related to the force of an event). Militantism is important, but it can only be temporary and cannot be reduced to slogans. In Guattari's words, one has to be 'analytically militant.' In *The Three Ecologies*, he argues that singularities come together temporarily to militate for certain short- or long-term objectives, such as the rights of women, of gays and of the flora and fauna composing the environment. Guattari does not provide an economic strategy but focuses rather on the reinvention of the subjects or, on 'effects of subjectivation' to foment a change in thinking and social exchange that will yield a more just but also a more enjoyable world where, just as Judith Butler has it, life is worth living.

The philosopher makes it clear that ecology, a way of addressing and governing one's *oikos* or the earth as habitat, bears at once mental, social and natural components. Nature is not something 'to go back to' (if it ever has been), but something that must be considered carefully in terms of the way it is 'occupied.' In consort with Claude Lévi-Strauss he recognizes the impossibility of separating nature from culture. With the help of Gregory Bateson's *Steps to an Ecology of Mind* (1972) (that had been a bible for the generation of 1968), he notes the importance of the feedback loop that can (as well as it cannot) assure change, alteration, and a dynamically corrective operation of the environment. Yet, as with the social and built environment, natural environments must be dealt with from today's conditions, where new and other dynamisms are at stake. To be dealt with properly, Guattari argues, the environment requires another sensibility and intelligence.[3] Life, he claims, has always been at war with nature. Defending himself against the accusation made by François Dosse of being utopian, he writes elsewhere, and presciently (in view of the ineffectiveness of today's governing institutions), that the conservatives, that is, those who insist on a return to 'an older, simpler way' of living are those whose politics are regressively 'utopian.'

With a distant memory of the sixties, a decade that saw a generalized 'becoming-minoritarian' in the midst of many uprisings all over the world, today a belief persists that a dynamics can be lifted from that era. However, with further demographic explosions, a continued intensification of capitalism, the changes wrought by the electronic revolution, and the very real and rapid depredations of the environment, our world seems light years away from what he knew or envisaged. Already in 1983, Guattari wrote that 'what is terrifying is our lack of collective imagination in a world that has reached such a boiling point, our myopia before all the "molecular revolutions" which keep pulling the rug out from under us at an accelerated pace' (Guattari 2009: 307). And this pace has accelerated over the last few decades with molecular revolutions in myriad areas. How then can we use the philosophers' toolbox while updating its implements that had been made perhaps for a slower world that, both thermally and figuratively, is now at boiling point? What kind of collective imagination can we muster to tackle social, political and environmental problems?

A sense of an answer may be in the here-and-now. Glimpses of such an updating of Deleuze and Guattari's dynamism have come, and continue to come, with Occupy. With popular uprisings, from the Arab Spring and the Indignants in Spain to the recent mass protests in Greece, Turkey, Brazil and again in Egypt in June 2013, new diagrams have been charted, novel occupations of space essayed and worldwide demographic shifts undertaken. The liberal euphoria of 1989 seems to be giving way to another sensibility and, hopefully, a new form of intelligence that does not simply speculate on the equivalence of material, natural and cultural goods in terms of the augmenting flow of capital.[4] New and spontaneous preoccupations have arisen among groups at the grassroots levels. Others, engaged in fields pertaining to the creation of subjectivities – educators, urban planners, artists (including many media artists) – have developed a sense of social responsibility that makes preoccupations perceptible. As Žižek warned the participants of Occupy Wall Street, to be sustained, the movement has to go beyond self-congratulation. The movement has to continue to resound as a compelling imperative, and as an aphorism of action and not only a slogan or a piece of shorthand. It is incumbent upon militants to be analytical and, in turn, to tactically revise and correct their positionings, and to shift the loci of their occupations. The revolution cannot, in Deleuze and Guattari's terms, become the object of its own history. Its success depends on the becoming-revolutionary of the people in order to be part of a short- and long-term transformation. As they remind us, beginnings are difficult and outcomes uncertain. Yet, as Samuel Beckett, through the ambulation of his personages show us, one needs to go on.

In the 1960s, a generalized 'becoming-minoritarian' was unified in its fight against capitalism, as well as a dying colonialism and rights for blacks, women and gays, as well as a return to 'nature.' Today, issues are more complicated and their scales are different. While Occupy can be seen as a global movement in its struggle against economic and social injustice, its virtue and its success are found in its variety. 'Mediatized, securized and represented subjectivities' are more easily found in certain areas of the globe than in others. Occupy is aiming to reach the theoretical plateau on which the philosophers moved about by urging local groups to reterritorialize subjectivity and to advocate an active prying open of myriad microspaces that can bring about new sensibilities, indeed, other forms of intelligence that, in the words of Jacques Rancière, do not associate economics with politics and that, as Guattari and Butler noted, make the earth habitable and life worth living. It is perhaps in the opening of micro-spaces that the movement has its most resounding success.

More delicately, however, when thinking from today's conditions, proponents of the movement understand and contend with infinite modes of expansion and subtle smoothing of spaces that capitalism otherwise continually coopts. Occupy must deploy a strategy of civility to engage long-term transformation. As Deleuze and Guattari put it, the becomings that it seeks are difficult to obtain and their results always uncertain. Over the last few years, a preoccupation, however faint, that reintroduces idealism has become perceptible. In addition to the occupation of microspaces, it is in fields such as education, urbanism, architecture and the environment that a shift has become noticeable among a newer generation seeking to redirect its thoughts and energies for the sake of social justice, the rights of fauna and flora or simply put, for a life worth living and a habitable world. These issues are often local and require coordination of analysis and careful exercise of militancy by which preoccupation becomes occupation – occupation such that new affects generate percepts and concepts.[5] In this light, Occupy's aphorism of action has to be carried out in the accompaniment of an ongoing question on how to occupy a space, that is, how to open and distribute it, and how to develop a different sensibility and intelligence that, although situated within capitalism, runs against its grain. A different sensibility calls for ways of existing that both embrace singularity and collectivity and recognize both transversality and interdependence. It thinks change from today's conditions, from the standpoint of a global scale and from that of locales in their many-faceted and ever-changing conditions. A different intelligence does not measure the state of things in terms of profit alone. Its condition of difference seems at times difficult to generate in the present 'climate,' notwithstanding Occupy's success that is yielding hints of what it can be. As Deleuze and Guattari had argued, a kind of 'preoccupation' that rises spontaneously, *autopoietically*, is the pre-condition of the creative intelligence of singular and collective occupation. In addition, those who are in a position to affect subjectivities share the responsibility of introducing a wedge in people's thinking and open spaces for charting new lines of inquiry.[6]

The question Occupy asks today is how to reorient social, economic and artistic production for collective benefit. And for the two philosophers 'artistic' did not mean a vaguely creative act (that, in fact, they dismissed as 'vitamin induced,' or *bien vitaminé*). They noted then what needs to be noted now: in a state of occupation in the economy in which it is born, art has to do with invention and experimentation and not just with testing and bigger markets. In the wake of Deleuze and Guattari and the artists they championed, we can say that Occupy aims to produce a different type of singular and collective existence. Retrospection tells us that they ask to create an *oikos* or habitat in dynamic process. The type of occupation for which Deleuze and Guattari had virtually argued would change awareness. To be preoccupied is to be aware of occupation before occupation 'takes place.' Preoccupation is a situated place at the level of affect, a sense of something that stirs, turns into a percept and eventually becomes a concept. As the philosophers had underscored over and again, a new sensibility is fostered under the influence of other forms of intelligence; added to the intuitive sort of the artist, are those of scientists and philosophers who too create new plateaus and new dynamisms.

Occupy thrives on creativity in an era of new modes of communication, but also on creatively passive militancy. It is hopefully part of a long-term projection that can be measured in terms of duration. Occupy began with a sudden and contagious preoccupation, that has inspired a desire to occupy space otherwise. Like the philosophers of 1968 before them and with their tools refashioned for use in the twenty-first century, occupiers of mettle are those who rethink and refashion space by means of new distributions and redistributions: who value *nomos* against *logos*; who, refusing refuge in the fort, circulate in both real and electronic streets. Occupation always begins with an event, a rupture, a sudden surge of affect. It begins with preoccupation.

Works Cited

Barthes, Roland. 1972. *Mythologies*. Trans. and ed. Annette Lavers. New York: Hill and Wang.

Butler, Judith. 2011. 'Precarity, Embodiment and the Politics of Public Space'. *Tidal* (December 12). Accessed January 1, 2013 from: http://occupytheory.org/Tidal_7.html

Deleuze, Gilles. 1995. *Negotiations 1972–1990*. Trans. Martin Joughin. New York: Columbia University Press.

Deleuze, Gilles and Félix Guattari. 1983a. *On the Line*. Trans. John Johnston. New York: Semiotext(e).

Deleuze, Gilles and Félix Guattari. 1983b. *Anti-Oedipus: Capitalism and Schizophrenia*. Trans. Robert Hurley, Mark Seem and Helen R Lane. Minneapolis: University of Minnesota Press.

Deleuze, Gilles and Félix Guattari. 1986. *Kafka, Toward a Minor Literature*. Trans. Dana Polan. Minneapolis: University of Minnesota Press.

Deleuze, Gilles and Félix Guattari. *1987. A Thousand Plateaus: Capitalism and Schizophrenia*. Trans. Brian Massumi. Minneapolis: University of Minnesota Press.

Doherty, Gareth and Moshen Mostafavi (Eds). 2010. *Ecological Urbanism*. Baden: Editions Müller.

Dosse, François. 2007. *Gilles Deleuze et Félix Guattari: Biographie croisée*. Paris: Éditions La Découverte.

Guattari, Félix. 1986. *Les années d'hiver, 1980–1985*. Paris: Barrault.

Guattari, Félix. 2000. *The Three Ecologies*. Trans. Ian Pindar and Paul Sutton. London: Athlone.

Guattari, Félix. 2009. *Soft Subversions: Texts and Interviews 1977–1985*. Ed. Sylvère Lotringer. New York: Semiotext(e).

Guattari, Félix. 2012. *Un amour d'Uiq*. Ouvrage dirigé par Silvia Maglioni and Graeme Tomson; avec la collaboration d'Isabelle Mangou. Paris: Éditions Amsterdam.

Hardt, Michael and Antonio Negri. 2013. 'Declaration'. *Jacobin Magazine*. Accessed May 4, 2015 from: https://www.jacobinmag.com/2012/05/take-up-the-baton/

Harvey, David. 2000. *Spaces of Hope*. Berkeley: University of California Press.

Khatibi, Kate, Margaret Killjoy and Mike McGuire. 2012. *We Are Many, Reflections on Movement Strategy from Occupation to Liberation*. Oakland: AK Press.

Žižek, Slavoj. 2012. 'Occupy Wall Street: What is to be Done Next?'. *The Guardian*. Accessed May 5, 2015 from: http://www.theguardian.com/commentisfree/cifamerica/2012/apr/24/occupy-wall-street-what-is-to-be-done-next

Notes

1. 'In the Cage' is included in MD Zabel (Ed.), *Henry James: Eight Tales from the Major Phase* (New York: Norton, 1969). Deleuze and Guattari make little mention of the cage as a prison, composed of crisscrossed wires, in which the female is traditionally (and iconically) confined. One set of lines is thus opposed to that of another, the heroine's that crosses the barrier.

2. Footnote letter to Réda Bensmaia.

3. Massive technological interventions alone, Guattari speculated, will alter the environment for the better, including worldwide installations of oxygen-producing space stations. He traced a line of reflection between science and fiction, and he even wrote a film script, *Un amour d'Uiq* (Guatarri 2012). In their introduction to his posthumous publication, "Uiq, Un cinéma de l'infra quark," the editors, Sylvia Maglioni and Graeme Tomson, write that Guattari cherished Ridley Scott's film *Bladerunner*, especially the scene in which two replicants, Roy and Pris, hide in the apartment of a genetic engineer, JF Sebastian. Guattari is said to have seen in this scene a kind of Spinozist drifting of their intelligence and a desire to transform their life into a field of experimentation.

4. In *Spaces of Hope*, David Harvey (2000) could be in fact the geographer of vacuoles that in their later writings Deleuze and Guattari were advocating.

5. If after what was perceived as the Arab Spring and the protests in Spain and Greece, the widespread and sudden success of Occupy suggested the beginning of another worldwide wave of protest as in the nineteen-sixties, the movement has, for the time being, often been more immediately successful at the local levels. For example, in "Occupy Utica, Occupying a Small Rustbelt City," the authors show how for reason of its precise, concrete and attainable demands that include local school programs, extension of social services (of which a psychiatric clinic would be a part) and even the organization of a May parade in honor of labor, Occupy was successful and produced change. The members involved realized the importance of moving past the celebratory moment of occupation and toward an active occupying of a space (Khatib, Killjoy and McGuire 2012, cited in *Le Monde diplomatique*, January 2013).

6. In 'The Third Ecology,' in *Ecological Urbanism*, (Doherty and Mostafavi 2010), Sam Kwinter argues that the sixties were not all that bad even if it is now fashionable to say so. Deleuze and Guattari did recognize the decade as important when people were briefly animated by a desire to militate for social justice, the lowering of production and a more just distribution of the renewable wealth the world can provide. They had a sensibility that acknowledged beauty in the nature of things.

Chapter 6

Minor Politics, Territory, and Occupy

NICHOLAS THOBURN

This chapter is the amended text of a talk given at Occupy London's School of Ideas as part of a workshop called 'Deleuze and Guattari and Occupy,' February 25, 2012.[1] A little context may be instructive. Having moved from the Bank of Ideas in an occupied UBS office, the School of Ideas was situated in a spacious and attractive school building that had been left vacant for three years prior to its occupation. Two days after this workshop the School of Ideas was evicted in a coordinated move with the eviction of the main Occupy London camp at St Paul's Cathedral (at over four months, the world's longest running of the 750 camps that sprung up in the wake of Occupy Wall Street, the Spanish *indignados*, and the Arab Spring).[2] Upon eviction, the School of Ideas was immediately bulldozed – a fitting emblem of the wanton destruction that characterizes the current round of neoliberal restructuring and public service cuts.

Westminster local authority, just down the road from the School of Ideas, encapsulated the boorish swagger of the new culture in its promotion of the cuts to Housing Benefit: 'To live in Westminster is a privilege, not a right' (Westminster Council press officer quoted in Gentleman 2012). Inner London is indeed to be the class-cleansed home of the privileged, a middle class enclave serviced by a newly suburbanized and ever more precarious working class – Westminster's own figures project that 17% of primary school pupils could be forced by the cuts to move out of the borough. Meanwhile, at the other pole, the 2012 'millionaire's budget' cut taxation for the rich – those on incomes of £1m will benefit annually to the tune of £42,500.[3] No wonder recent years have seen the police and law courts shift up a gear in the discipline, punishment, and brutalization of student demonstrators, anti-cuts activists, and the young people involved in the 2011 riots – a move undoubtedly driven by concern that the normalization of this grotesque inequality can't hold indefinitely.

In repurposing the vacant UBS office and abandoned school, Occupy London spun such critical threads as these through neoliberalism, cuts, housing, and the city, and did so in ways both analytical and practical. But the Bank then School of Ideas also had a distinct pedagogical dimension. In Chile, California, Britain, and elsewhere, direct action against neoliberal education policy has been a leading edge of the current cycle of struggles. These education struggles have been largely defensive, fighting for the last remnants of a model of liberal education that is far from perfect, albeit that it is vastly superior to the emerging neoliberal model of debt-financed vocationalism. But the composition of this struggle has also been characterized by new critical knowledges and solidarities, as funding cuts in tertiary and higher education, creeping privatization of educational institutions, student debt, the casualization of academic labor, and graduate unemployment have drawn together a diverse range of actors that have interrogated the forms, functions, and possibilities of education at a new level of intensity. The School of Ideas, like other autonomous educational endeavours, was interlaced with these developments, as participants in various struggles cycled through the building and shaped it in their own ways. But it was also something that 'stood up on its own,' to make use of an expression I discuss below. Equal parts co-learning school, workshop, community center, organizational base, public interface, and home, one might say that the School of Ideas amplified (not isolated) the critical intellectual function and culture of Occupy London, and it was in that context that a sizeable group gathered on a bright winter's morning to discuss Deleuze, Guattari and the politics of Occupy.

Minor Politics

With the UK government itching to criminalize squatting, it's a real pleasure to be speaking in a building that is undergoing 'public repossession,' so I'd like to thank Andrew Conio for organizing this workshop and the

School of Ideas for hosting us.[4] What I want to do in this talk is work through three of Deleuze and Guattari's concepts that are helpful in thinking about Occupy. What do I mean by 'helpful?' My aim is deliberately not to try and *explain* Occupy, to sew it up in a theory – that for Deleuze would be to negate what is inventive in a movement, but also to lose the inventive quality of theory, making it merely a *representation* of a state of affairs. Instead my approach will be to use theory to reflect upon certain themes or problems in Occupy, looking at how these problems can be approached with Deleuzian concepts in a way that may help shed light upon them and aid their further development. It's a recursive relation, for reflection upon Occupy's themes or problems should also help extend Deleuzian concepts, lending them a contemporary vitality.

Given that this workshop is concerned in equal measure to bring Deleuze and Guattari's concepts into relation with Occupy and to offer an introduction to Deleuze and Guattari as political thinkers, I'm going to try and strike a balance between concept and Occupy, leaving space for us to expand upon the points I make about Occupy in the discussion. The concepts and problems that I address in turn are: minor politics and the 99%; territory, expression, and occupation; and fabulation and agency.

I will start with 'minor politics' and fold in some comments about the 99% – though bear with me, the relation may not at first be apparent. Running throughout Deleuze and Guattari's philosophy is a notion that politics arises not in the fullness of an identity – a nation, a people, a collective subject – but, rather, in 'cramped spaces,' 'choked passages,' and 'impossible' positions; on the condition, that is, that *'the people are missing'* (Deleuze and Guattari 1986: 15–16; Deleuze 1989: 216; Deleuze 1999: 133). To understand how this anti-identitarian formulation works, we need to consider their concepts of the majoritarian and minoritarian.

As Deleuze and Guattari have it, *majority* describes a system of identities that are constituted and nurtured by social relations to the extent that 'the social milieu serv[es] as a mere environment or a background' (Deleuze and Guattari 1986: 17). The *minoritarian* condition, on the other hand, is one where social relations no longer facilitate coherent identity, for they are experienced as riven with competing imperatives and constraints. As such, the social ceases to be mere background and floods individual experience, as life becomes a tangle of limits or 'impossibilities' – let's say, the experience of poverty, precarity, debt, racism, but also the spatial arrangements of the city, the gendered divisions of labor, the partitions of public and private, dominant linguistic forms, in their myriad combinations in each particularity. It is a condition that 'forces each individual intrigue to connect immediately to politics,' for without an autonomous identity, even the most personal, individual situation is always already comprised of social relations. And vice versa: this immanent relation to the social is not a flattening of particularity, quite the contrary. For the mesh of complex and contradictory social relations in every particularity is such that '[t]he individual concern thus becomes all the more necessary, indispensable, magnified, because a whole other story is vibrating within it' (Deleuze and Guattari 1986: 17). Particularity, then, is constituted by and interlaced with social relations, and it is on this condition, not some kind of minority *identity*, that minor politics is founded. So, what Deleuze and Guattari call 'major' or 'molar' politics expresses and constitutes identities that are nurtured and facilitated by a social environment, whereas minor politics is a *breach* with such identities, when the social environment is experienced as constraint, as perception is opened to what is 'intolerable' in social relations (Thoburn 2003).

Deleuze uses an appealing image to convey a sense of this minor condition. He says that to be on the Right is to perceive the world starting with identity, with self and family, and to move outward in concentric circles, to friends, city, nation, continent, world, with diminishing affective investment in each circle, and with an abiding sense that the center needs defending against the periphery. On the contrary, to be on the Left is to *start* one's perception on the periphery and to move *inwards*. It requires not the bolstering of the center, but an appreciation that the center is interlaced with the periphery, a process that undoes the distance between the two (Deleuze and Parnet 2012).

It is clear thus far that the minoritarian is a structural condition. And it is one that is very much entwined with developments in global capitalism. For the imperative of capital to set and overcome limits (an appreciation of which is the basis of Deleuze and Guattari's Marxism)[5] has produced an ever more fragmented, variegated, and mutable patchwork of unequal exchange, exploitation, and poverty, where the identity structures of Fordism no longer hold and 'peripheral zones of underdevelopment' become constitutive features of the 'center.' 'Ours,' as they say in 1980, 'is becoming the age of minorities' (Deleuze and Guattari 1988: 469).

But, if structural, the minoritarian is also something that is actively *affirmed*, constituted as a politics through a certain 'willed poverty' – a persistent deferral of subjective plenitude that forces ever-new critical engagement with social relations – such that, as Deleuze and Guattari quote Kafka, 'one strives to see [the boundary] before it is there, and often sees this limiting boundary everywhere' (Deleuze and Guattari 1986: 19, 17). And here we encounter a second aspect of Deleuze and Guattari's relation to Marx. For the minoritarian is framed as the contemporary condition of the *proletariat*, provided that we understand the proletariat, with Marx, not as a substantial subject but as the immanent critique of capital, and, hence, of itself, insofar as the working class is itself a functional product of capital, the subjectivity of labor:

> The power of minority, of particularity, finds its figure or its universal consciousness in the proletariat. But as long as the working class defines itself by an acquired status, or even by a theoretically conquered State, it appears only as 'capital', a part of capital (variable capital), and does not leave the *plan(e) of capital*. (Deleuze and Guattari 1988: 472)

What does all this mean in practice? Politics can no longer be a question of self-expression, of the unfurling of a subjectivity or the self-assertion of a people, because in this formulation there *is* no identity to unfurl. Instead, minor politics is the critical engagement with the social relations that traverse each particularity, the relations through which life is experienced as cramped and intolerable. By social relations I mean the whole gamut of economic structures, urban architectures, gendered divisions of labor, personal and sovereign debt, national borders, housing, policing, workfare – whatever combination it might be in any particular situation. And there is an important propulsive or motive aspect to this formulation. For, rather than allow the solidification of particular political and cultural routes, forms or habits, the active deferral of identity works as a mechanism to induce continuous experimentation, drawing thought and practice back into a field of problematization, where contestation, argument, and engagement with social relations ever arises from the experience of cramped space. The constitutive sociality of this 'incessant bustle' dictates that there can be no easy demarcation between conceptual production, personal style, concrete intervention, tactical development, or geopolitical events, and there is plenty of space for polemic (Kafka 1999: 148) – it is a vital environment well expressed in Kafka's seductive description of minor literature:

> What in great [or 'major'] literature goes on down below, constituting a not indispensable cellar of the structure, here takes place in the full light of day, what is there a matter of passing interest for a few, here absorbs everyone no less than as a matter of life and death. (Kafka, quoted in Deleuze and Guattari 1986: 17)

The Grid of the 99%

What has this account of minor politics got to do with Occupy? I want to consider that question through the theme or problem expressed in the Occupy slogan: 'We are the 99%.' It is a complex problem with competing formulations, some of which articulate a troubling tendency toward identity.[6] But it also contains progressive political content, which is my point of focus here. First, 'We are the 99%' is an assertion that the vast majority of the world's population are exploited by and for the wealth of a small minority. It names, in other words, a relationship of exploitation and inequality. The intervention of minor politics here would be to follow those in Occupy who push for an understanding of this formulation of inequality and exploitation as an intrinsic feature of capitalism. Framed in this way, inequality and exploitation signify not so much the *control of one group, the 99%, by another, the 1%*, nor even the *distribution of wealth*, but the very *form that life takes* in such a system, where the 'we' (as well, indeed, as the '1%') is wholly a product of the social relations of that system, its political potential lying not in asserting its collective identity, but in perceiving and challenging its intolerable conditions. Second, in naming this inequality and exploitation, 'We are the 99%' simultaneously designates a *breach* with such social relations, or pushes for such a breach. Let me stress again that in neither aspect does the slogan name a substantial *identity*; rather, it at once names and cuts the *social relations* of exploitation, among those who feel cramped by these relations, feel their intolerable pressure.

This naming and breach in capital is of course very general, without immediate purchase on concrete particularities. And here lies the risk of a tendency toward identity, as the generality is mistaken as naming a coherent group of people, a political subject. But 'We are the 99%' is, rather, something like a 'formula' or, to use a term with more spatial connotations, a 'grid.' It lays out the abstract principle that can be taken up and extended by any person or collective that would embody or express it in their concrete experience; indeed, it is an abstract principle that only has any meaning or purchase insofar as it is expressed in particular circumstances. In order to see how this grid functions, I want to compare it to one that Occupy is more or less directly opposed to, the grid of parliamentary democracy. Parliamentary democracy is, for Deleuze, a grid laid out across social space that seduces and channels political activity through its specific forms and structures:

> Elections are not a particular locale, nor a particular day in the calendar. They are more like a grid that affects the way we understand and perceive things. Everything is mapped back on this grid and gets warped as a result. (Deleuze 2007: 143)

Politics in this way gets 'warped,' as he puts it, because everything is reduced to and formatted by the status quo, to the perpetuation of that which gave rise to politics in the first place. A fundamental aspect of this warping is the exclusion of problems of inequality and exploitation from the realms of political interrogation. This was of course Marx's insight,[7] but the condition is currently so *acute* that it has widespread, even popular recognition, as Greece and Italy have unelected technocrats imposed on the populace to force through hitherto unknown assaults on living standards, as the ConDems slice up the National Health Service while claiming that it matters *not 'one jot'* whether it is run by the state or private capital.[8] This is why Occupy's much remarked upon refusal to make demands is so important and so much a product of our times. A demand is a mechanism of seduction into the grid of democratic politics, a means of channelling the political breach with capital right back into the institutions that perpetuate it.

In contrast, the grid that is constituted by the slogan 'We are the 99%' is very different. Rather than a mechanism of seduction into the status quo, it is a means of *multiplying points of antagonism*, or, in more Deleuzian terms, it extends the process of perceiving the intolerable and politicizing social relations. As I said, this does not occur *in general*, but from people's concrete and situated experience – it is a variegated field, where the points of problematization are housing repossession, the laying waste of public services, privatization of common resources, debt, police violence, workfare, and so on, and the tactics range from occupying social space, through the Oakland general strike, to direct actions against eviction from foreclosed housing, non-payment of debt, the hacking activities of Anonymous, or 'public repossessions' as we have in this building. Put another way, the grid is a *catalyst* across the social, not an aggregating body extending ever-outwards from Zuccotti Park but a zigzag, a discontinuous and emergent process. Again, it's not a catalyst because people come to recognize themselves in it as an identity – even a *collective* identity – but because they come to embody and express its abstract problematic in concrete circumstances.

Before moving on I want to directly address two points that are implicit in what I've said so far. First, it is not infrequently said by those involved in Occupy that it in some sense is creating the new world in the shell of old; that practices of collective decision, direct action, cooperation and care, global association, and so on, are a kind of communism in miniature. Certainly, all of these collective practices are crucial to understanding the unfurling of Occupy, to its effectivity and affective consistency, to the complex pleasures and pains of being a part of it. But from a minor political perspective, the risk with this formulation is that Occupy turn inwards, valorizing its own cultural forms at the expense of self-problematization and an ever-outward engagement in social relations. Occupy's vitality lies in its extension and intensification of the problematic of the 99% through an open set of sociopolitical sites and events, in what is of course a highly segmented and stratified terrain (where, to return to my earlier point, the fact of segmentation negates any notion that the 'we' of the 99% could designate a coherent subjectivity). For it is in and through these sites and events that the world's population exists, and from which an unknown set of possible futures will emerge. To identify those futures with the cultural forms discovered in Occupy camps would be naïve at the least, and risks a conservative reduction of the movement's minor political potential, a reduction to identity.

Second, refusing to make demands is not a refusal to *speak* – to formulate and express our anger, hopes, and desires, to name the particular problems of which we are concerned – and to seek *practical effects*. On the contrary, to work through the problems of Occupy requires an incessant production of critical knowledge and practice, knowledge and practice that needs to be circulated in the extension and development of these problems. The point is that this critical production is *immanent* to Occupy, or to the social relations that Occupy politicizes, not a pleading for recognition from an external power or a transposition of its problems into the grid of parliamentary democracy. We have seen Occupy developing slogans and concrete decisions that move toward defining what the movement wants, as part of reflection on how it may get it – and this of course is encouraging. But such formulations need to have a minor political 'efficiency,' as Guattari has it, they must be adequate to the specific and mutating problems of Occupy and its world, not reproduce themselves at the level of cliché: 'either a minor language connects to minor issues [which should not be taken to mean 'small' or exclusively 'local' issues], producing particular results, or it remains isolated, vegetates, turns back on itself and produces nothing' (Guattari 1995: 37). All this knowledge production will involve critique, contestation, and the development of divergent positions. Deleuze and Guattari are certainly interested in the way group consistencies emerge from distributed decision – let's say, the process of 'consensus' in Occupy's General Assemblies – but a good problem is not best extended in thought and practice by pretending that we all agree: 'The idea of a Western democratic conversation between friends has never produced a single concept' (Deleuze and Guattari 1994: 6).

Territory and Expression

I will move now to my second main concept and problem – on this and my third point I will be more concise. I want to look at an aspect of the tactic of *occupation*, specifically the *tent*, and explore their relation to Deleuze and Guattari's concepts of 'territory' and 'expression.'

The tent in an Occupy camp is first of all a practical object. It enables space to be taken and occupied for a certain duration. In this respect it has a family resemblance to the tripod as was used by Reclaim the Streets in the 1990s, an object that worked at once to cut the flow of traffic and act as a catalyst in the occupation of a road and the emergence of a street party. In Deleuzian terms, both tent and tripod play a part in 'deterritorializing' the space in which they operate – that is, in undoing the patterns of behavior, laws, sensory structures, and economic forms that determine that space as a road, stage for commerce and governance, or municipal park. But if the tent and tripod deterritorialize in this way, they simultaneously generate a *new* territory, they *re*territorialize into an Occupy camp or a street party.

To construct such a territory is of course difficult. It requires considerable knowledge of the territory that is to be undone: the governing legal situation, movements of traffic, an intuition about likely police tactics, potential solidarities and enmities of the locale, and so on. The constructed territory is thus a finely balanced constellation and can be easily botched. Things in London might have been different, for example, if Paternoster Square hadn't been barred and Occupy had not instead ended up on land owned by the Church.

But let's turn to consider the characteristics of Occupy's territory. Deleuze and Guattari make a rather intriguing argument that the construction of territory goes hand in hand with *art*, that art is a question of *home* or *habitat*: 'Perhaps art begins with the animal, at least with the animal that carves out a territory and constructs a house.' Such territory is functional, of course, but it is simultaneously sensory and expressive, that is, *artful*: 'the territory implies the emergence of pure sensory qualities, of sensibilia that cease to be merely functional and become expressive features, making possible a transformation of functions' (Deleuze and Guattari 1994: 183). These tangled aspects of habitat and expression are apparent, for example, in the 'art' of the Bowerbird, whose courtship rituals involve the production of elaborate decorated structures.

What are the components of this constructed territory? Well, they are drawn from the environment, from existent materials – in the case of the Bowerbird, twigs, berries, bottle-tops – but they are also qualities and forms that emerge in the process of construction:

> This emergence of pure sensory qualities is already art, not only in the treatment of external materials but in the body's postures and colours, in the songs and cries that mark out the territory. It is an outpouring of features, colours, and sounds that are inseparable insofar as they become expressive. (Deleuze and Guattari 1994: 184)

The St Paul's occupation is very much this kind of constructed territory. It comprises practical materials, the tent of course, items of furniture, cooking equipment – but also placards and signs, books, newspapers, drums, assemblies, hand signals, the people's mic, photographic images, livestreams, YouTube clips, the OccupyLSX website and Twitter feed, and so on. My point is not to proclaim that Occupy is 'art' exactly, but to suggest that alongside the *practical* tactics of occupation, the construction of territory through these functional components also includes an *expressive, sensory* quality that becomes an inseparable aspect of the occupation.[9] This is one explanation, for instance, of the production of newspapers at the Occupy camps, when online production and distribution is clearly more practicable. As well as being an object of news, discussion, and practical politics, the newspaper in this regard is also a *bloc of sensation*, an aesthetic expression of Occupy.

Tent as Monument

You might ask, 'What's the relation between this sensory or expressive quality of Occupy and its *meaning* or explicit *politics*?' For Deleuze and Guattari the two are different modalities of composition that come into a mutually sustaining encounter. They sometimes use a surprising word for these works of art or works of territory – they call them *monuments*:

the monument is not something commemorating a past, it is a bloc of present sensations that owe their preservation only to themselves and that *provide the event with the compound that celebrates it*. The monument's action is not memory but fabulation ... [It] confides to the ear of the future the persistent sensations that embody the event: the constantly renewed suffering of men and women, their recreated protestations, their constantly resumed struggle. (Deleuze and Guattari 1994: 167–8, 176–7; emphasis added)

So, the monument, the bloc of sensation, *celebrates* the event of which it is a part. In our case, it celebrates the suffering and struggle that is named and enacted by the slogan or grid of the 99%.

I have mentioned the range of artefacts that constitute the work of territory, the monument, but the tent is a special case. It is of course a habitation, that's what distinguishes it from the tripod I mentioned earlier. As habitation it has great tactical value in the endurance of Occupy camps, even through the winter. But it also comes with particular sensory associations or expressive qualities. A tent pitched in the inner city conveys something of the *fragility* of life, the precariousness of existence – 'bare life,' if you will, an impersonal quality of *all* life. And this impersonal, precarious life is filtered in our time through the specific condition of homelessness, as soaring rents, mortgage foreclosures, evictions, benefit and wage cuts, debt, and unemployment tip the home into a state of crisis. Indeed, as we're seeing with the rise of 'tent cities' in the US and elsewhere, the tent has become a very real habitation for a considerable volume of displaced people, a feature of Occupy camps themselves: 'a part of the homeless has become Occupy London, and a part of Occupy London has become the homeless.'[10]

This quality of life – fragile, impersonal, damaged – is central to the tent as monument, lifting 'suffering' to the level of aesthetic expression without losing any of its 'struggle.' Even in its expression of suffering, then, the tent is no *abject* object. And it also conveys a rather joyous quality of mobility. At risk of playing to a cliché, it is the dwelling of the *nomad* so dear to Deleuze and Guattari, where dwelling is part of an itinerant process, tied not to land but subordinated to the journey – the production of a 'movable and moving ground' through 'pitching one's tent'

(Deleuze and Guattari 1994: 105).[11] With the tent, then, we see something of the tactical or practical aspect of Occupy interlaced with its sensory or expressive quality: a tactic, and a sensory bloc – both, for Deleuze and Guattari, are constitutive of its territorial form.

The nomadic tent – this production of a movable and moving ground – orients our attention to a final aspect of the territorial form of Occupy. In constituting its territory, Occupy needs to remain open to a strong degree of deterritorialization of its own. Indeed, the relation should be reversed – Occupy's reterritorializations need to play only a 'secondary' role to the onward and open process of deterritorialization if it is not to become blocked, bogged down, identified in its new territory (Deleuze and Guattari 1988: 508). Deterritorialization in this way lends an evental quality to a social formation, the ungraspable and often highly seductive character of a formation whose directions remain unmapped, indeterminable, full, as Deleuze has it, of *virtuality*. But what does deterritorialization mean in more practical terms? You can think of deterritorialization here as the spatial dimension of that minor political opening to the social that I began with, the process of warding off identity and problematizing social relations. It is a central problem of Occupy, as well expressed in one editorial of *The Occupied Times*:

> [The eviction of Occupy Wall Street from Zuccotti Park] triggered a period of self-examination about how the Occupy movement might best move forward beyond its signature tents and into communities, enacting the movement's core message through practical action rather than symbolism. It is a journey that has seen American occupiers leave tents behind in favour of defending the homes of those about to be foreclosed ... Thanks to equal measures of adroitness and serendipity, Occupy London's initial encampment at St Paul's Churchyard has now far outlived Zuccotti Park in duration ... It would be a bitter irony – and a failure of enormous proportions – if we allowed our comparative security to stop us seeing some of our more distinctive tactics for what they are: a tool to be employed only for as long as they remain useful. Useful tactics generate change. They inspire others

to act. To do that we must look outwards. (The Occupied Times 2012: 2)

This process of deterritorialization concerns not only the dynamics of the one territory, but also the relation or *reverberation* with other territories or social formations. The obvious example is the relation with St Paul's itself. There's a clear sense in which Occupy subjected St Paul's to a force of deterritorialization, Occupy's *minor* monument undoing at the borders Wren's rather more major monument and the Church's structures of authority. Hence we witnessed the resignation of the canon chancellor, Giles Fraser, and Occupy's forcing of the Church to reflect upon the politics of Christianity and its relation to the city's banks. In turn, this strange reverberation between Occupy and St Paul's had some effect on the territory of the popular imagination, if we can call it that, even on its dominant media representation. The obvious hypocrisy of the Church in its initial dealings with Occupy seemed to lift and project the image of Occupy in the popular imagination, lending it a degree of popular support that it may not have had if it had been in a straight face off with bankers and police (for despite all that we have witnessed since 2008, when the lines are drawn between police and resistance in this way, common sense, ever re-charged by news media, unfortunately still tends to prostrate itself to the truths of authority).

There are of course other points and possibilities of reverberation: other Occupy camps, the hacker activities of Anonymous, precarious workers, rootless graduates, assailants of workfare, those involved in education campaigns and struggles against public service cuts, and so on. The aim of political theory informed by Deleuze and Guattari would be to consider the specific qualities or features of these interlaced points, all of them groping toward some sort of *patchwork* of politicized relations.

Fabulation and Agency

Thus far I have worked through two sets of concepts and problems: minor politics and the 99%; and territory and occupation. I want to end now with a brief sketch of a third concept and problem. This is Deleuze and Guattari's concept of *myth* or *fabulation* and the problem of the collective *agency* of Occupy. In theory circles at the moment and in some commentary on Occupy there are indications of a return to voluntarism, with talk of the people's 'will' as driver of change. From a Deleuzian perspective, such voluntarism abstracts an integrated subjectivity from what are in fact multiple and disjunctive levels of subjective determination (in dimensions that are economic, libidinal, semiotic, organizational, etc.), and so fails to ascertain from where politics comes, or to address the realities of conflict and reaction amidst and between social formations. Deleuze and Guattari would counter this voluntarism with the minor political emphasis on practical problematization that was the focus of the first part of this talk – political composition not formed of a generic quality of human will to overcome all contradictions, but arisen amidst the specific and multiform material conditions of 'the present state of things,' as Marx has it (Thoburn 2013). But there is an additional aspect of Deleuzian philosophy that is helpful for getting at the issues of collective agency or force that those who appeal to the people's will are, rightly, interested in.

Concepts, problems, territories, and so on are constructed by their human and non-human participants in the kinds of ways that I have been discussing. But they also have a *self*-positing character – they are created by participants, and they simultaneously create *themselves*, they have a life of their own: 'Creation and self-positing mutually imply each other because what is truly created, from the living being to the work of art, thereby enjoys a self-positing of itself, or an autopoietic characteristic by which it is recognized' (Deleuze and Guattari 1994: 11).

This isn't easy; most created entities collapse without becoming self-positing. But if an entity *does* achieve this, if it can 'stand up on its own,' as Deleuze and Guattari put it, then you have something interesting, something with an *agency* all of its own (Deleuze and Guattari 1994: 164). You have a revolution, an art work, a concept, or in our case, you have the Occupy movement. What does it mean to say that Occupy is self-positing? It means that as well as being generated by the people, tactics, objects, slogans, sounds and so on that are a part of its territory, it also takes on a life of its own, a life that pulls its constituent parts along, creating *them* as parts of its event.

Now, when Deleuze and Guattari discuss this self-positing process in the context of politics, they sometimes describe it as a process of 'fabulation.' It's a word you might have noticed earlier in the quotation about the monument. Fabulation or myth-making occurs when the shock of an event – be it an earthquake, a work of art, a social upheaval – produces visions or hallucinatory images that substitute for routine patterns of perception and action and come to guide the event. In Deleuze and Guattari's reading, fabulation is a weapon of the weak, a means of fabricating 'giants,' as they put it – germinal agents with real world effects in the service of political change (Deleuze and Guattari 1994: 171). What is perhaps most appealing in the context of Occupy is that these fabulations or myths are not so much located in individual *people* – the cults of personality, for instance, of Lenin, Mao, Churchill, what have you – but have a *desubjectified* or *anonymous* quality, generated and held in the fragmented *bits* of events, stories, medias, affects, material resources, and are associated as much with 'mediocrity' as with the grandiose (Deleuze and Guattari 1994: 171). In this way Deleuze describes myth as a 'monster,' it '*has a life of its own*: an image that is always stitched together, patched up, continually growing along the way' (Deleuze 1989: 150; Deleuze 1997: 118; Thoburn 2011).

Occupy has had something of this mythical quality, an agential power of its own that exists among and between us, and that pulls its particularities along. I'll end by pointing to one small (and by no means unproblematic) artefact in this myth: the Guy Fawkes mask. Think how different these two images of political myth are. Mao, a concentrated myth centered, in demagogic fashion, on an individual and the truth of his infallible thought. And the Guy Fawkes mask, an anonymous, distributed power – a part of the myth of Occupy, open to anyone, signifying a resistance to closure in a leader, vaguely menacing, a little bit silly, mediocre even, and pop-cultural to boot. The mask's impersonal mythical power is well expressed in a cartoon in *The Occupied Times*, a cartoon that takes its words from Subcomandante Marcos (and Thomas Müntzer in turn) and so forms a red thread across to another political myth of our time: it's not 'who we *are*' that's important, but '*what we want*': 'everything for everyone' (The Occupied Times 2011: 2).

Works Cited

Gilles Deleuze. 1989. *Cinema 2: The Time-Image*. Trans. Hugh Tomlinson and Robert Galeta. London: Athlone.

Deleuze, Gilles. 1997. *Essays Critical and Clinical: 1968–1990*. Trans. Daniel W Smith and Michael A Greco. Minneapolis: University of Minnesota Press.

Gilles Deleuze. 1999. *Negotiations 1972–1990*. Trans. Martin Joughin, New York: Columbia University Press.

Gilles Deleuze. 2007. *Two Regimes of Madness: Texts and Interviews 1975–1995*. Ed. David Lapoujade. Trans. Ames Hodges and Mike Taormina. Los Angeles: Semiotext(e).

Deleuze and Félix Guattari. 1986. *Kafka: Towards a Minor Literature*. Trans. Dana Polan. Minneapolis: University of Minnesota Press.

Deleuze, Gilles and Félix Guattari. 1988. *A Thousand Plateaus: Capitalism and Schizophrenia*. Trans. Brian Massumi. Minneapolis: University of Minnesota Press.

Deleuze and Guattari. 1994. *What Is Philosophy?*. Trans. Hugh Tomlinson and Graham Burchill. London: Verso.

Deleuze, Gilles with Claire Parne. 2012. *Gilles Deleuze: From A to Z*. Dir. Pierre-André Boutang. Trans. Charles Stivale. Los Angeles: Semiotext(e).

Gentleman, Amelia. 2012. 'Housing Benefit Cap Forces Families to Leave Central London or be Homeless'. *The Guardian* (February 16). Accessed May 4, 2015 from: http://www.guardian.co.uk/society/2012/feb/16/housing-benefit-cap-families-central-london

Guattari, Félix. 1995. *Chaosophy*. Ed. Sylvère Lotringer, New York: Semiotext(e).

Kafka, Franz. 1999. *The Diaries of Franz Kafka: 1910–1923*. Ed. Max Brod. Trans. Joseph Kresh and Martin Greenberg. London: Penguin.

Marx, Karl. 1975. *Early Writings*. Trans. Rodney Livingstone and Gregor Benton. Harmondsworth: Penguin.

Marx, Karl. 1976. *Capital*. Trans. Ben Fowkes. Harmondsworth: Penguin.

The Occupied Times. 2011. *The Occupied Times* 6. Accessed May 4, 2015 from: http://issuu.com/theoccupiedtimes/docs/ot_issue_6_issuu/1?e=0

The Occupied Times. 2012. *The Occupied Times* 8. Accessed May 4, 2015 from: http://issuu.com/theoccupiedtimes/docs/ot_8_issuu/5?e=0

O'Sullivan, Simon. 2006. *Art Encounters Deleuze and Guattari: Thought Beyond Representation*. London: Palgrave.

Thoburn, Nicholas. 2003. *Deleuze, Marx and Politics*. London: Routledge.

Thoburn, Nicholas. 2011. 'To Conquer the Anonymous: Authorship and Myth in the Wu Ming Foundation'. *Cultural Critique* 78: 119–50.

Thoburn, Nicholas. 2013. 'Do Not Be Afraid, Join Us, Come Back? On the "Idea of Communism" in Our Time'. *Cultural Critique* 84: 1–34.

Zepke, Stephen. 2005. *Art as Abstract Machine: Ontology and Aesthetics in Deleuze and Guattari*. London: Routledge.

Notes

1. A different version of this article was published previously in *Mute*. Many thanks to *Mute* for allowing its republication here. See http://www.metamute.org/editorial/articles/minor-politics-territory-and-occupy

2. See Simon Rogers, 'Occupy protests around the world: full list visualised', *The Guardian* (November 14, 2011), available at: http://www.guardian.co.uk/news/datablog/2011/oct/17/occupy-protests-world-list-map#data

3. See Patrick Collinson, 'Budget 2012: Earning £1m? Your Tax Cut Will Pay for a Porsche', *The Guardian* (March 21, 2012), available at: http://www.guardian.co.uk/uk/2012/mar/21/budget-2012-earning-1m-tax-cut-pay-for-porsche

4. Since this talk took place, the ConDem administration has enacted what Tory regimes have long threatened, making squatting in residential properties a criminal offence. The government and media bogeyman, as ever, was the squatter who moves into an occupied family home; a clear ruse to deflect from the disgraceful situation where people sleep on the streets when 610,000 homes lie empty in England alone. See Empty Homes Agency, 'Statistics' (October 2014), available at: http://www.emptyhomes.com/statistics/ Attacking working class housing on another front, central government has set rents for local authority and housing association tenants to rise to 80% of those in the private rental sector, a move that in many parts of the country effectively brings to completion the destruction of council housing that began with Margaret Thatcher's policy of 'right to buy.'

5. 'Félix Guattari and I have remained Marxists, in our two different ways, perhaps, but both of us. You see, we think any political philosophy must turn on the analysis of capitalism and the ways it has developed. What we find most interesting in Marx is his analysis of capitalism as an immanent system that's constantly overcoming its own limitations, and then coming up against them once more in a broader form, because its fundamental limit is capital itself' (Deleuze 1999: 171).

6. The critique of the formulation of the 99% is well made in Clinical Wasteman, 'No Interest but the Interest of Breathing', *Mute*, Available at: http://www.metamute.org/editorial/articles/no-interest-interest-breathing

7. It is worth sketching Marx's thesis here, and keeping in mind Deleuze and Guattari's distinction between major and minor politics while doing so, for the correspondence is striking indeed. Rather than engage with the human as social animal – as 'species being' in all the socioeconomic complexities and antagonisms of its production – bourgeois politics abstracts an isolated individual – a 'partial being,' the 'individual withdrawn into himself, his private interest and his private desires' – and devotes all its energies to securing this subjectivity. Here, 'the whole of society is there only to guarantee each of its members the conservation of his person, his rights and his property', and, as such, the political 'sphere in which man behaves as a communal being [*Gemeinwesen*] is degraded to a level below the sphere in which he behaves as a partial being.' This is not a mere ideological ruse, but a structural feature of the inverted subjectivity of capital, where the worker, who is wholly a product of capitalist social relations, experiences life as an individual 'free' to sell her labor-power on the open market. It is upon these conditions that Marx can proclaim with every reason – and some irony – that capital, for all that it 'comes dripping from head to toe, from every pore, with blood and dirt', is indeed a 'very Eden of the innate rights of man' (Marx 1975: 2301; Marx 1976: 926, 280).

8. See 'To be honest I don't think it should matter one jot whether a patient is looked after by a hospital or a medical professional from the public, private or charitable sector', Tory health minister Lord Howe, quoted in Nick Triggle, 'Private Sector Have Huge NHS Opportunity', *BBC News* (September 7, 2011), available at: http://www.bbc.co.uk/news/health-14821946

9. The bowerbird is certainly not the last word on 'art' in Deleuze and Guattari. I should point out that despite possible indications to the contrary here, their writing on art is not best viewed through the avant-garde lens of the subsumption of art and everyday life, for they invest considerable import in the exacting forms and techniques of modernist practice, in painting and cinema especially (see O'Sullivan 2005; Zepke 2005).

10. See the 'Occupy London Homelessness Statement', available at: http://occupylondon.org.uk/homelessness-statement/

11. Many thanks to John Bywater for pointing out this passage on the 'English' taste for camping, which helps counter any Orientalism in Deleuze and Guattari's concept of nomadic dwelling.

Chapter 7

September 17, 2011: Occupy without Counting

IAN BUCHANAN

The events of September 2011 will probably go down in history in much the same way as the events of May 1968, with no-one being able to decide what, if anything, actually happened.¹ Zuccotti Park in New York City briefly flickered in the global consciousness as the spark that threatened to ignite a global revolution, just as the Latin Quarter of Paris had four decades earlier (Buchanan 2008: 7–12). Within a month over 150 Occupy events were taking place all over the world and as one expects these days the movement was even more prominently and diversely represented on the internet. The message the occupiers wanted to relay was both simple and complex. 'We are the 99%,' they said: the part that in Rancière's terms effectively has no part because the other 1% control a profoundly disproportionate share of national – global – wealth (the top 1% in the US have a greater net worth than the bottom 90%), (Rancière 1999: 9). They demanded nothing except to be noticed. Although they received support from a number of labor unions, including teachers and health workers who marched in solidarity with them on October 5 and November 17, 2011, they were on the whole chary of being too closely identified with established political groups. Partly this was out of a fear of being coopted, but largely it had to do with the collective desire to create a new kind of political organization that was 'leaderless and directionless' (Greenberg 2011: 12). The occupiers confounded virtually every attempt the mainstream media made to understand what was going on. Their silence about what they wanted made the point that there is no democratic agency in the US that their concerns could be addressed to because all of them are in some way or another beholden to the corporate world. And it was this basic fact of American – global – life that they wanted to draw attention to and initiate a change in what environmental activist Bill McKibben usefully refers to as 'the political consciousness' (Greenberg 2012b: 47).

Occupy Wall Street and the corresponding Occupy movement that sprang up in its wake was premised on the idea that change is not achieved by violence or extortion, but rather by presence and permanence. The occupiers put their bodies on the line in order to make their point. Situated in Lower Manhattan, literally on the doorstep of Ground Zero, Zuccotti Park is anything but a park, if by that we mean lush green spaces like New York's own Central Park or Hyde Park in London. It is rather just over 3,000 square meters of concrete interspersed by a few sapling trees that in time may give it at least the appearance of a park. There are no toilet facilities or any other basic amenities needed to sustain life in a reasonable degree of comfort. So the occupation called for hard living and ingenuity. They were fortunate that the weather remained mild for the first couple of weeks but by late October the first snows had fallen, making life very uncomfortable indeed. Because generators weren't permitted, electricity had to be produced using pedal power. It was the drive in the legs of determined occupiers that heated frozen bodies and kept the media center going and recharged all the cell phones and laptops. Amplifiers weren't permitted either, so public meetings were facilitated via a call and response process in which the speaker's words were relayed, person to person, from the front of the audience to the rear. The occupiers were aided by the fact that Zuccotti Park is a private park controlled by Brookfield Properties, who were far from supportive. This meant it was exempt from curfew laws that would have applied in a public park. Occupying Zuccotti Park was never easy and the City of New York did everything it could to make it as difficult as possible. It directed homeless people towards the park and dropped off released prisoners there and infiltrated the occupiers and spied on them, with the result that several were put on charges. Then on November 15, 2011, the police cleared the park and brought the occupation to an end.[2] The occupiers produced a manifesto of sorts, 'The Declaration of the Occupation of New York City,' as well as a kind of newspaper, *The Occupied Wall Street Journal*, which published ideas put to and ratified by the General Assembly, an ad hoc group of occupiers who listened to and voted on proposals presented to them by anyone with the interest to do so. Some of the proposals were practical – such as Adbuster editor Micah White's call for the reinstatement of the Glass–Steagall Act, which from 1933 until 1999 separated commercial and investment banking, thus protecting America from precisely the kind of speculative lending that led to the global financial meltdown of 2007 – but many were not, at least not in a straightforward sense. Calls that corporate influence on government should be ended cannot easily be enacted.[3] But the manifesto was never really that important as far as the wider public was concerned. It functioned simply as a chronicle of what the people were thinking in those heady weeks of the occupation, rather than a carefully thought out and precisely articulated position statement, much less a utopian vision of the future. The true legacy of Occupy Wall Street will not be found in its pages. It was rather the process of putting the manifesto together that was important not the end result. Its production was an example of participatory democracy in action – the set of principles the occupiers wanted to live by was created and embraced by the occupiers themselves. All proposals required the support of at least 90% of the General Assembly in order to be ratified, which is far more onerous than parliamentary democracies anywhere else requires. And of course that was precisely the point: it demonstrated that democracy as we know it, that is, democracy as it is practiced in the United States and elsewhere is a pale shadow of 'true' democracy, which is open to all and premised on the notion that only near-consensus can be regarded as representative of the will of the people. As impractical as this model of democracy might be, its symbolic value should not be underestimated. It bespoke a powerful hunger for social justice, for a political and economic system that represents the needs of the many not the greed of the few that not even President Obama could fail to perceive.[4]

One may put it even more strongly than that. It could be said that the occupiers staging of 'real' democracy revived the idea that, as Rancière argues, political society is at its core, in its very foundation, consensus driven: '[B]efore becoming the reasonable virtue of individuals and groups who agree to discuss their problems and build up their interests, [consensus] is a determined regime of the perceptible, a particular mode of visibility of *right* as *arkhê* of the community' (Rancière 1999: 107). Consensus is not the goal of politics, but its starting point, its possibility, because it stipulates that everyone has the right to be counted, to count, in the formation of political ideas and decision. But as Rancière also argues, consensus is in some ways the end of politics precisely because it demands/assumes that everyone is, has been, counted and therefore leaves no place for the part who have no part. It obscures, then, the place of dissent (Rancière 1999: 116). The staging of a regime of consensus within a political environment such as twenty-first century USA that does not even pretend to be motivated by or interested in consensus as a political ideal escapes this double bind because it simultaneously performs consensus as an idea but does so in a context in which the performers continue to be viewed as belonging to the part who have no part. Occupy Wall Street was in this sense a highly complex piece of political theatre, but it was also more than that because the effects of its performance were not purely symbolic, but completely real.

There are of course obvious political reasons why certain commentators would want to deny that anything takes place in these kinds of events in which a populace suddenly and without warning or obvious provocation decides to express its dissent, and does so in a way that isn't aimed at either bringing down a particular regime or taking power. It is hardly surprising that pundits who generally identify with the hegemonic regime would tend to claim that events like Occupy Wall Street are ultimately inconsequential, that is more or less their reason for being. It is a bread-and-butter move for someone like Niall Ferguson to claim that Occupy Wall Street is a giant, misguided waste of time because the real issue of the day isn't the fact that the top 1% control the bulk of the nation's wealth, it is fact that there are so many baby boomers around getting ready to hoover up all that free money from social security and government health insurance (Mills 2011). What is surprising, though, is that the number of basically sympathetic observers, including Michael Greenberg (who otherwise does such a marvellous job of reporting on Occupy Wall Street for *The New York Review of Books*) should find the movement wanting. In an article that documents the way the New York police infiltrated and harassed the occupiers, Greenberg describes the occupiers as corrupted by their own 'inviolable purity of principle ("We don't talk to people with power, because to do so would be to acknowledge the legitimacy of their power").' I do not want to suggest that the occupiers should somehow be seen as immune to criticism. But I do want to suggest that the political frameworks in place today are in many ways conceptually inadequate to deal with events like Occupy Wall Street, which falls outside most people's standard paradigms for understanding political interactions between the manifestly powerful and the apparently powerless. Usually power is equated with violence and more especially the control of the right to violence. The fact that non-violent movements like Occupy Wall Street challenge that very idea, indeed that basic assumption, that politics ultimately boils down to who has the best weapons and the most troops is in many ways the most overlooked (in the media, I mean) aspect of political activism today.

Conceptual advances are, in this sense, political acts in themselves, because they open a space, or more precisely, create the form of the expression for new political ideas (as the content of the expression) and thereby enable political voices to be heard that would otherwise be presumed silent or adjudged irrelevant.

This is one of the key reasons that the concept of the event has been so central a preoccupation for critical theory for the past decade or more; it is starting point for any inquiry about 'what happened?' Of the several philosophers who have given thought to the concept of the event, the most influential – in critical theory, at least – are undoubtedly Alain Badiou and Gilles Deleuze. The event is a crucial concern for both, but they each approach it quite differently. At the risk of grossly oversimplifying their respective arguments, I will try to generalize the difference between them as follows. For Badiou the event gives rise to truth (it is truth's condition), whereas for Deleuze it gives rise to sense (it is sense's condition). Badiou's event, as a truth-event, demands our commitment – it therefore hovers on the border between conscious and unconscious, voluntary and involuntary, that which we choose to do and that which we feel compelled to do. Our commitment to a particular truth is not so much a rational decision based upon the weighing up of evidence as a lightning strike, an epiphany that hits us and in an instant reshapes our view of the world. Badiou tends to give mathematical examples to explain what he means by truth because for him the real quality of a truth is its inarguable nature: a triangle has three sides, a square has four, and so on. Similarly, one could look to physics, and the various laws formulated there: gravity means everything must fall. It is an open question, it seems to me, whether any political idea can attain a comparable status, but for Badiou this is what conviction would mean in a political context: the unshakeable belief in the rectitude of a particular idea and the concomitant clarity of perception this conviction affords (Badiou 2012: 60–61).

For Deleuze, too, the event is a kind of lightning strike, but it demands only that we adapt to it. It does not demand our conviction, or even our belief. The event for Deleuze is an eruption of immanence, if you will, a bursting forth of a kind of immanent time-space continuum in which something transcendent (sense) appears. In a late essay, published after his death, Deleuze even called this type of eruption of immanence 'life' (Buchanan 2006). In his work with Guattari, space was usually referred to as smooth space (but it had other names as well – the body without organs, the plane of immanence, the plane of composition, the plateau and so on). This life-sense as we may perhaps call it (to distinguish it from ordinary or semantic sense) has a structuring effect inasmuch as it gives shape to the world as we live and experience it. F. Scott Fitzgerald's notion of 'the crack' is, for Deleuze and Guattari, something of a touchstone example of what they mean by the event. It is a kind of mental 'clean break,' a 'brain snap' as some people say, after which nothing is the same. Examples of cracks might include the realization that one's job is worthless and not deserving of the effort you put into it, or that you aren't as talented as you once thought (which was Fitzgerald's feeling), and so on (Deleuze and Guattari 1987: 198–200). This is by no means at odds with anything Badiou says about the event, except that for Deleuze this eruption of immanence (the opening up of a smooth space in other words) does not necessarily correlate with an idea of truth. It is also worth noting that the event for Deleuze and Guattari is not measured by a change in the state of things – a large crowd gathering in a public square in Cairo or camping out in New York City is not intrinsically an event in Deleuze and Guattari's thinking. It only becomes recognizable as an event if it brings about a transformation of thought itself, if it yields a new idea, a new way of acting.[5] And I would argue that is precisely what Occupy did: it opened up a new space of thought.

In contrast to Badiou's truth-event, Deleuze and Guattari's smooth space of thought, or life-sense, is not universal or universalizable. The crack Fitzgerald experiences is a truth for him, but not for anyone else, not even Zelda Fitzgerald, who experienced her own crack. It is *his* sense of *his* world, not anyone else's. That's why we call it his life. And even if we empathize with his outlook on things and feel that it somehow describes our own world too, that it has something to say about our own life, it is a not a truth we can be faithful to in Badiou's sense (as he applies it to ideological worldviews like communism, for instance). I can believe in the existence or occurrence of the crack ('clean break,' 'brain snap', etc.) in someone's life, but only in a formal sense. The specific content of someone else's crack will always elude me because as Tolstoy more or less said we're all unhappy, that is to say, broken or cracked, in our own way. What pushes me over the edge does not have to be the same as whatever pushes another person over the edge for us to both say we've experienced a crack. Yet for that very reason our respective experiences of cracking are only comparable in an abstract way. This is not to say that for Deleuze and Guattari there are no such thing as collective events, or events that affect more than one person, but it does mean that universality cannot be one of its defining criteria, as it is for Badiou. The other difference is that for Deleuze and Guattari the life-sense event is involuntary – Fitzgerald doesn't choose to accept or adhere to the crack, it comes up upon him without him knowing about it in advance and leaves him a changed man in its wake. For Badiou, in contrast, the event requires our fidelity, we have to choose to believe in it and place it at the center of our lives.

The event for Deleuze and Guattari is a radical break with the normal continuity of things that at once interrupts the usual flow of daily life and initiates its own counter-flow.[6] This was precisely what Occupy Wall Street did: it brought about a radical break with the normal continuity of daily life, not just in lower Manhattan, but globally, as the whole world stopped to see what was happening there. That it could do so without violence or even the threat of violence is remarkable, particularly in an era that is in many ways defined by the so-called 'War on Terror,' which had its beginnings – Ground Zero – a short distance from Zuccotti Park.

Having said that, it is important to see that Occupy Wall Street's non-violent approach, the so-called passive resistance it exercised, is anything but passive. It is a misnomer that robs the non-violent approach to protest of its core, namely the galvanizing effect of a desire for change. As Perry Anderson writes, Ghandi himself translated *satyagraha* as 'truth-force' rather than passive resistance. Inspired by Tolstoy, Ghandi coined this neologism himself to conceive a vision of non-violent resistance infused with a religious idea of transcendence (Anderson 2012: 6).[7] For Badiou, this is precisely how an event like Occupy Wall Street works. It ignites what he calls a 'truth process' – it makes apparent to all that 'human animals are capable of bringing into being justice, equality, and universality (the practical presence of what the Idea can do). It is perfectly apparent that a high proportion of political oppression consists in the unremitting negation of this capacity' (Badiou 2012: 87).

The fact that people take the trouble to interrupt their own lives to commence and participate in an occupy movement and do so in substantial numbers is living proof that in the words of the anti-WTO protesters from the decade before Occupy Wall Street, 'another world is possible.' What counts is the act, the willingness to disrupt one's own life and beyond that the lives of others, and beyond that the life of the social machine itself. As Badiou puts it, speaking of the occupation of Cairo's Tahrir Square in January 2011, which sparked the Arab Spring: even if the occupiers 'are a million strong, that still does not represent many of the 80 million Egyptians. In terms of electoral numbers it is a guaranteed fiasco! But this million, present in this site, is enormous if we stop measuring the political impact (as in voting) by inert, separated number' (Badiou 2012: 58). Deleuze and Guattari call this space one occupies without counting 'smooth space,' which they contrast to 'striated space.' In what follows I will argue that Occupy Wall Street can usefully be thought of as having created a new kind of smooth space. Ironically, it is perhaps Badiou who, while severely critical of Deleuze's attachment to the concept of the virtual, gives us the most useful illustration of precisely what is meant here by smooth space. Speaking of Spain's *indignados*, the loose social movement which arose in response to the 'austerity measures' the Spanish government was forced to impose by the European Central Bank as a condition of its debt relief (following the global financial crisis of 2007 and the resulting meltdown of the euro), Badiou argues that as noble as their cause is, because it is fuelled only by negative emotions – a desire for 'real democracy' to replace the 'bad democracy' they have to live with – their movement isn't as powerful or as sustainable as it would be if it were underpinned by an 'affirmative Idea' (Badiou 2012: 97). The Idea, Badiou says, is blind to the self-evidence of what is before it – the local defeats, as in the case of Occupy Wall Street, which was rousted out of Zuccotti Park after only two months – and far-sighted concerning the future that no-one else has eyes to see – it isn't concerned with results, with counting in the here and now, what it awakens is the force of History itself, the certainty that nothing – not even capitalism – is forever (Badiou 2012: 98–9).

Now, I would not want to say that smooth space is identical with Badiou's conception of the Idea, but I do want to make the point that it is both conceptual and historical in nature. Take for example Deleuze and Guattari's key exhibit, Paul Virilio's concept of the 'fleet in being.' At a certain point in history, naval commanders arrived at the idea that the ocean could be dominated by the superior mobility of forces and the power to interdict the mobility of others rather than through the control of fixed positions. This idea, which was fully an event in both Badiou's and Deleuze's terms, was communicated from sea to land to air to space. Now war in all its modalities is informed by this idea. There have been moments when this idea has seemed out of step with history. Germany's Schlieffen Plan to sweep across Western Europe came horribly unstuck in 1914 when their planned war of mobility was unseated by the twin powers of the machine gun and barbed wire and turned into a standstill war of attrition claiming the lives of millions. But almost as soon as the first trenches were dug the opposing forces began scheming to regain the power of mobility and within the space of a few years solutions were found: tanks and airplanes rendered the gridlocked space of the battlefield smooth all over again. In this way a new pattern of action was set in motion: striated space was to be defeated by technological advancement. But within a few decades, by the time of the Vietnam War, if not sooner, this model was also brought unstuck. Today, the incredible mobility of high-tech weapons is countered by the fluidity of the identity of the enemy. The unseen and unknown enemy compels the one who seeks them to give up at least some of their mobility for the apparent security of checkpoints and surveillance procedures. In each instance, the Idea of space dominated by mobility remains very much alive (Deleuze and Guattari 1987: 480).

It is this power – the power of an Idea as a force that shatters or cracks the status quo and lets in a new kind of light, one that hasn't shone there before – that is the key to understanding Deleuze and Guattari's concept of smooth space. Let me offer a different example that will hopefully bring it into even sharper relief. I would claim that smooth space is comparable to David Harvey's conception of the urban commons. He argues that the 2011 occupations of Syntagma Square in Athens, Tahrir Square in Cairo, and the Plaça de Catalunya in Barcelona transformed these public places into latter day variations of the medieval idea of the commons. Importantly, although these spaces are all physical places that one can go and visit, the urban commons itself is not, it is a social relation, and that is precisely how smooth space should be understood I believe. Harvey writes: 'The common is not to be constructed, therefore, as a particular kind of thing, asset or even social process, but as an unstable and malleable social relation between a particular well-defined social group and those aspects of its actually existing or yet-to-be-created social and/or physical environment deemed crucial to its life and livelihood. There is, in effect, a social practice of *commoning*' (Harvey 2012: 73). The key to commoning, as Harvey sees it, is that it removes the relation between a group and a space from commodity exchange: the commons is off-limits to the market. This amounts to saying the commons is a virtual space as Deleuze and Guattari would put it and that the virtual space of the commons is produced by the occupiers of that space, which is an important clarification of what Deleuze and Guattari mean by smooth space.

Virtual does not mean unreal, as Deleuze and Guattari often remind us. The virtual is fully real, as real as an idea, an image, and an innovation, is real. It is real because its effects are real. Here one might think of Jameson's frequently made point about the need to keep alive what he calls the utopian imagination: without bold ideas for the future, that is, ideas which envisage a break – a disruption, as Jameson calls it – with the present state of affairs we are condemned to simply let things continue as they are. And this, as Walter Benjamin rightly said, is the real emergency.

The smooth space may not suffice to save us, as Deleuze and Guattari caution, but it does at least apply the handbrake to history and that may just be enough.

Works Cited

Anderson, Perry. 2012. 'Ghandi Centre Stage'. *London Review of Books* (July 5): 3–11.

Badiou, Alain. 2012. *The Rebirth of History: Times of Riots and Uprisings*. Trans. Gregory Elliott. London: Verso.

Buchanan, Ian. 2008. *Deleuze and Guattari's* Anti-Oedipus. London: Continuum.

Buchanan, Ian. 2006 'Deleuze's 'Life' Sentences'. *Polygraph* 18: 129–47.

Greenberg, Michael 2011. 'In Zuccotti Park'. *The New York Review of Books* (November 10). Accessed May 4, 2015 from: http://www.nybooks.com/articles/archives/2011/nov/10/zuccotti-park/?pagination=false

Greenberg, Michael. 2012a. 'New York: The Police and the Protesters'. *The New York Review of Books* (October 11). Accessed May 4, 2015 from: http://www.nybooks.com/articles/archives/2012/oct/11/new-york-police-and-protesters/?pagination=false

Greenberg, Michael. 2012b. 'What Future for Occupy Wall Street?'. *The New York Review of Books* (February 9–22): 46–8.

Harvey, David. 2012. *Rebel Cities: From the Right to the City to the Urban Revolution*. London: Verso.

Mills, Nicholaus. 2011. 'Occupy Wall Street: A Primer'. *The Guardian* (November 7). Accessed May 4, 2015 from: http://www.guardian.co.uk/commentisfree/cifamerica/2011/nov/07/occupy-wall-street-primer

Rancière, Jacques. 1999. *Disagreement: Politics and Philosophy*. Trans. Julie Rose. Minneapolis: University of Minnesota Press.

Notes

1. In November 2011, Nicholaus Mills from *The Guardian* in the UK helpfully published a cross-section of opinions from prominent cultural and political pundits, spanning the spectrum from Naomi Klein to Niall Ferguson. See also the April 2, 2012, issue of *The Nation*, which similarly carries a round-up of opinion on the occupy movement, albeit all from a left perspective.

2. Details of living conditions are drawn from Greenberg (2011).

3. Examples drawn from Greenberg (2011).

4. In a speech given on December 6, 2011, at Osawatomie, Kansas, President Obama said that the issues identified by the Occupy Wall Street movement were the 'defining issues of our time' (Greenberg 2012b: 46).

5. As they observe, following Gabriel Tarde, the French revolution began when peasants stopped doffing their caps to the aristocracy, not when the heads began to roll (Deleuze and Guattari 1987: 216).

6. In their book on Kafka, Deleuze and Guattari describe this counter-flow as a 'witches' flight.'

7. In an interesting twist of history, the Phillip Glass opera based on the life of Ghandi, *Satyagraha*, was playing at the Lincoln Center in New York for much of the period of Occupy Wall Street's tenancy at Zuccotti Park. See Greenberg (2012b: 46).

Chapter 8

Negative Space War Machines

David Burrows

'Suck My Kutzs'[1]

With the first cuts, the first voids appear. The first negative spaces appear. A window in London's Milbank is kicked repeatedly, cracks radiate from a hole – filmed and photographed by much of Britain's news media. The following day, footage of a fire extinguisher dropped by a student from the roof of the Conservative Party's HQ is uploaded to YouTube. The fire extinguisher scatters ranks of police who survive unscathed except for minor injuries. Nervous systems are stimulated by the first day of mass protest against plans to charge full fees for undergraduate education in England and Wales. The mass media twitch and pulse anticipating the conflict to come.

Day X. The stepson of a millionaire rock star – 'out of his mind' on LSD, whiskey and valium – swings on a flag poll at the Cenotaph in Whitehall, London. Kettles are sprung like traps on unsuspecting protestors. Some though are prepared. The Book Bloc batter police lines with scaled-up cardboard replicas of *Our Word is Our Weapon* (2002) by Marcos, *End Game* (1957) by Beckett, *One Dimensional Man* (1964) by Marcuse and *Just William* (1921) by Compton. Others improvising with metal barriers join them and punch holes in the cordon at Parliament Square. As evening descends, the government votes to increase university fees for home and European students and confrontation between protestors and police escalate. Television news leads with stories of violence in the streets of Westminster, an attempted storming of the Treasury and a group of students sitting in the National Gallery, refusing to leave, surrounded by 'millions of pounds worth of paintings.' Later, a chaufferdriven Rolls-Royce limousine in London's West End is splattered with paint. One of the vehicles windows is breached and an aristocrat sitting in the back seat of the car is poked with a stick.

On an overcast day in March, swarms of protestors peel off the Trade Union Congress (TUC) march to Hyde Park in London to occupy Oxford Street. A giant, ramshackle horse representing the TUC lumbers towards the center of Oxford Circus and is sacrificed. The pantomime horse is set on fire. Dense, black plumes of smoke are visible for miles around and the smell of melting tar fills the air. As does the sound of whirring electric motors closing shutters, signalling the area is closed for business. Rather than join the zombie-shuffle from point A to point B (the prearranged rallying point from which a message to the powerful is to be sent), a few thousand protestors transform the West End into a carnival of refusal. UK Uncut occupy the luxury goods shop Fortnum and Mason and police form a ring around the store, serving as a membrane for a vacuole of discontent.

At first, the UK's news media equated protests against austerity measures with violent confrontation – the sought-after photograph was a smashed window. Soon another tale emerged, told by journalists close to the action: the birth of a new kind of protestor, the networked individual connected through social media. This declaration was followed by another: a new kind of protest movement was identified by commentators, presented as an alliance forged through weak links, rapid collective decision-making and organization without hierarchies. But there is another story to be told about this period of unrest and protest. As with other manifestations of refusal around the world in 2010 and 2011, protesting against the coalition government's austerity measures involved producing the space for protest. This took the form of occupations, protest swarms, teach-ins and gatherings; collective actions that rejected representational politics and embraced pragmatism and protocols and tactics developed by anti-globalization activists. All of which contributed to the production of protest as an occupation of space and time different to that sanctioned by orthodox political organizations and traditions. Protestors experimented with producing negative spaces that traversed and bored holes into the representations of organized politics and the mass media. By 2011, for many the issue of education fees was succeeded by a focus on the 1% whose spiritual home is the square mile governed by the City of London Corporation, targeted by Occupy London. By then, opposing austerity was no longer equated with violence in the UK, rather it was equated with a group of people who met daily on the steps of St Paul's Cathedral, experimenting with ways of living in tents in a small patch of ground in the heart of the capital.

This essay is concerned with this recent period of unrest and opposition to student fee increases in London, in particular the occupations, teach-ins and gatherings that not only manifested protest but the space of protest. It is an account that draws upon my involvement with Arts Against Cuts during this period, and thus will be a partial account and include an assessment of the role art played in producing the negative space of protest, experiments named here as negative space war machines. In this, the essay is specifically concerned with three interrelated problems.

1. **Saying no**. Protestors said no or expressed refusal in different ways, something mirrored in the discussions concerning negativity, refusal and affirmation that took place during this period of protest in various scenes or circles, many of which overlapped. Often views were polarized; actions and discussions included a militant rejection of affirmation as well as an exploration of the relationship of dissent and affirmation. A constellation of names, that include Marx, Deleuze, Negri, Marcos and Badiou, plotted different, competing political and philosophical ideas circulating during this period of unrest. However, to frame this period of protest with a political or philosophical concept or name would be unwise. Better to view recent protests as a testing ground for competing orientations, better to focus on the modes of operation employed than present the concepts and ideas of philosophers as providing meaning for events. To that end, this essay charts various instances of refusal and reflects upon the relevance of philosophical concepts and orientations. Two orientations in particular are addressed: (a) total refusal to produce anything that might hinder collapse or

facilitate business as usual; and (b) dissent as the space from which something new might be produced.

2. **Space**. Protestors were concerned with occupying places of commerce, institutions and (so-called) public space, and with the sphere of media communication and social network technology. A corollary of opposing the government was a questioning of hierarchical organizations and forms of decision-making. Movements formed which knotted together two modes of address: the physical (face-to-face address) and the mediated (face-less or Facebook address). It is the latter mode of address that has received most media attention – producing the much-heralded networked individual already mentioned – but this is to misunderstand the role and importance of mass communication technology for many protestors, which as an important aspect of protest culture might best be considered as a tool rather than a *point de capiton* for protestors. A more accurate account of the role of communication technology in this period of protest would focus on the knotting of the seemingly infinite, inhuman scale of cyberspace and communication technology with the space and time of occupation and protest. This knot of cyber and physical space enabled individuals who may have previously felt atomized to discover the joys of collective action. While the majority of protestors were far from class conscious, many shared a class identity of a kind: the educated without a future apart from the promise of debt slavery and precarious work if they could get it. One of the contentions of this essay is that it was physical space that served as the medium through which protestors produced a collective expression of refusal and commonism.

3. **Art**. While many artists and art students were involved in the protests, very little was produced by protestors that could be described as conventional art, or what style magazines and newspapers would term contemporary art. For the most part, banners and slogans were produced that articulated statements of opposition to the powerful. In addition to this, there were

performances, writing and art produced for the like-minded – art for others involved in the movement. Both these approaches addressed what the role of art could be in this period of protest. Within gatherings of protestors, conventional art was not welcome or did not surface, not least because the hierarchies (and ideologies) of the business of art were at odds with the non-hierarchical ideals of the movement. It is significant that anyone wanting to make art, perform or write can do so by protesting and find an audience at protest events. In fact, in the context of protest, it might be true to say anyone and everyone can be an artist if they wish to claim this mantle. In addressing the role of art during protest, alternatives to market and institutional conventions became tangible for many artists and students. Reflecting on this, this essay argues that it is art that turns its back on the powerful and public opinion to address or engender a collective that is most worthy of attention, for such impermanent and contingent productions function to open up new horizons or perspectives beyond opposition in the spaces produced by protest.

Saying 'no,' occupying space and the production of art: three problems relating to this recent period of protest. It is no easy task to address them all and arrive at a coherent conclusion or overview. Instead this essay addresses the various ways protest challenged existing and dominant subjective and discursive formations by experimenting with the production of negative spaces.

Just Say No!

In the novel *Chevengur* (1978), a story by the Russian writer Andrei Platonov, about a troubled utopia (a collectivized village), a man frightens himself with a dream in which he thinks his heart has stopped and on awakening sits on the floor and asks, 'Where then is socialism?' He peers into a murky room but cannot find it. It seems to him that he had this thing already but wasted it in sleep amongst strangers. Fearing punishment he runs off 'into his own distance.' The reader senses that this precious thing had already been lost before the man was visited by this disturbing dream or perhaps the precious thing was only ever an elusive idea of a thing yet to be produced.

Many involved in the protests have voiced similar feelings of disquiet. It is not that a precious thing has been lost exactly; rather, it is the feeling that the act of saying 'no,' an act that should be simple and straightforward, is more complex than it once was. No doubt, this is due in part to many lacking a faith in any politics of representation. No doubt too, globalization has made opposing or reforming capitalism, the goal of many protestors in UK, a much harder task. During the print union and miner's strikes in the UK in the 1980s, the unions identified a clear goal and course of action: stop the transportation of newspapers or coal by drawing a line, a picket line, across a gate or road. Action was envisaged as taking place on a local scale and having a national impact. In the 1990s and 2000s different spatial configurations were produced. Anti-capitalist movements traveled the world and converged on the gathering points and summits of global powers within various cities. In response, governments created secure lines or corridors between protected cordons or sealed vacuoles, so as to allow business to be conducted without interruption. The protestor's actions, though often spectacular and confrontational, had little effect or influence. In recent times, occupation rather than confrontation has become prevalent, leading some to declare 'Bartleby, the Scrivener' (1853) by Herman Melville to be the model for a new kind of protestor, and the first occupier of Wall Street.[2]

'Bartleby, the Scrivener' is a strange tale of a man staying put and refusing to do anything. Whenever his employer makes a request, including asking the scrivener to vacate the attorney's office in Wall Street, Bartleby replies, 'I prefer not to.' When asked about a change of employment or environment he indicates he would 'prefer not to' as he is not particular; that is, he has no specific desire to do anything in particular. What is confusing for the attorney, who means the scrivener well, is that Bartleby's statement 'I prefer not to,' as Gilles Deleuze (1998: 68) argues, is asymmetrical grammar or *agrammatical*; it is the affirmation of a negative that withdraws from dialogue.

Paul Mason, in *Why it's Kicking Off Everywhere* (2011), continually remarks upon how, in his encounters with European protestors, he rarely encountered anyone willing or concerned with identifying with a political ideology or set of demands. It might be the case that he didn't try hard enough (the recent protests brought many class warriors out of the shadows and the websites of various protest collectives carry numerous statements and lists of demands); but Mason's observation was echoed in oft-heard criticism of the movement's refusal to identify as one mass or group promoting an agreed political doctrine, program or set of demands. When asked to articulate the political doctrines of various protest movements many replied 'I prefer not to.' Mason understood something that others critical of the protestor's lack of identification with a named or historic political position did not. The refusal to identify is a refusal of representation, a refusal of the modes and organizations of mainstream media and politics mentioned earlier. 'Speak with us, not for us,' as the popular refrain goes.[3] And this approach is effective to a point; without a head to speak to or a name to cite or negotiate with, the conventions of representational politics fails.

Comparing Bartleby's acts of refusal with recent protest might not be inappropriate though. The scrivener ends his days in a prison or asylum refusing to eat and rejecting all assistance and kindness. Eventually he dies: a sad end but, as suggested by the narrator, perhaps one ensuring Bartleby's freedom or sovereignty until his last breath. Perhaps this is where the analogy of Bartleby as contemporary protestor seems limited, the scrivener's silence and inactivity towards death would have been out of place in the camps occupying the steps of St Paul's Cathedral in London and Zuccotti Park in New York. Bartleby's asymmetrical grammar and occupation of space is, however, a compelling example of a refusal that forecloses exchange and dialogue. Such refusal is relevant when analyzing recent dissent and also when differentiating between protests that demand the powerful accommodate or afford specific interests from the refusal that does not afford representation or dialogue, and declines accommodation by the powerful. In this latter mode of protest, the refrain 'we prefer not to' plays out in many different ways.

The voices that articulated the most militant forms of refusal argued that creative solutions and actions addressing the crisis of capitalism do nothing more than breathe life into the failing organizations and economies of capitalism. To explore this idea I turn to perhaps a surprising source, the thoughts of Nick Land, the neo-reactionary philosopher whose early interpretations of Deleuze and Guattari's writing were delivered with a negative charge. In the essay 'Machinic Desire' he states:

> Capital is not an essence but a tendency, the formula of which is decoding, or market driven immanentization, progressively subordinating social reproduction to techno-commercial replication. (Land 2011: 480)

Land's statement suggests that creative acts and social productions, even those deemed alternative or oppositional, feed capitalist and technological development: the crumbling edge of capitalism is also the cutting edge of capitalism. Many would agree with Land's assessment even if they reject his politics. Some protestors argued that only action (or inaction) that contributed to a catastrophic collapse of capitalist economies (for which no creative solution is produced) could arrest or resist this tendency of market-driven immanentization.[4] The protestors' refusal to develop hierarchical organizations and identifications and a fixed program of actions echoed another aspect of Land's (1997) early thinking, expressed in a short interview published online by *Wire*, in which he is asked about why the internet reproduces dull organizations and relations of power. He replies:

> You have to understand that organisation involves subordinating low level units to some higher level functional program. In the most extreme cases, like in biological organisms, every cell is defunctionalised, turned off, except for that one specialised function that it is allocated by the organic totality. And hence the preponderant part of its potential is deactivated in the interests of some higher-level unity. That's why the more organised things get, the less interesting their behavior becomes – "interesting" simply meaning here how freely they explore a range of possible behaviors, or how "nomadic" they are ... Organisation is suppression. It's more accurate to say that systems which avoid self-organisation whilst maintaining trajectories of productive innovation end up parasitically inhabited by organisms of all kinds, whether those organisms are biological organisms, corporations or state systems.

> The history of life on this planet right through to Microsoft is of the successive suppression of distributed, innovated systems. (Land 1997)

This concern was not limited to a small community of protestors and philosophers. The documentary filmmaker Adam Curtis has expressed similar reservations about the internet and social media technology, driven by narcissism and the ideologies of selfhood and selfishness. In talks and interviews he suggested that to advocate for self-organizing societies empowered by new forms of connectivity and communication was foolish. His example of a game of *Pong* being controlled by 'a hive mind' is chilling (Curtis 2011). In 1991 in California, scientist Loren Carpenter invited a group of people to take part in an experiment. The group quickly perceived that by waving paddles with red and green faces they could control the virtual bats projected on a large screen in front of them. They do so as two groups, spontaneously playing the game without communication or instruction from a leader. Curtis hints that this so-called hive mentality or organization may just be articulating a pre-designed system; participants delight in their collective cleverness but ultimately they may be nothing more than an expression of that system. Curtis feels the same way about the internet, which he feels will be seen in years to come as an expression of powerful systems of control, Facebook being seen as similar to the social realist paintings produced in the era of Stalinism (Curtis 2011).

But rejecting collective action and communication, renouncing desire and doing nothing, as we learn from Bartleby, is perilous; it is after all an unaffordable path, and does not necessarily challenge existing relations. To avoid nihilistic paths or noble suicide, refusal must produce new horizons. In the interview Land suggests that while organization produces hierarchies and curtails potential, self-organization may counter parasitic inhabitation by various agencies, allowing bodies and minds to freely 'explore a range of possible behaviors, or how "nomadic" they are.' Perhaps Land articulates here something that many UK protestors valued: self-organization or autonomy as opposed to majority rule or hierarchical organization of bodies and minds.

While it would not be true to say that protest groups eschewed organization or preparation, as stated earlier, many protestors did refuse to create organizations with fixed and hierarchical roles in favor of gatherings convened by facilitators. These gatherings proceeded through spontaneous organization producing weak links between groups and individuals and consensus voting (allowing people to opt out of actions).

The role of facilitator was often taken up or adopted by individuals in relation to the demands of a situation or event on the understanding that the role lasted for the duration of that event. Not only this, events and gatherings were arranged without a set program or agenda. At such events, the order of activities and items for discussion were decided on the day or through open space technology.[5] The use of facilitators and open space modes of programming expressed an ambition to avoid fixing symbolic mandates and to produce a political movement that was multiple, flexible and peripatetic in action and word.

To further develop this discussion of movements that are not only nomadic in thought and deed but that foreclose dialogue with the powerful, the thoughts of Gilles Deleuze are helpful. Deleuze, in conversation with Toni Negri, argued that it was better to produce 'a vacuole of non-communication,' to produce circuit breakers, 'to prefer not to' communicate rather than connect (Deleuze 1990: 175). For Deleuze, creating was something different from communication. He argued that resistance and communism has nothing to do with minorities or masses 'speaking out,' not least because speech and communication, which has become corrupted by money and unable to evade control, has to be hijacked (Deleuze 1990: 175).

What is a vacuole of non-communication? Perhaps it is merely a noisy arrangement, or a piece of nonsense? In the same conversation, Deleuze allows us to understand the potential genesis of this vacuole when he discuses the term 'war machine,' a term that has nothing to do with waging war as such (Deleuze 1990: 172). Rather, it is a term that refers to a particular occupation of space, an experiment within space and time, an invention of space and time. Deleuze makes this term concrete by suggesting that the way the Palestinian Liberation Organization (PLO) had to invent 'space-time' in the Arab context has been underestimated. To do so, the PLO became a war machine, marking out a territory where previously none existed, opening up gaps and negative spaces in the discourses and organizations of local and international government and the mass media (Deleuze and Guattari 2003).

Franco Berardi aka Bifo (2009a) has proposed a similar idea when proposing that communism today is found in the production of singularities (experiments with time) born from the necessity of collective action as means of survival and as the refusal of control and exploitation. Berardi argues that such singularities manifest as 'the creation of an economy of shared use of common goods and services and the liberation of time for culture, pleasure and affection.' Without dismissing Berardi's arguments, the war machine can be defined as similar but different, in that it is not a singular experimentation with time and relations, or merely that, but an illegal or dissenting occupation and use of space and time too; a movement that rejects existing hierarchies or representations and produces its own space and time where none existed before, as a direct challenge to the policing – the management and ordering – of existing space, resources and relations.

A Place Called Space

Before addressing detailed examples of how refusal is linked to the occupation of space and time, and before examining the ways protestors knotted cyberspace and occupied (physical) space, a clarification of the different modes of protest so far considered is necessary. There are at least four modes of protest worth attending to.

1. **Refusal through identification.** Refusal as an act that demands the reform of existing laws or relations. This statement produces identification with a specific narrative or representation (an identification made with a cause or group that engages with representational politics, such as UK Uncut.)

2. **Refusal through connection and detachment: the didvidual.** Refusal that leaves individual choice open by maintaining weak identifications with groups and causes or deferring identification. This gesture engenders a post-continuity subjectivity, contemporary with a post-continuity consumer culture. The networked individual,[6] or what Deleuze (1990: 180) terms 'the

dividual,' is a connection between other connections; dividuals can articulate and be articulated by an organization, such as electronic media.[7]

3. **Refusal through producing nothing.** Refusal as an act that is not affordable (for an individual or others) and that welcomes the collapse or suspension of existing organizations without proposing anything but the destruction of existing relations: a refusal of affirmation, solutions or production of any kind.

4. **Refusal through producing something different.** Refusal as an act of dissent and as an experiment with producing a different space and time from that produced by existing organizations of relations: a refusal that is unconcerned with communicating or negotiating with existing hierarchies.

Of course, the four modes of refusal are not four different kinds of people; they are four statements that can be articulated by the same person or group. The statements can be found in the testimonies of different occupations, three of which, issued in 2010, are cited below.[8]

> ***Slade School of Fine Art Occupation Statement:*** We vehemently oppose the transformation of the university system into market based model; education should be a public debate, not a private economy. Therefore we the students of the Slade are offering a space for the assembly of all art colleges in England in order to organise non-violent direct action against what we view as an attack by the government on the arts. This is not a virtual exchange, this is a physical assembly. We are demonstrating the value of physical space for art education through the continuation of our day-to-day activity, as well as by inviting other colleges to participate in open events, lectures and workshops. Our occupation is not designed to be disruptive, nor will it engender any damage to the building. Rather, we want to highlight the value of intellectual and cultural exchange within art courses. This is not a boycott, it is an act of support (Slade Occupation 2010).

At Goldsmiths College a less affirmative, more militant statement was posted – and staff were not allowed to work in the university's occupied library.

> ***Goldsmiths Occupation Statement I:*** We have taken over Goldsmiths' Library, the most publicly visible and accessible physical space in the college. We are opening it as a center for organization, available 24 hours a day to students and all those on the receiving end of the government's assault in the Lewisham community. We support library staff at Goldsmiths and public libraries across Lewisham. The proposed changes in Higher Education represent a historically unprecedented attack on society. In response, we have taken the exceptional step of deciding that no staff shall work in the library building, although students are welcome to come and join us. Until our demands are met, there will be no business as usual at the college. (Goldsmiths Occupation 2010a)

Finally, a statement representing a group of people who occupied the library for a second time and shut it down.

> ***Goldsmiths Occupation Statement II:*** I was among those supporting a real occupation of Goldsmiths this week. A large group of students, staff and supporters agreed before the library was occupied that only a significant disruption of the normal functioning of the university would contribute to blocking the govt's plans and forcing action from the university management. For me the idea that symbolic protests with banners, or more innovative tokens of opposition, are the only 'positive' forms of protest is regressive aesthetically and politically ... In a society in which just doing our jobs and carrying out our tasks – whether writing essays, teaching, or stacking (book)shelves – is the main way in which social relations are reproduced, it may be that NOT doing anything is our real weapon ... So sitting in a library doing paid teaching or studying work (like those attending radical teach ins with their radical paid teachers yesterday and today) is a purely symbolic gesture which refutes and undoes itself ... They want to shut

down our society? Fine, we'll shut it down. And not just for a few moments, or for a day, but for as long as it takes to reverse their decision to axe our services, our jobs, and our futures.
(Goldsmiths Occupation 2010b)

Three statements, three negative spaces, three different expressions of refusal. The first and most affirmative statement proposes an occupation in which the university remains open but is run by the students as a platform for national resistance and as a space to experiment with what the university could become. The last statement is damning of most of the actions carried out by the majority of protestors at this time and proposes that all universities, and society itself, should be shut down as a means of striking at the government. We can discuss who is right and wrong, which statement is the more idealistic, and whose actions are more symbolic or pragmatic but this would require a second piece of writing. In citing these statements, the intention here is to draw attention to the ways in which space became the material of protest, and how the production of negative space became a means of resistance.

By examining the statements produced by the occupations we can see how refusal relates not just to the political and ethical orientations but the production of space. This should not be a surprise. First, the protests addressed the problem of who can afford to attend the institutions of education and culture, and which people and logics administer and organize these spaces. Secondly, protestors, by marching and occupying, discovered or confirmed that much so-called public space was constantly surveyed and policed in London, if not run by or owned by private companies. Kettling, the restraint of groups of people as a means of containing protest or as a means of intimidation by the police, turned out to be a defining and politicizing experience for many. Finally, protest (in producing the space and time of protest) necessitated the occupation of space through swarms, teach-ins, disruption of business and the staging of spectacles. All of which required preparation – time and space – that for groups such as Arts Against Cuts and their fellow travelers took the form of direct action planning weekends at various student unions. For many, these were the encounters that mattered. Contrary to commentators who have focussed critically on the use of social network technology by protestors, face-to-face meetings in physical space were the medium that forged collective action and occupations. The majority of protestors at these meetings, if employed, were mostly precarious workers or students whose withdrawal of labor would make little difference. In this context, where union muscle is not what it once was and marching toward violent confrontation a dead-end, the occupation of space as a means of forming collectives and resistance makes sense. Beyond refusing debt slavery, the occupation and use of space could be considered a key political problem or project of anti-austerity protestors.

Space is the Place

There is one more aspect of the production of negative space (as war machine) that needs examining, one already touched upon in comments proposing that cyberspace and actual space were knotted together through protest swarms and occupations. The different scale and intensity of relations (the different kinds of feedback) engendered by occupation meant that experimentation, collective action, and the formation of community were understood as more than a symbolic gesture. Protestors formed new subjective attachments through producing a space with an operational scale that facilitated affective and transformative action.

To explore this question of scale it is helpful to examine how commentary on modes of attention and cyberspace has changed over recent years. Before the internet had become a common form of communication, Frederic Jameson, in *Postmodernism, or, the Cultural Logic of Late Capitalism* (1991), argued that human perception was unable to deal with the invasion of mass media and communication technology in everyday life and environments, an event he announced as the dawning of a postmodern hysterical sublime. Jameson refers to the character Jerome Newton, played by David Bowie in the film *The Man Who Fell to Earth* (1976), an alien who can watch 57 televisions all at once; something that Jameson suggests the human is unable to do (1991: 31). Franco Berardi (2009b: 89) has alluded to this discrepancy between the limited time and capacity that humans have to process information, messages and potential connections and the attention demanded by a seemingly limitless cyberspace that can dominate our attention at work and play. For Berardi, fatigue and atomization rather than a hysterical sublime is the most likely result. Clearly, though, Berardi points to how we have evolved from the postmodern primitives described by Jameson, but to do so we have evolved into networked individuals – dividuals – continually making connections. The use of social network media by the occupations, while never fully cutting out the 'middle man' of mass media broadcasters and communications corporations as some claimed, allowed networked individuals to plug into collective culture and space, and to broadcast from and about the actual spaces that they affected, controlled and transformed through action. This radicalization of the dividual went far beyond the act of creating Facebook pages. Two key examples of the knotting together of cyberspace and physical space to produce the negative space of protest are the creation of the smartphone application *Sukey*, developed by University College London students, to track the movement of the police through gathering Twitter information and the use of text messages and other social media to amass and disperse swarms and occupations at rapid speed. Whilst remaining dividuals (connecting, circulating information and responding to messages) the protestors used cyberspace to physically manifest negative spaces within the city.

Mise en abyme

To address the role of art as negative space war machines during this period of protest it is important to clarify further what the term 'negative space' refers to in the context of art. The term is borrowed from an art school exercise that encourages abstract thinking and drawing. This is not a process of opposition or of producing opposites; drawing the 'space of the negative' is different from developing a piece of film as a negative for a positive photographic print. Rather a negative space drawing counters figuration, habits of seeing and thinking, and our perceptions of what exists. Negative space is produced through a process of experimenting with composition, a process that begins with observation (of things and the unoccupied space around things), but produces new and abstract arrangements (though a drawing might still bear the trace of the observed or recognizable world that has all but disappeared in the final image). By drawing empty space, by drawing nothing rather than things, the transcription of outlines and spaces onto a two-dimensional surface creates a composition that is ambiguous, one that could be viewed in multiple ways: shapes can be viewed as forms or spaces, as having depth or as being flat, as something or nothing. In this way, negative space drawings are experiments that lead to new combinations and relations of forms.

The association of negative space drawings with occupation and protest came to mind not just because the occupations countered the *status quo* but also because the process of occupation and swarming relied on spontaneity and a new counting or use of objects, environments and space. In this way, the art of protest, as the production of a negative space war machine, is understood as a performance or action that marks or inscribes a negative space. It is for this reason that negative space war machines are four-dimensional, operating beyond the one-dimensional ideologies of capitalist realism, the two dimensions of opposition and speaking to power and the three dimensions of pragmatic or direct action.

To expand upon the four-dimensionality of art as (negative space) war machines, five examples of art from this period of protest are presented below (though there are many other examples to choose from). All are unlikely to make their way into any archives or galleries of museums.

1. **Society**. Two artists produce a simple banner, red in color, baring the word 'Society.' The banner is unfurled and carried around London during the protests against austerity. The banner is carried by different people and taken to different locations where photographs are taken amongst protestors, next to a soldier standing guard in Whitehall and next to a fountain. Everywhere the banner is displayed a question is raised, 'What constitutes society?'

2. **Funeral March for the Liberal Party**. On the day following the passing of the bill to increase students' fees, a small group walk from High Holborn to Trafalgar Square in crow masks, howling and carrying wreaths. The event is best captured by Paul Mason in his book, *Why It's All Kicking Off Everywhere*:

> Whitehall and Parliament Square are still strewn with rubble and missiles … Suddenly out of the dark comes the sound of drumming and wailing. Seven or eight figures emerge, dressed in black and wearing elaborate crows' head

masks. They do a dance across three lanes of traffic into the middle of Parliament Square and approach the statue of David Lloyd George. And they lay a black wreath ... "We're here to mourn the death of the Liberal Party," croaks the guy holding the drum, as he beats out a tocsin surrounded by the masked, mainly female, wailers. This goes on for about five minutes. At no point do they attempt to photograph, film or otherwise record the performance. It is purely gestural, vanishing into obscurity the moment it is over. (Mason 2012: 53)

Throughout the march the mourners are spat at, sworn at and abused. The performance gauges that levels of anger and fear are high, and upsets the process of things quietly getting back to normal.

3. **The Hive Manifesto (Arts Against Cuts 2010).** A text produced spontaneously and collectively, by all who occupied the National Gallery on the night of Day X. As stated by Paul Mason, who also comments on the manifesto, no great work of literature perhaps, but a working through of protocols for refusal and modes of protest different to those sanctioned by representational politics (Mason 2012: 54). Protestors refused to leave the gallery until the manifesto was complete.

4. **Long and Direct Weekends[9] (and the Notice Boards, Maps of Spaces and Timetables They Produced).** On several weekends, Arts Against Cuts and their allies held talks, discussions and workshops at various universities, each weekend producing intense collaborations and encounters. The protocols of open space technology were employed, so that all could stage a workshop, discussion or presentation or produce props, banners and posters. Maps, notice boards and timetables indexed rapid transformations of space and discussion; the timetables and notice boards bore the residue of intense encounters in the form scribbling, drawings, arrows, crosses, strikethroughs, felt-tip and ink smudges, erasures, notes and tape.

5. **Merz Summer School**.[10] Perhaps inspired by the free schools of London and feeling they needed time to process all they had seen and done, perhaps needing time to work through the problems of collaboration and collective and individual action, and perhaps dissatisfied with universities as they existed and discussions dominated by lecturers and experts, a group of students involved in the occupations and protests left London for the Lake District to run their own summer school, open to all who wanted to attend, at the invitation of Kurt Schwitters' Merz Barn.

Negative Space War Machines

In conclusion, it is important to acknowledge the protests and occupations discussed above failed to halt austerity measures (whether due to lacking critical mass or effective tactics) but the protests have a legacy of a kind. While it is true that the five examples above and the occupations in general posed no serious threat to the order of things, these negative space war machines experimented with specific problems concerning affirmation and negation, autonomy and collective action and the relation of cyberspace and physical space; all are problems relevant to politics and protest concerned with refusing existing relations and exploring alternatives. Through actions and productions that were more than a communication of opposition, the occupations and the examples cited above share four attributes that define negative space war machines:

- Negative space war machines are not representational machines but address a problem.
- Negative space war machines are made in the moment for the moment.
- Negative space war machines contest space and its relations.
- Negative space war machines are produced collectively for a collective (not as a political communication to a public or power).

Works Cited

Arts Against Cuts. 2010. 'The Nomadic Hive Manifesto' (December 9). Accessed 8 May, 2015 from: https://artsagainstcuts.wordpress.com/2010/12/10/after-the-national-gallery-teach-in/

Berardi, Franco. 2009a. 'Communism is Back But We Should Call the Therapy of Singularization'. *Generation Online* (February) Accessed May 4 2015, from: http://www.generation-online.org/p/fp_bifo6.htm

Berardi, Franco. 2009b. *Precarious Rhapsody: Semiocapitalism and the Pathologies of the Post-alpha Generation*. Ed. Erik Empson and Stevphen Shukaitis. Trans. Arianna Bove, Michael Goddard, Giuseppina Mecchia, Antonella Schintu and Steve Wright. London: Minor Compositions.

Curtis, Adam. 2011a. *All Watched Over by Machines of Loving Grace*. Episode one. BBC2 (May 23).

Curtis Adam. 2011b. 'Untitled paper'. *The Story Conference at Conway Hall* (February 20). London: Storythings. Podcast available on iTunes at: https://itunes.apple.com/gb/podcast/storythings/id439627244?mt=2#

Deleuze, Gilles. 1990. *Negotiations 1972–1990*. Trans. Martin Joughin. New York: Columbia.

Deleuze, Gilles. 1998. 'Bartleby; or, The Formula'. In *Essays Critical and Clinical: 1968–1990*. Trans. Daniel W Smith. London and New York: Verso.

Deleuze, Gilles and Félix Guattari. 2003. 'Treatise on Nomadology – War Machines'. In *A Thousand Plateaus: Capitalism and Schizophrenia*. Trans. Brian Massumi. London: Continuum: 387–467.

Foucault, Michel. 1974. *The Archaeology of Knowledge*. Trans. AM Sheriden Smith. London: Tavistock.

Goldsmiths Occupation. 2010a. 'Goldsmiths Occupation Statement'. *Mute* (December 7). Accessed May 9, 2015 from: http://www.metamute.org/community/your-posts/goldsmiths-occupation-statement

Goldsmiths Occupation. 2010b. 'Statement on the Goldsmiths Occupation. *Mute* (December 8). Accessed May 9, 2015 from: http://www.metamute.org/community/your-posts/statement-goldsmiths-occupation

Jameson, Fredic. 1991. *Postmodernism, or, the Cultural Logic of Late Capitalism*. London and New York: Verso.

Land, Nick. 1997. 'Organisation is Suppression: Interview by James Flint'. In *Wire* (February). Accessed April 1, 2013 from: http://dialspace.dial.pipex.com/town/park/di21/art_tech_ec_files/land.htm

Land, Nick. 2011. 'Machinic Desire'. In *Fanged Noumena: Collected Writings 1987–2000*. Cornwall: Urbanomic: 340–41.

Mason, Paul. 2012. *Why It's Kicking Off Everywhere*. London and New York: Verso.

Platonov, Andrei. 1978. *Chevengar*. Trans. Anthony Olcott. Michigan: Ardis.

Slade Occuption. 2010. 'Our Statement'. Accessed 8 May, 2015 from: https://sladeoccupation.wordpress.com/our-statement/

Notes

1. Slogan printed on an Arts Against Cuts sticker.
2. Journalist Hannah Gersen, commenting on Bartleby and Occupy Wall Street suggests, 'If Occupy Wall Street has any goal, it should be to have the same effect that great literature has to unsettle,' see 'Bartleby's Occupation of Wall Street', *The Millons* (October 11, 2011), available at: http://www.themillions.com/2011/10/bartleby's-occupation-of-wall-street.html Other websites linking Bartleby to the occupations include Nina Martyris, 'A Patron Saint for Occupy Wall Street', *The New Republic* (October 15, 2011), availabe at: http://www.newrepublic.com/article/politics/96276/nina-martyris-ows-and-bartleby-the-scrivener and Jonathan Greenberg, 'Occupy Wall Street's Debt to Melville', *The Atlantic* (April 30, 2012), available at: http://www.theatlantic.com/politics/archive/2012/04/occupy-wall-streets-debt-to-melville/256482
3. See Occupy London, 'Statement on Autonomy' (December 14, 2011), availabe at: http://occupylondon.org.uk/about/statements/statement-of-autonomy/
4. In relation to the problems of art and creativity, Reza Negarestani articulated a similar position in a discussion at the event 'The Medium of Contingency' at Thomas Dane Gallery, London on February 23, 2011, the day that protests against workfare and EMA (education maintenance allowance) cuts took place in the capital. In his talk Negarestani argued for artists to be complicit rather than creative with their materials and await contingencies or collapse. He urged artists to do nothing creative.
5. Open Space Technology (OST) is a mode of staging meetings that begin with no formal agenda other than an agreed theme, aim or problem. Such gatherings develop through bulletin boards and flexible timetables stipulating spaces or slots that are filled as the event progresses. Participants attend workshops or discussions depending on whether they feel they can contribute or the sessions are productive. OST was developed by individuals involved in business studies.

6. Paul Mason describes such a protestor, @littlemisswild who joins an occupation by accident (she didn't want to be alone and she is told she can twitter all she likes). She doesn't know the history of the term 'solidarity' though she ends every tweet with the greeting, and she does not read books on politics if she can help it but reads twitter flows, blogs and websites to know what is going on, and she does know what is going on (Mason 2012: 41–2).

7. Mason (2012: 79) describes another (mythical) figure in the same book, sitting in Starbucks, face colored blue from the reflected light of a laptop. She may be facebooking, designing, gaming, tweeting or planning protest and revolution, or all of these things at once. Mason suggests that this marks a shift in culture from a generation steeped in collectivism to a generation concerned with the expansion of the individual.

8. The term statement is used here to refer to performed or performative roles, as outlined by Michel Foucault who argued that a statement 'is not a unit, but a function that cuts across a domain of structures and possibilities and unities, and which reveals them, with concrete contents, in time and space' (Foucault 1974: 79–118).

9. See Arts Against Cuts, 'Arts Against Cuts: The Long Weekend' (December 2, 2010), available at: http://artsagainstcuts.wordpress.com/2010/12/02/arts-against-cuts-the-long-weekend/

10. See Kurt Schwitter's Summer School, available at: http://kurtschwitterssummerschool.wordpress.com/

Chapter 9

Occupy America and the Slow-Motion General Strike

EUGENE HOLLAND

I see three areas of significant overlap between the Occupy movement and Deleuze and Guattari's political philosophy, and I will examine them under the rubrics of the war machine, ahistorical becomings, and the minor. Given that their first collaborative work, *Anti-Oedipus*, emerged at least partly as a reflection on the unanticipated political events of May 1968, it would be very surprising if Deleuze and Guattari's perspective turned out not to be relevant to the equally unforeseen resonance of the Occupy Wall Street movement throughout the United States (and indeed around the world) some forty years later. And it is the unforeseen quality of both these political movements that leads into the first two of the three topics under consideration in what follows.

War Machines

Although the term itself is in many ways misleading, the concept of the war machine is central to Deleuze and Guattari's understanding of politics and society, and especially to their conception of micro-politics, which is one of their most important contributions to political theory. While it is true that war machines do in certain specific circumstances make war, their essential characteristics are that they operate by means of a very particular kind of social cohesion, and that they produce change: in this respect, they would be better known as 'mutation machines' (Deleuze and Guattari 1987: 229) or, as Paul Patton (2000) has suggested, 'metamorphosis machines.' In order to evoke the kind of social relations characteristic of mutation machines, we can draw on Deleuze and Guattari's distinction between pack and herd animals. Herd animals form an undifferentiated mass, and they all follow a single leader; this for Deleuze and Guattari is the epitome of the State form of social relations. Pack animals such as wolves interact very differently: for wolves on the hunt, there is a significant degree of role specialization, and the pack operates via the collective coordination of members' activities rather than via obedience to a single leader. (While it is true that the dominant alpha-male and alpha-female of a wolf pack unilaterally determine the distribution of food *after* the hunt – as well as the distribution of mating opportunities, for that matter – they do not serve as leaders of the hunt itself, which operates instead via spontaneous or horizontal coordination.) The kinds of change produced by mutation machines, meanwhile, vary widely. Deleuze and Guattari even go so far as to say that the war machine 'exists only in its own metamorphoses; it exists in an industrial innovation as well as in a technological invention, in a commercial circuit as well as in a religious creation' or 'in specific assemblages such as building bridges or cathedrals or rendering judgments or making music or instituting a science, a technology' (Deleuze and Guattari 1987: 366). Finally, and perhaps most important, mutation machines operate via contagion, enthusiasm, *esprit de corps*, and solidarity (Deleuze and Guattari 1987: 241–9, 267–9, 278, 366–7, 384, 390–93) rather than strict obligation or duty.

Certainly much of what happened during the events of May 1968 in France can be accounted for only in terms of enthusiasm and contagion rather than duty: a small student protest against corporate sponsorship of war gradually spread to become a general strike against the dissatisfactions of French society as a whole. The Occupy Wall Street movement of 2011 (OWS), in a similar way, spread rapidly to cities and campuses around the country, and eventually to groups and places around the world. It operated by contagion rather than by obedience to a single leader or even a single platform or program. OWS also quickly developed both a remarkable degree of role specialization and very effective horizontal modes of cooperation and coordination. And although it was initially conceived and organized by an identifiable group of activists (as was the initial French student protest), it very quickly grew beyond the bounds of anything they had imagined, and certainly grew far beyond anything they could control. Yet the fact that OWS can be said to have taken the form of a mutation machine does not make it a panacea: the contemporaneous right-wing Tea Party movement operated according to quite similar dynamics – although it did benefit from funding by the likes of the Koch brothers and from media hype provided by the likes of Fox cable news. As Deleuze and Guattari point out, the Nazis operated as an autonomous war machine before they took power and integrated that machine into the apparatus of state rule. Ultimately, then, the form of organization or of the social dynamics of a given group says relatively little about the content of their positions or activities. The value of the concept of the war machine is rather that it directs our attention to the manner in which these social groups or movements actually operate. And in OWS and the Tea Party movements, we have chosen rather extreme examples: it may be that elections in so-called liberal or representative democracies are always won or lost on the basis of which party can mobilize more numerous and more energetic war machines operating on its behalf – from student volunteers going door-to-door, to volunteer housewives stuffing envelopes, to donors and campaign operatives themselves. Much like the stock market, electoral politics depends far more than is usually recognized on the kind of enthusiasm and contagion that are key elements of the war machine.

Since war machines operate on the Right as well as the Left, and everywhere in between, the fact that OWS took that form, or started out that way, cannot be considered decisive in evaluating its impact. But the same was true of the events of May 1968 for Deleuze and Guattari: within the span of a few months, the French movement had been re-absorbed into macro-politics as usual, with President de Gaulle receiving broad-based and strong support in the ensuing elections. But that doesn't mean nothing changed on the level of micro-politics. Deleuze and Guattari describe deep-seated effects on countless individuals, for one thing – in a portrait that might just as well suit a generation of young Americans who would soon participate in OWS:

> The children of May '68, you can run into them all over the place, even if they are not aware who they are, and each

> country produces them in its own way. Their situation is not great. These are not young executives. They are strangely indifferent, and for that very reason they are in the right frame of mind. They have stopped being demanding or narcissistic, but they know perfectly well that there is nothing today that corresponds to their subjectivity, to their potential of energy. (Deleuze 2006: 235)

And for another thing, the kind of movement that May 1968 was gets registered in the concepts (such as the war machine, micro-politics, etc.) that Deleuze and Guattari (and others) created in order to better understand it and hopefully relay its potential to future generations. Finally, even when a social movement produces no apparent immediate results – as was the case with May 1968, and appears to be the case with OWS as well – it may have produced what Deleuze and Guattari call 'incorporeal transformations' whose real or corporeal effects only become apparent at some later time. Thus a judge's sentence doesn't in and of itself physically kill a condemned person on the spot: it produces an incorporeal transformation, changing that person's social and legal status from accused to condemned, which only later, barring unforeseen mitigating circumstances or disruptions, leads to corporeal death. But history is rarely (if ever) as clear-cut as a judicial proceeding: incorporeal transformations may occur without our even being aware of them at the time, such that it is only later that we ask 'What happened?' – what must have happened x months or y years ago, to lead up to the unforeseen changes we are witnessing today? In a famous 1984 magazine article (later re-published as an essay in *Two Regimes of Madness* (2006)), Deleuze and Guattari even went so far as to claim that 'May 68 did not take place' ('Mai '68 n'a pas eu lieu'); they characterize it instead as a 'visionary phenomenon' and a 'pure event' whose realization depends on society's ability to develop 'collective agencies of enunciation' to institutionalize the changes foreseen by the event: 'French society has shown a radical incapacity to create a subjective redeployment on the collective level, which is what '68 demands' (Deleuze 2006: 234). But the fact that no such agencies were found in the two decades following May 1968 doesn't mean that they couldn't develop in the future. And in the same way, incorporeal transformations put into motion by OWS may yet bear fruit; there can be no question that the movement has at least already completely transformed the social meaning of an otherwise anodyne figure, 'the 99%.'

Ahistorical Becomings

In order to better understand the sense in which Deleuze and Guattari can say that May 1968 did not take place and yet call it a pure event, we must learn, along with them, to distinguish between history and becoming, that is to say, between linear history and the potential alternatives to historical development they call becomings. History for Deleuze and Guattari is always a mixture combining linear development that is causally determined with bifurcation points that are unpredictable both as to when they occur and where they will lead. May 1968 in France, as we have seen, was a potential bifurcation point that could have led French society in a very different direction, but it didn't (or hasn't yet) because the requisite collective agencies of enunciation weren't available. One of the important roles for political philosophy is to diagnose the becomings inherent in historical events, to extract what is 'untimely' (as they say, borrowing the term from Nietzsche), from linear historical determinacy. If Deleuze and Guattari were able to extract a concept of micro-politics from May 1968, is it possible today to extract concepts from OWS? We will return to this question below. But first we need to further examine the relation of becomings to history.

Conceiving of history as non-linear poses at least three kinds of problem. One is that historical achievements are never permanent. Deleuze and Guattari contrast May 1968 in France with the mid-twentieth century American New Deal, inasmuch as the New Deal was able to institutionalize the solutions it envisioned to address the Great Depression. Yet those institutions have not survived decades of Republican attacks, so that now, even when confronting the worst economic crisis since the Great Depression, a new New Deal has not been possible. A second problem arising from non-linear history is the impossibility of identifying bifurcation points, or even assessing their potential when they are recognizable. May 1968 may have set in motion deep-seated transformations in French society that will take decades to become visible – and the same may be true of OWS: perhaps it will have been a bifurcation point, and we just don't know it yet. Finally, in the context of non-linear causality, effects may be wildly disproportionate to causes – as in the famous (if fanciful) illustration of a butterfly flapping its wings and thereby contributing to a hurricane on the other side of the globe. Such disproportionality adds to the difficulty of identifying bifurcation points in the first place, and to the impossibility of assessing their future potential with much confidence. What all this suggests for political strategy is a new way around the hoary reform–revolution conundrum. Given the non-linear view of history, there is no point in waiting around for the right moment to make the revolution: we might miss any number of opportunities because we didn't recognize them as tipping points. At the same time, there is no reason to shy away from reforms, even those that at the moment seem unlikely to produce widespread change, because with effects being disproportionate to causes, any one or combination of them might be or become a tipping point before or without our realizing it in the short-term. Political action must be worthwhile in its own right, in the short-term, as well as hold out reasonable prospects for contributing to significant and wide-ranging social change in the medium-to-long-term. This was one of the most striking features of the Occupy movement in practically all of its incarnations: rather than simply calling for a more democratic society, as many political demonstrations tend to do, it actually enacted one. Food was collectively prepared and distributed; lending libraries and small discussion groups were established; most important, a whole set of informal discussion and decision-making procedures were developed for the General Assemblies (particularly in the face of police injunctions against the use of megaphones and PA systems). OWS tried to instantiate and illustrate what true – participatory – democracy looks like, rather than merely make demands of a supposedly democratic system that it knew to be hopelessly corrupt. Yet at the same time, its propensity was emphatically not to 'turn on, tune in, drop out' (as it was for a portion of the 1960s counter-culture movement), but rather to take the example of more truly democratic social relations to the very 'heart of the beast' – Wall Street. So OWS had both a long-term or systemic large-scale target (Wall Street) and an immediate small-scale goal (instantiating democracy), and satisfying this double requirement is one aspect of what I have called (Holland 2011) the slow-motion general strike, which we will discuss below. But it poses some problems for the politics of the war machine, as discussed above. How do you make political action that is not obviously revolutionary into something contagious? How does the felt need for social change become urgent? In the 1960s United States, it was anti-war protest, and the prospect of dying in a war we didn't believe in, that lent the counter-culture movement its sense of urgency; in 1960s France, however, there was no such focal point, and yet the French student movement proved far more contagious than its American counterpart, and ended up mobilizing a far greater proportion of the French people than were mobilized by the American counter-culture and anti-war movements combined. The Occupy movement certainly became contagious, but despite the name 'Occupy,' it never had concrete long-term ambitions: what will become of 'Occupy 2.0' is a pressing question that so far remains unanswered. One of the unfortunate difficulties of the war machine and non-linear history is that they are so unpredictable – practically by definition. It is just as impossible to produce enthusiasm or solidarity at will as it is to predict the timing or extent of a bifurcation point in advance. But it was certainly no accident that 'ground zero' for the Occupy movement was none other than Wall Street.

The Minor

And it may be just as revealing that the single most enduring, significant and vigorous off-shoot of the Occupy movement has been the (inaptly named) 'Occupy Student Debt' movement. To help explain why this might be so, we can turn to Deleuze and Guattari's adaptation of Marx's analysis of capital, which I call their 'minor marxism' (Holland 2011). The key difference between most 'major' or dialectical Marxism and this minor or structural marxism is that while the former focuses on the results of the dialectical process of capital accumulation, the latter focuses on the structural preconditions for capital accumulation – also known as 'primitive accumulation.' The watchword of major Marxism follows from the dialectical precept of the negation of the negation: expropriate the expropriators; confront the power of accumulated capital head-on, and wrest it from its illegitimate private owners by force. The approach of a minor marxism is different: address the structural preconditions for capital accumulation rather than the power of accumulated capital itself; disrupt and reverse the process of primitive accumulation. This is the basis of the strategy I call the slow-motion general strike. It is a *general* strike in that it is not directed against a single industry, but against capitalist industry as a whole; and indeed, following the example set in France in May 1968, it could be considered to be a strike against many or all facets of social life, not just industry – and in particular a strike against a nominally democratic political system that, then as now, has clearly not served the interests of the majority (the 99%). But the slow-motion general strike is also distinctive because, unlike the traditional or major general strike, it is not punctual and not confrontational: it unfolds gradually over the long haul rather than provoking (or hoping for) immediate wholesale changes in social life; and rather than confronting the power of accumulated capital, it seeks to undermine that power by subtracting greater and greater areas of social and economic activity from capitalist markets through the development of alternative economies and social networks that provide alternative means of life outside the circuits of capital. As the work of Gibson-Graham has amply demonstrated, economic activity already actually takes many different forms, even 'under' or 'within' capitalism, and many of them are in fact non-capitalist, if not explicitly anti-capitalist. The political strategy of a minor marxism thus centers around people gradually extricating themselves from dependence on capitalist markets, goods, and means of life, by instead relying on and further developing alternative means of life – community-supported agriculture, open-source software, DIY (do-it-yourself), fair trade, the list goes on and on – until a tipping point or bifurcation point is reached where capitalist markets begin to starve and then eventually wither away. This is what it would mean to reverse the process of primitive accumulation from which capitalism first emerges and on which it continues to depend.

As Marx points out – although he waits until the concluding part of *Capital, Volume One* to do so – the process of 'so-called primitive accumulation' (called so by Adam Smith) is better understood as a combined process of accumulation and destitution. For capital investment to emerge, there must be a prior accumulation of wealth in liquid form (not land), available to be invested. But equally important, there must be a population stripped of their traditional livelihood, who thus have no way of surviving other than by selling their labor-power for a wage. 'So-called primitive accumulation,' Marx insists, 'is nothing else than the historical process of divorcing the producer from the means of production' (1887: Ch. 26, Para. 3). Capitalism emerges on the basis of this fortuitous encounter between liquid wealth and destitute labor, which Deleuze and Guattari call the primary axiom of capital accumulation. Innumerable other axioms can be added and subtracted – consumer tastes, production technologies, state forms, and so on – but the axiom that converts wealth into investment capital and work into dependent wage labor remains at the heart of the capitalist mode of production. Major Marxism focuses on accumulation; minor marxism focuses on dependency. In the course of capitalism's historical development, dependency has taken three basic forms. The first form of dependence to predominate was work: destitute workers were forced to sell their labor-power to survive. But this form was from the start inextricably linked to a second form, involving consumption: workers were obliged to buy means of subsistence from capitalists (rather than producing them independently). Availability of non-capitalist ways of procuring the means of life would aggravate capital's 'realization' problem: capitalists can't make a profit if the goods they produce are not bought back in sufficient quantities. As brute starvation (in some parts of the global economy) declines in importance as a way of enforcing dependency, marketing and advertising intervene to make people psychologically dependent on the purchase of capitalist commodities. Even leisure time gets commodified, as people become increasingly unable or unwilling to entertain themselves and purchase mass-produced entertainment instead. Even worse than the subsumption of production, consumption and leisure time by capital, however, is the third form of dependency, which is debt. As Deleuze puts it in his prescient essay on 'control society,' 'modern man is no longer a man confined, but a man in debt' (Deleuze 1995: 181). This context renews and heightens the significance of the fact that the first known word for freedom is an *economic* rather than a political term: it meant freedom from debt peonage. Trading the unfreedoms of disciplinary confinement for the unfreedom to go into debt in neoliberal society of control is hardly a bargain: while capitalist production and consumption certainly subsumed huge portions of social life, the debt to capital weighs 'like a nightmare' on every decision in every minute of every day, 24/7/365: for those in debt, each and every moment of their entire life must enter a calculus of whether it reduces, merely defers, or actually increases their debt burden.

But modern debt itself takes several different forms. Modern debt-financed capital investment, of course, dates back to the early days of mercantile capitalism, and continues unabated under industrial capitalism. 'The public debt [was] one of the most powerful levers of primitive accumulation' from early on, according to Marx (1887: Chap. 31 Para. 15). But as capitalist production develops and massifies, the 'realization problem' emerges, as we have seen, and debt-financed consumption arises alongside debt-financed production. Indeed as long as profit gets extracted from the entire sum of exchanges between wages and commodity prices, capitalism requires debt-financed consumption in order to survive. But debt-financed consumption itself takes two very different forms. The first was the great Keynesian-New-Deal-Fordist-welfare-state gambit, whereby states would go into debt in hard times to bail out capital through deficit spending, with the expectation, supposedly, that the debt would be repaid in good times. Except that, as we know, the debt never does get repaid; instead, it continues to grow and grow and eventually goes through the ceiling – until or unless the ceiling itself is conveniently moved, as it has been repeatedly by bipartisan acts of Congress. But the debt ceiling can't be moved forever, at least not without exposing the whole capitalist accounting system as a massive hoax or Ponzi scheme. The inevitable conclusion is that capitalism has been living on borrowed time for at least the last 83 years – or on borrowed money, which as we know is more or less the same thing. Nation states around the world, and not just the United States, face this long-term 'sovereign debt crisis,' as it is called – Argentina, notoriously, a decade ago; Greece, Italy, Spain, and Ireland more recently – with no final solution in sight. As the Occupy movement spread around the world, it often focused on this form of debt. But in the United States, the 'original' OWS focused on the other form of debt, which we can call neoliberal debt or indentured debt peonage – the kind that Deleuze associates with what he calls control society (Deleuze 1995: 177–822). In this form, some of the debt required to keep capitalism afloat gets displaced from sovereign states onto private individuals (home mortgages, car loans, student loans, credit card retail debt, and so on). While private consumer debt is hardly new, the scale of predatory abuse of consumers perpetrated by finance capital, including most notably in home mortgages and student loans, went through the roof, and were a key motivation for OWS, and for the choice of Wall Street as the place to occupy in the first place.

Minor marxism offers another kind of explanation for OWS choosing Wall Street as its prime target, which has to do with the nature of debt to begin with. Marx likens the role of 'so-called primitive accumulation' in bourgeois political economy to that of original sin in theology: it is crucial to everything that follows, but it itself remains unexamined and/or unexplained. Deleuze and Guattari offer a very different account of 'primitive accumulation': on their account, pre-capitalist accumulation is responsible for the appropriation of surplus-labor long before the rise of capitalism, and the consolidation of capitalism as a mode of production entails the transfer of what had been an infinite debt from gods or despots to capital itself. What had been owed to them in various forms of tribute or taxation is henceforth owed to capital in the form of interest. This means that finance capital has not just a historical precedent (as most Marxists will admit, from the period of mercantile capitalism), but a theoretical precedence as well. For major Marxism, credit becomes possible because of, and out of, the surplus generated by capitalist production; the dialectical account occupying the first few hundred pages of *Capital, Volume One* shows how through a process of increasing abstraction money emerges from in-kind exchange, and then how the commodification of labor-power enables money to become capital, and finally how interest on money represents a share of the surplus-value generated through the production process owed to finance capital. Deleuze and Guattari, by contrast, insist that finance capital is prior to industrial capital not just at the historical emergence of capitalism, but in principle and throughout the history of capitalism. This is so in principle because Deleuze and Guattari follow Nietzsche in understanding money to be primarily a vehicle for debt and the establishment and enforcement of unequal power relations rather than a vehicle for the exchange of equivalents among equal parties. For minor marxism, then, ownership of capital is first and foremost the power to create value *ex nihilo*, if only for the purpose of subsequently introducing it into the production process in order to appropriate even more surplus-value. Modern state regulations, it is true, require what's called a 'cash reserve ratio' – which means that banks must hold some modicum of assets against which to make loans; recently, these ratios have been found to be scandalously low, and have in some cases led to bankruptcy: but the point is that the cash reserve ratio for banks is never anywhere near 100% – so even if technically speaking capital is not being created *completely ex nihilo*, it is nonetheless the case that most of it is, and that a major function of the finance sector is, in the strongest sense, to invent or create fictitious capital for investment in productive enterprises, with the expectation that surplus-value will be generated and some of it paid back in interest. With Wall Street's development of complex derivatives and markets for insuring them, the disparity between actual 'industrial' value and fictitious 'financial' value became too great and too obvious – yet another reason for choosing Wall Street as the prime target for the Occupy movement.

Minor marxism focuses on the dependence or 'precarity' generated by so-called primitive accumulation, and particularly by the degree of dependence accompanying the wholesale fabrication of ubiquitous debt relations by contemporary finance capital, among which the home mortgage and student debt crises became the most visible, and therefore became precipitating factors in the Occupy movement. A student debt-strike is one of the most important ideas to emerge from the aftermath of OWS – but there is no reason to limit such a strike to students, when practically everyone suffers from the imposition of debt in one form or another. But eliminating or reducing debt is by no means the only laudable goal of the Occupy movement: its sights were set on far more than that. By modeling post-capitalist and post-representative social relations, OWS points to a more far-reaching and thoroughgoing transformation of contemporary society, which perhaps only a slow-motion general strike, based on principles similar to those instantiated in OWS, will be able to bring about.

Works Cited

Deleuze, Gilles. 1995. *Negotiations 1972–1990*. New York: Columbia University Press.

Deleuze, Gilles. 2006. *Two Regimes of Madness: Texts and Interviews 1975–1995*. Los Angeles: Semiotext(e).

Deleuze, Gilles and Félix Guattari. 1987. *A Thousand Plateaus: Capitalism and Schizophrenia*. Trans. Brian Massumi. Minneapolis: University of Minnesota Press.

Gibson-Graham, JK. 1996. *The End of Capitalism (As We New It): A Feminist Critique of Political Economy*. Cambridge: Blackwell Publishers.

Holland, Eugene W. 2011. *Nomad Citizenship: Free-Market Communism and the Slow-Motion General Strike*. Minneapolis: University of Minnesota Press.

Marx, Karl. 1887. *Capital, Volume One*. Trans. Samuel Moore and Edward Aveling. Accessed May 8, 2015 from: https://www.marxists.org/archive/marx/works/1867-c1/index.htm

Patton, Paul. 2000. *Deleuze and the Political*. London and New York: Routledge.

Chapter 10

Savage Money[1]

Andrew Conio

The process by which banks create money is so simple that the mind is repelled.
JK Galbraith (1975: 29)

Banks create money. That is what they are there for ... Each time a Bank makes a loan ... new Bank credit is created – brand new money.
Graham Towers, Governor of the Bank of Canada 1935 to 1955

The analyses of the banking system and prescriptions for repairing it by the monetary campaign group Positive Money have received a remarkable degree of attention.[2] The group has been party to policy discussions with governments, think tanks and research groups, has a reputable board of advisors,[3] and has established a significant political presence, as well as attracting large public audiences, widespread media coverage and book sales unprecedented in the history of monetary reform campaigns.

Expressed with undue brevity their argument runs something like this: Our current economic problems stem largely from the fact that the banks have the ability to create endogenous money – money that they can then charge for. Almost the entire money supply is on loan from the banks: only 3% of the money in the system is notes or coins or reserves of the central bank, with the remaining 97% being created by the banks as debt. By paying interest on virtually every dollar or pound in circulation, we are, in effect, renting a privatized currency from the banks.

This single feature impacts upon every aspect of economic and political life. First, it is difficult to overstate the role that bank money played in the creation of the housing bubble. The rise in house prices was not a supply and demand issue: over the last 20 years US housing stock grew by 16%, meaning that the number of houses grew faster than did the number of people, whilst mortgage lending grew by almost 600% over the same period. Subprime mortgage lending increased from $30 billion a year to $600 billion a year in 10 years, leading to an effective doubling of house prices.

This endogenous form of money creation has distorted the UK national economy and cannot be disassociated from the gigantic Ponzi scheme that brought the world economy to its knees. It was the transformation of debt into tradable securities that made possible the invention of securitization and the armory of 'financial weapons of mass destruction,' as Warren Buffet dubbed them.

Bank-created money provided the base fuel for unrestrained money creation – taking into account the $1.5 quadrillion derivatives market, it is safe to say that in effect money creation became infinite. This is a system whereby so-called fiat money, money that is not backed by reserves of another commodity, became virtual.

In a speech to the Committee on Monetary and Economic Reform, Michael Rowbotham (2013) dissects most clearly how a debt-based economy squeezes disposable income; it also squeezes the profit margins of businesses creating the need for cheaper and cheaper products and higher levels of mass production, which in turn creates increased impoverishment of the labor force, thousands of tons of cheap and disposable goods, and the unpayable social and environmental costs of production and distribution. Money creation is the main driver behind the imperative for growth that is in essence the driver of ecological destruction.

As Ross Jackson notes, 'the most important single factor that is driving our civilization toward ecological collapse is the promotion of great per capita consumption as the primary goal of every nation state at a time when we are already over-consuming' (2012: 73). The stark reality is that if we continue to pursue the economic growth required to pay off the debts then runaway climate change is all but guaranteed.

When banks create money they realize the stuff of wizards and legends. The magical power to create your own money in the form of an asset out of thin air is expressed by Paul Fisher (2013) thus:

> When you start printing money, you create some value for yourself. If you can issue a thousand pounds worth of IOUs to everybody, you've got a thousand pounds for nothing.
>
> From 2003 to 2013 the banks created £1trillion, netting interest of between £108bn to £217bn every single year. The financial system has effectively held the political system hostage. As banks create money they have the power to shape the economy and decide the economic priorities of the nation.

With little bearing on any sensible measure of what counts as economic development and wealth creation, between 1980 and 2007 the assets of the banking sector grew from $2.5 trillion to $40 trillion. In 1980 banking assets were worth 20 times the then global economy; by 2006 they were worth 75 times (according to the UN). Due to this wizardry banks have an undue influence on the development of the economy. Asset-stripping, off-shoring and speculative trading are now favored over the steady growth that emerges out of a commitment to manufacturing and long-term business-development. As a result, new money is often more likely to be channelled into property and financial speculation than into small businesses and manufacturing, with profound economic consequences for society.[4] Given that five banks control 85% of the money in the UK economy, a total of 87 board members (or 30 to 40 key decision makers) have effective control over the nation's money supply.

Government has to gear its policies to keeping the money (debt) supply working, and because the banks are essentially responsible for that supply, when they get into trouble, government – that is, taxpayers – have to bail them out. We have no choice. We find ourselves in a position where the banks' lending is higher than all government spending. Further, each and everyone of us now has to shoulder the burden of this debt; the natural human propensity to take responsibility for oneself, to shoulder one's burden, is exploited and masochistically internalized as we take upon ourselves the costs and risks of the economic and financial disaster.

Financial markets became integral to the administration of public debts, accompanied by an expansion of their logic, their rules, their imperatives and interests. This implies, finally, the shifting of the reserves of sovereignty. The financialization of government structures, the mediation between public and private debts have mechanized political decisions as market-driven decisions; the markets themselves have become a sort of creditor-god, whose final authority decides the fate of currencies, social systems, public infrastructures, private savings, etc. (Vogl 2012: 5)

The overall effect of this cycle was a colossal transfer of wealth from the poor to the rich. Far from creating jobs, and prompting the miraculous 'trickle down effect,' this wealth concentration created a restriction of real demand. The owners of assets (property, stocks and shares, private equity, complex financial products, works of art, race horses, etc.) were able to use easy credit to inflate the value of those assets. By these means were they obscenely enriched. Those without assets and therefore without access to 'easy credit' were correspondingly impoverished. Thus did the rich get richer, and the poor poorer. The repugnant effects spread across household, regional and global scales as debt repayment was used to justify outcomes that would be intolerable in other circumstances: an avalanche of people losing their homes, who also can no longer afford healthcare; countries losing their economic sovereignty and devastating their social provision; cancellation of healthcare programs leading to the deaths of tens of thousands and, on a global scale, the hunger, even starvation, of vast numbers and the immiseration of millions.

The link between the housing bubble and money creation is clear, as is the relationship between the creation of the shadow banking system, the huge swathes of predatory products, and the 'vulture,' 'voodoo' or downright quasi-criminal speculative trading schemes that brought the world economic system to the brink of collapse. Bank credit provided the fuel, deregulation the environment, and algorithms the velocity required to create colossal sums and to some extent shield the players from their responsibilities.

For the Positive Money campaign group, the effect endogenous money has had on the banking sector betrays *the* structural flaw at the heart of the financial system in the form of ceding control of the nation's finances to private interests. What has become clearer is the central role money creation has played in this, along with the staging of a financial *coup d'état* by the financial services industry. A rogue, predatory industry, bereft of moral values, has been bolstered by an idiotic idiom that models 'only objective illusions' (Goodchild 2013: 55) perpetuated by an economics profession that has captured the debate to the exclusion of any consideration of the values of life, ethics, species, planet, community, compassion, or the future of life itself.

However, whilst from the perspective of mainstream (neoliberal) economic theory, Positive Money's thesis may be considered unorthodox, from a philosophical or anthropological perspective they rely on a set of conventional and unexamined predicates, particularly around the nature of money, which they take to be relatively colorless or frictionless instead of originativily and structurally riven with power relations. With regard to the history, nature and function of money this paper questions whether there exists an unbridgeable methodological, ethical or ontological divide between speculative philosophy and political economy.

To answer this question, I propose a journey from the empirical policy-driven world of Positive Money to the experimental empiricism of Gilles Deleuze and Félix Guattari, in order to test one against the other. I will examine the theory of money presented in *Anti-Oedipus*, which is coming to be regarded as a prescient and prophetic reading of contemporary capitalism.

In conclusion, I suggest that the philosophical speculations of Deleuze and Guattari and Positive Money's empirical approach to debt-based money can, despite emerging from wholly different epistemologies and methodologies, be overlaid, one atop the other like tracing paper, each ultimately saying the same thing. The political, economic, and philosophical consequences of this are far reaching. Not least in the identification of a potential meeting place for the most intensive critiques of capitalism as a totalizing 'abstract machine' and the political demands of policy formation and reform.

Credit and Debt

The following discussion is framed by four works that have the strongest purchase on the issues at hand: Friedrich Nietzsche's *On the Genealogy of Morality* (1887), David Graeber's *Debt: The First 5000 Years* (2011), Deleuze and Guattari's *Anti-Oedipus*, and Maurizio Lazzarato's *The Making of Indebted Man* (2011). The first three books each delineate differently the same formative period in the development of humanity before the emergence of societies that were structured chiefly through the interaction of church, money and state. The period is outlined with different emphases but with substantive details in common as the 'The Axial Age'[5] (Graeber), 'Primitive Society' (Nietzsche), or 'Primitive/Territorial Society'[6] (Deleuze and Guattari). Lazzarato's work offers a reading of a new stage of capitalist development (contemporary finance capital) and the concomitant emergence of a new subject, 'the indebted man,' by way of the Nietzsche-inspired thoughts of Deleuze and Guattari.

Graeber accumulates extensive anthropological and historical evidence going back millennia to take issue with the conventional view that money emerged in order to expedite barter and to demonstrate that coins were used in the Agrarian Age[7] which preceded the Axial Age but were made to suit the needs of small city states, and acted as a currency of last resort – when informal credit systems became too unwieldy. They had few of the features which we would today associate with money.

This concurs with Deleuze and Guattari's description of 'primitive territorial' societies where debt was plural, finite and based on systems of alliance. Indeed, in a recent International Monetary Fund (IMF) paper Benes and Kumhof (2012: 12) pull together an even wider range of accounts which in their different ways show that money did not develop out of the need to trade or as a way of measuring equivalences.

Nietzsche's thesis in the *Genealogy of Morals* can be expressed in short order: man is innately aggressive, he expresses 'enmity, cruelty, joy in pursuit, in attack, in destruction,' and to think otherwise is naïvely to divorce man from his animal nature. In primeval times, within the 'original tribal cooperatives,' relations were principally relations of judgment and measure rather than cooperation and mutuality. Nietzsche (1998) outlines in his book *On the Genealogy of Morality* that man is 'an inherently calculating animal,' and selling and buying, together with their psychological attributes, are the oldest forms of social organization.

The character of the system for the measurement and collection of debts determined the logic of social exchange and relations. With regard to non-payment of debts, punishment was not sought as a kind of revenge; instead, *payment*, even in another kind, was calculated for non-payment. The debtor was not cast as somehow in breach of a moral code or as having fallen short of some moral value. What was owed was not guilt, gratitude or supplication but the debt itself. Thus, as objective compensation for a crime, an eye could be taken for an eye. Debt was measured according to custom, payment due and taken; a pound of flesh or a child taken away could amount to a debt executed and payment measured precisely. Whilst savage means for exacting payment were used – amputation for example – they were measured without rancor or enmity as they allowed for a 'natural discharge' of anger, executed with a disinterested, enjoyable and affirmative malice. This was for Nietzsche a naïve and innocent type of cruelty unencumbered by sentimentality and piousness. Crucially, because they were dischargeable, debts in this sense were finite.

According to both Norman Brown in *Love's Body* (1966) and Graeber, such debts owed to the gods were discharged periodically. Instead of an overarching concept of 'indebtedness' or guilt there existed a palimpsest of debts and credits as well as a multiplicity of systems for the collection of payment. Following Deleuze and Guattari's account in *Anti-Oedipus*, Eugene Holland (1999: 65) writes that debt 'was sporadic and reciprocal, remain[ed] immanent to the kinship system of blood-lineages and marriage-alliances comprising savage social organisation, and function[ed] to prevent power from accruing to any one family or clan.'

In social relations, natural sadism and aggression could be aligned with and expressed through the collection of debts. A creditor's balance could be taken in the form of his pleasure in the infliction of pain and his enjoyment of violation of the debtor. In this way, anger was not associated with unkindness but was an appropriate manifestation of an instinctual expression of power upon gaining the entitlement to mistreat another.

Clearly, today, human aggression is no longer expressed in this way – and, in Nietzsche's terms, with good conscience. Instead, it is veiled behind malevolent sympathy or expressed in other dissimulated forms. What are a 25-year mortgage, homelessness, or the circus-like spectacle of *The Jerry Springer Show* if not forms of institutionalized cruelty? Mostly, though, the failure to exhibit natural aggression results in self-hating and supplicant men bent over in prostration or, in Nietzsche's contemptuous dismissal, 'enjoyable self-flagellation.'

The ancient systems of debt, credit, calculation, measurement and collection were fundamental processes in the development of the process of thinking: 'the very oldest form of astuteness was bred here' (Nietzsche 1998). Indeed, the debtor/creditor relation is the fundamental and primal psychological tendency, and the measurement of debts, obligations and payment was the driving force behind the development of thinking and consciousness. According to Nietzsche (1998): 'To set prices, measure values, think up equivalences, to exchange things – that preoccupied man's very first thinking to such a degree that in a certain sense it's what thinking is.' Central to this was the understanding and administration of pain, and the psychological impact of the imprint of suffering. For Nietzsche, whatever is impressed through pain is remembered. Hence the highly ritualized individual and tribal enactments of tributes, sacrifices and punishments that were formulated to sear into the mind the 'morality of custom':

> there is perhaps nothing more fearful and more terrible in the entire pre-history of human beings than the technique for developing his memory. 'We burn something in so that it remains in the memory. Only something which never ceases to cause pain stays in the memory.' (Nietzsche 1998)

Interestingly, only five or six of these seared memories have to be made ineradicable, as the subject will create the ties and connections sufficient to bind such wounds together into a whole conscious landscape.

For Nietzsche then, the individual's capacity to participate in society was not born out of mutuality, sympathy or the modern psychology of identification, but from the violence used to secure the creditor–debtor relation. Out of this originating process emerges a man able to honor debts: 'Man' (*manas*), as Nietzsche points out, denotes a being that 'values, measures and weighs,' capable of reason and the capacity to 'live by their word with the advantages of society.'

Clearly this is an account fundamentally at odds with the Levinasian model of a social bond borne out of a mutual recognition between individuals whereby both are dependent upon the Other for their own sense of identity – a mutuality that *ipso facto* creates an ethical bond, as both are constitutive of each others' sense of self. Such a model has the whiff of an infinite obligation about it. As captured by Couze Venn's pithy paraphrase of Levinas:

> Such an ontological debt, arising from one's inherent condition as a social being, entangled in a world of other beings, and as an essentially vulnerable and fragile being, necessarily leaves us bereft because of the burden of responsibility for the other which it places upon us, a responsibility which can never be completely discharged since it calls for a generosity that entails the abnegation if not sacrifice of the self. (Venn forthcoming)

Nietzsche would denounce as idiotic the argument that the development of society, guilt, conscience and honor arose out of an innate human tendency to share, commune and cooperate. For him, this is but the symptom of a wilful ignorance of history and human nature. Indeed, it may be possible to ascribe the concern for 'mutuality' and 'just' relations between co-dependent equals merely to a superannuated calculation whereby those who measure a grievance calculate a 'moral' revenge that takes the form of malicious sympathy: 'Everything has its price, everything can be paid off – the oldest and most naïve moral principle of justice, the beginning of all "good nature," all "fairness," all "good will," all "objectivity" on earth' arises when man measures himself against another.

Certainly, without rational thought, anticipation and prediction, man would not survive; but memory is more than that. It lays the foundation for the formation of will by the creation of a link between 'I will' and the actual manifestation of the will in action. In this way an infallible psychological law leads to predicable subjects who, in turn, provide the infrastructure for the social bond: not the other way round.

Money

'Primitive/territorial' society was characterized by multiple trading arrangements and various systems of record-keeping; sticks, shells and other simple devices were used to record debts. They were aids to memory and accounting tools, but did not have the functions normally associated with money as exchange value, stores of wealth, or commodity. Money in the form we know it today emerged out of conquest. It was the form in which the conqueror could extract tribute and/or facilitate expansion. A single currency replaced a myriad of logical currencies some of which were metal-based coinage. Here is Graeber:

> Coinage, certainly, was not invented to facilitate trade. It appears to have been first invented to pay soldiers, probably first of all by rulers of Lydia in Asia Minor to pay their Greek mercenaries. Carthage, another great trading nation, only started minting coins very late, and then explicitly to pay its foreign soldiers. (2009)

After the violence of conquest, populations were enslaved and tribute extracted, not least to pay for the campaign and to create a market in which the conquerors were sole controllers of a currency invented precisely for purpose of control and domination.

The credit systems of the Near East did not crumble under commercial competition; they were destroyed by Alexander's armies – armies that required half a ton of silver bullion per day in wages. The mines where the bullion was produced were generally worked by slaves. Military campaigns in turn ensured an endless flow of new slaves. Imperial tax systems, as noted, were largely designed to force their subjects to create markets, so that soldiers (and also, of course, government officials) would be able to use that bullion to buy anything they wanted (Graeber 2009).

The despot would impose his currency on the society, while local 'currencies' were downgraded in relation to a single representative of value, which served as the measure of power relations, hierarchy, social control and obligations.

Graeber puts this into sharp relief when he asks why the ruler created coins when he owned all the gold and silver mines anyway. The answer is that coins became not only the most efficient way of paying the troops and buying supplies, but also the main way of supplicating the population in bondage who were required to pay their taxes in coins, which were exchanged for the produce they made. A relationship of disequilibrium thus becomes exquisitely efficient, and a hierarchical form of social organization is sewn into the fabric of every exchange and relation. As Deleuze and Guattari note: 'Money is fundamentally inseparable, not from commerce, but from taxes as the maintenance of the apparatus of the State' (2000: 197).

Graeber's agrarian and Deleuze's primitive territorial worlds of finite dischargeable debts were thus gradually replaced – or in Deleuzian terms 'overcoded' – by monetized debts as tributes. In the subsequent despotic societies the subject became *ipso facto* dependent upon the state/despot for his life and existence – the subject lived at the behest of the state, and was subject to the state. As monetized debt was also a debt of a *life*, 'the infinite creditor and the infinite credit replaced the blocks of mobile and finite debts ... the debt becomes a debt of existence, a debt of the existence of the subjects themselves' (Deleuze and Guattari 2000: 197). The original palimpsest of multiple indebtedness within a horizontal mosaic of alliances that formed the community and weaved the social fabric was superseded by a system of vertical filiation to hierarchical powers: to God, the despot, money and the state.

The question as to which had precedence – despotic societies, world religions, states or money – may be impossible to answer; but that money and world religions emerged at the same time appears indisputable. Here it is worth quoting Graeber in full:

> The most remarkable pattern is the emergence, in almost the exact times and places where one also sees the early spread of coinage, of what were to become modern world religions: prophetic Judaism, Christianity, Buddhism, Jainism, Confucianism, Taoism, and eventually, Islam. While the precise links are yet to be fully explored, in certain ways, these religions appear to have arisen in direct reaction to the logic of the market. To put the matter somewhat crudely: if one relegates a certain social space simply to the selfish acquisition of material things, it is almost inevitable that soon someone else will come to set aside another domain in which to preach that, from the perspective of ultimate values, material things are unimportant, and selfishness – or even the self – illusory. (2012: 13–14)

We find support for this approximation in the *On the Genealogy of Morality*, where Nietzsche finds that there is no evidence of the reactive creditor nor the guilt-ridden, culpable, self-flagellating subject before the arrival of money, but plenty to show that money heralds 'the most fundamentally constitutive creation of them all, an eternal indebtedness to an omnipresent God to whom everything is owed: a God who sacrifices himself for the guilt of human beings (can you believe that?).' And when debts were finite 'guilt' was not a property of human emotion. Only, with the creation of God and money do we find guilt emerging as a manifestation of suffering, a suffering that is an absolutely interminable consequence of a debt that can never be repaid.

The effects of relinquishing the world of finite, payable debts were many and deep. Humans lost touch with their nature, their beginnings and their ancestors: they turned against the womb from which they arose and 'into whom from now on the principle of evil is inserted' (Nietzsche 1998: 62), and turned away from existence itself, which is thus felt to have little value. This turning away is in the first instance nihilism, and in the second, prompts the search for other states of being – particularly religious piety.

These shifts in the relations of credit and debt are first-order events in the development of a certain consciousness. The crucial point here is that with Nietzsche, Deleuze and Guattari, and Graeber, we have a materialist account of the development of thinking as such; and when we come to consider whether economic predicates are *a priori* or *transcendental*, we find, if sufficiently lengthy timescales are used, that historically, politically imposed precepts and narratives which suit the needs of the rulers over the ruled can be challenged. This includes what appears to be the most naturalized precept of them all: the neutral status of money.

There are, however, two problems with this view. Money is indeed all of the things described above. Money may have been forged out of calculation, it may have emerged with war and despotism, and it may, as Deleuze and Guattari contend, be 'first and foremost a power of command.' But money is also whatever we want it to be, because how something emerges is not the same as what it is. Money is a superlative tool for the calculation of obligations and debts; it makes the creation of markets possible and creates anonymity. It enables deterritorialization, freedom from bonds, class and the exhilarating freedom of all things to shed limiting meanings, purposes, uses or values. This is a tremendously productive development in human relations. To be able to borrow without sticky social or kinship obligations is an attribute of individual autonomy and existential capacity.

Money's emergence does mean that there is a tendency for personal, finite (that is, dischargeable) compassionate indebtedness, the binding among people borne out of mutual reliance, to give way to alienated and commodified relations, but the opposite is also the case; money can also be used to express love and compassion, to appease and facilitate human relations and forge the social bond.

Unquestionably, money creates hierarchies, changes the nature of obligation, monetizes relations and changes the value of everything, particularly subjective, social and ecological relations. But this type of thinking must not shelter *ressentiment* towards the innovations, entrepreneurial risks and expansion that capitalism affords. Money also creates new alliances, new soma, affects, desires and thoughts; polyplurient life is facilitated through money as pure flow. Capitalism forces us to be free, and this is an axiom, but, without question, millions of people find contentment through the opportunities, freedom and security that capitalism and the inherent ease of money affords. However, as Goodchild (2010: 33) points out, a specific historical process *has* taken place, from money as universal equivalent and exchange value to money as speculative capital, until 'finally money replaces itself as a differential, reflexive flow.'

Money has so many dimensions it is little wonder that no definitive theory of it exists. Such rhetorical statements as 'in capitalism the debt becomes infinite because one is submitted to a law and a system, but this law does not demand a particular body so much as empty and formal submission' (Colebrook 2006: 130) need to be balanced by the fact that the deterritorialization facilitated by exchange enables the transcendence of all bodies including God, the despot, the nation state, Oedipus, and class. Money is both capture and release: the deepest diastolic and systolic movements of the psyche and the bowels are manifested in the flows of the financial markets. The desolate capitalist system is also creative, innovative and facilitative of human needs and multiple layers of expression and joy. It is nothing short of arrogant to dismiss the hard creative work and self-determination of millions of economic actors that sustains the system as we know it, not least because *de*territorialization is not a facet of capitalism, but a life force that finds its expression in the exchange of equivalences, open systems and flexible forms of social organization facilitated by the market. This is at some remove from Nietzschean and Graeber-inspired accounts of money as despotic imposition and alienating abstraction.

For Nietzsche, to become a dependable man is a form of self-slavery, but we must concede that without dependable men who honor their debts society breaks down and chaos ensues. It is exactly this type of ethical demand to take responsibility for one's own debt that has been exploited by the financial sector. Debt to the homeowner means self-respect, personal responsibility and security. For the financier, it is merely an asset to be packaged, collateralized, securitized: an asymmetry of obligation that works only in the banks' favor. Venn captures the unequal relationship between debtor and creditor turned predatory and punitive:

> [A] historical shift [in] a chain of signifiers … has gradually come to link debt to fallenness through the idea of sin and its metonymies, such as wilful inadequacy, laziness, dysfunctional behaviour, underdevelopment, inferiority, and so on. It is a worldview (and an imaginary) which in the minds of policymakers authorises the criminalisation of indebtedness.
> (Venn, forthcoming)

Can this to-ing and fro-ing between what has the appearance of liberation/emancipation and repression/iniquity be resolved by returning to Deleuze's Marxist account of the development of capital and labor?

First we should review how Deleuze and Guattari set out the relationship between the emergence of labor-power and money in the development of capitalist production in *Anti-Oedipus* (2002: 226/228). Most importantly, abstract labor was not premised upon the production of capital, and an asymmetry of the relations between debtor and creditor precedes historically that of production and wage labor. Indeed, abstract labor existed independently of money and commodities and effected a decoding of flows in and of itself. However, it required the appearance of a double-sided monetary system of general equivalence and capital accumulation for the force of abstract labor to be fully unleashed. Money, having emerged semi-independently, imposed upon abstract labor the characteristic of exchange, and money became a value in its own right.

Once detached from the body and the socius, money enters into relations with itself and becomes the supreme value of society, assuming the capacity to concretize once again that which it abstracted into the plane of equivalence. This is a circular motion: as monetary equivalences liberate values from needs, money becomes its own force and money begets money. Money then determines the concrete processes, taking on the appearance of prime cause. Here Deleuze and Guattari (2000: 227) follow Marx:

> Value in process, money in process, and, as such, capital … value … suddenly presents itself as an independent substance, endowed with a motion of its own, in which money and commodities are mere forms which it assumes and casts off in turn. Nay more: instead of simply representing the relations of commodities, it enters now, so to say, into relations with itself. It differentiates itself as original value from itself as surplus value. (Marx 1887: 106)

This force, as capital, is then used to enforce a system for the maintenance of profit, but over time it effects this less through the extraction of surplus value than by rent or tribute and through command of the flows of life and production. Deleuze and Guattari expand Marx's thoughts in many ways: for them, control of the flow is power in and of itself, a type of omnipotence that can far exceed the satiations of acquisition and excess.[8] Through controlling investment, capital determines both what is done (investment in environmentally destructive industries, the endless production of rubbish) and what is not done (ethical care, stewardship of resources, genuine democracy, equal distribution of the common wealth).

We can see this model most clearly in the endemic criminality and amorality of the financial sector which demonstrates how capitalism under neoliberalism – after asset striping, off-shoring and wage reduction – ran out of assets to exploit and came to feed off itself. An avaricious and rapacious tendency unleashed the capitalist war machine against life.

It is much more than a coincidence that the New York Stock Exchange topped 15,000 for the first time ever just as it was announced that the atmosphere had absorbed 400 ppm CO_2. Such is the ruin that the only recourse open to it appears to be a return to much more savage social formations as increasingly 'modern capitalist and socialist states take on the characteristic features of the primordial despotic state' (Deleuze and Guattari 2000: 220). Think of drone strikes, the prison–industrial complex and direct tribute in the form of quantitative easing. It is more than a note in passing to comment that for Deleuze and Guattari history is not teleological, as primitive, despotic and civilized capitalist machines coexist in contemporary society.

The world as represented by capitalism is therefore seen through the wrong lens. Instead of a world of production, wealth, values, and social relations, the world as represented increasingly manifests the exclusive requirements of the monetary system, the first requirement of which is the production of more money. Labor processes and general production that were once the heartbeat of society are now used to produce only capital. The deployment of this quotation from Marx in *Anti-Oedipus* illustrates why Deleuze and Guattari refer to themselves as Marxists: 'Capital is dead labour that vampire-like, only lives by sucking living labour, and lives the more, the more labour it sucks' (Marx 1887: 160).

However, and this is the real matter at hand, such is the nature of money that any discussion of its historical development and the amorphousness of its form bears yet further contradistinction in a seemingly endless movement between adversative conjunctions such as 'also,' 'but' and 'however' that is logically unavoidable. This is not a problem because the defining feature of any Deleuzian analysis is its capacity to take into account the contradictions inherent in any issue. Deleuze, across his entire corpus, whether on painting or cinema, philosophy or science, develops systems that create dynamic relations between what other systems would treat as irreconcilable contradictions, paradoxes or dialectics. Hence, we live under the axiomatics of capitalism, yet life retains its vitalism; the society of control regulates social relations, yet across *A Thousand Plateaus* unexpected speeds and slowness traverse the machinic, human and organic, in expressions of social life composed of melodic refrains.

Thus, the free market *is* a powerful liberatory, schizoanalytic, force. Despite Nietzsche's protestations, money does create an equality of relations where none previously existed. And here we might add another corrective to Nietzsche. Certain thought processes may indeed have been instantiated by exchange, and unquestionably psychic structures and social realities are imprinted by violence, but thinking is an infinitely more varied and dynamic process that involves the senses, memory, imagination, recognition and misrecognition, as well as the sensible and insensible flows and limits of this world. There is certainly no norm or model that reifies experience into a stable and unchanging form.

Money also allows for temporal equivalence. What incalculable freedom is this to be released from the shackles of time, as money enables unprecedented investment that creates new temporal dynamics? Consider the Channel Tunnel.

Money is at once a *de*territorialization, which allows relations to extend beyond immediate exchange or barter, thereby extending a tendency of life to create or produce for what is not present; but it is also a reterritorialization, which introduces equivalence, sameness and a quantity of value through time, an attempt to contain and master the disequilibrium of time (Colebrook 2006: 86).

The system of equivalences and the power to make the dissimilar comparable is freedom. As across time so also in space, a process captured by Philip Goodchild with his usual perspicacity:

> money is ... a quantum flow, facilitating an exchange of goods and services between heterogeneous cities, where interests, values, and codes lack a common measure. Money retains value and facilitates communication where the coding breaks down, where one encounters indeterminacies and intervals. It bridges the chaos. (2010: 29–30)

As well as being flow, money is also a thing. You can use it, it has direct objectivity. However, this very objectivity accounts for the perpetuation of an irrational system because it places an 'objective' value on things, which invokes a sense of trust and a semblance of objectivity (a loaf of bread is worth more than a slice). Money extends the illusion that we all participate in the system as equals: the money earned by the wage earner is the same as that amassed by the billionaires. But the stability provided by the idea that money is a determinate quantity entered on bank statements and balance sheets is based only on faith, as are the distortions, specious premises, bogus methodologies and mathematical tautologies of the dismal science known as economics. Economic 'rationality' only makes sense within a system that is irrational and is divorced from other measures that would include rudimentary values for life.

Everything is rational in capitalism, except capital or capitalism itself. The stock market is certainly rational; one can understand it, study it, the capitalists know how to use it, and yet it is completely delirious; it's mad (Deleuze and Guattari 2001: 215).

The other 'objective' part to this system is the sense that money is the fabric of life that we all have equal access to. It is approachable: it exists right there in front of you, not actually outside of you but as part of your very constitution; your processes are exactly the processes you have inherited. Hence:

> this principle of convertibility – which is enough ... to ensure that the desire of the most disadvantaged creature will invest with all its strength, irrespective of any economic understanding or lack of it, the capitalist social field as a whole. Flows, who doesn't desire flows, and relationships between flows, and breaks in flows? (Deleuze and Guattari 2000: 229)

Accordingly, an appearance is given of a medium of exchange that is fair, and able to provide a quantitative determination of all things as a price; yet in and of itself, it is neutral. Moreover, we can position ourselves wherever we wish in relation to it, and should take responsibility for our autonomous choices. Yet the effects of the price mechanism are also pernicious, it creates an illusion of a primary equivalence at the heart of society, and inurs us to a fundamental disequilibrium, as Shaviro (2011: 8) observes: 'The "price system" continually forces us into debt. And thereby it confines, restricts, and channels our behavior far more rigidly, and effectively, than any compulsion based upon mere brute force would be able to do.'

Neoliberalism as Infinite Debt

Possibly second only to Graeber's best-selling work in terms of impact in political activist circles is Lazzarato's *The Making of the Indebted Man* which is essentially an application of the 'prophetic' (Kerslake 2009) *Anti-Oedipus* to contemporary neoliberal society. However, there are distinct problems with this account, the resolving of which will allow sharper distinctions be drawn regarding the relationship between control societies and debt. Lazzarato presents a litany of effects of the concretization of the paradigm of debt in neoliberalism, including increased immiseration, the takeover of the common wealth, and the commandeering of public, social and psychic space. Lazzarato takes the Deleuzeo-Guattarian conceptual apparatus further by arguing that our expectations of what might be socially possible and the extent to which we can imagine the future have been effectively colonized by debt. For him, the archetype of social relations, and its violent substrata, is being concretized in real historical conditions. He attempts neither a critique nor an analysis, but aims to show, in an ardent call to arms, how the warnings of *Anti-Oedipus* have been realized.

Debt-based subjection takes all the forms discussed hitherto, it is as material as it is existential, as it suffuses our minds, sensibilities, languages and psyches. Infinite debt is the primary social bond and is now the material and subjective condition of our lives. To paraphrase Lazzarato: the subject of debt is in an existential condition, at once responsible for his own fate, and for the debt of the banks, society, the sovereign state and by extension the whole world.

For Lazzarato, this is at once a return to the logic of capitalism's originative form, the extraction of rent or tribute, and a new stage in its development whereby debt acts as a 'capture,' 'predation,' and 'extraction' machine on the whole of society, as an instrument for macro-economic prescription and management, and as a mechanism for income redistribution and a return to its originative form as tribute. For example, Mattera et al (2012) have tracked how 19 states have passed laws that allow 2,700 large corporations (every brand name company you know – Goldman Sachs, General Electric, Proctor and Gamble) to keep the state income taxes paid by the workers at their factories in those states. Put another way, 2,700 companies get to pocket the money paid by their employees in tax. Five-and-a-half billion dollars has been diverted from workers' paychecks in this way. US pipeline companies are exempt from corporate income tax but they are allowed to include the tax on the rates they charge customers. Energy customers are thus paying a tax that does not exist and this increases the ultimate return to the owners of these pipelines by as much as 75%. Recent research shows that in the UK welfare support functions as a 'failure to pay a living wage subsidy' to the employers of 5.5 million workers, and private sector housing benefit serves as a direct transfer of public funds to property owners and banks. This shift from profit to rent is also noted by Lofgren (2012), who writes that the super rich 'aim to create a "tollbooth" economy, whereby more and more of our highways, bridges, libraries, parks, and beaches are possessed by private oligarchs who will extract a toll from the rest of us.'

All of the accounts discussed above confront us with the same question: are we dealing with an anthropological invariant or a historically specific assemblage of forces? The answer is that the disequilibrium inherent to relations of exchange, which came to be expressed in money, is the originative paradigm of the social, *and* that the debt paradigm has displaced or superseded other forms of capitalist development (cognitive capital, financial capital, and so on). The neoliberal form is a specific form of debt relation in which this paradigm of 'capture, predation and extraction forms the very basis of social life. The creditor–debtor relationship constitutes specific relations of power that entail specific forms of production and control of subjectivity – a particular form of *homo economicus* the "indebted man"' (Lazzarato 2012: 77–8). Thus, in neoliberalism, the creditor–debtor relationship encompasses all other relations: capital/labor, business/customer, workers/consumers. Everyone is a debtor, accountable and guilty before capital. Capital has become the Great Creditor, the Universal Creditor.

The question arises as to the relationship between an abstraction, a seemingly amorphous ubiquitous indebtedness, and specific material acts such as the invention of new financial products, new computer algorithms, and the pre-crash wave of deregulation. The question often directed to Deleuze's articulation of the society of control (and to his wider politics) similarly concerns the relationship between the indefinite and the specific. In answer we should note that a significant feature of the Deleuzean and Guattarian political landscape is their tendency to avoid giving specific examples of (and indexes to) even their most productive and worthwhile political concepts – capitalist axiomatics, schizoanalysis, the war machine – requiring the reader to experiment with them each time they are used. To prevent ossification concepts must remain mobile, work in multiple circumstances and be brought into relations with other concepts in the manner of creating new understandings and potentials for political thought, and have an inherent resistance to subsumption and cliché. Most importantly, though, is that a level of abstraction must operate as a necessary counter-force and weapon: 'we must rise to this level of abstraction and deterritorialisation if we want to avoid being swept away or crushed by the Great Creditor' (Lazzarato 2011: 161).

Exchange Money, Credit Money

Accepting, indeed welcoming, all the paradoxes inherent to this statement: Deleuze and Guattari's identification of a profound dualism at the heart of money is the rock bottom of all of the matters at hand. For them we cannot underestimate:

> the extreme importance in the capitalist system of the dualism ... between the formation of means of payment and the structure of financing, between the management of money and the financing of capitalist accumulation, between exchange money and credit money (2000: 229).

Credit money and exchange money are tendencies; the multiple interactions between the two use the same coin, and banks facilitate both financing and payment transactions with one continually flowing into the other. Even so, the fundamental difference between the two is of inestimable importance. 'There is a profound *dissimulation* of the dualism of these two forms of money, payment and financing – the two aspects of banking practice' (Deleuze and Guattari 2000: 229). In this sense, it is decidedly *not* the same coin that is counted as credit on the balance sheet and in the pocket of the wage earner. Credit money is where the flow of exchange is arrested, where values are assigned, and divinations of purpose, rent and ownership are made according to the axiomatics of capitalism.

On the one hand, exchange money has no value in and of itself: it is 'an impotent sign of exchange value,' it could be a theatre token, a shell or a notch. On the other hand, credit money traverses a particular circuit where it assumes, then loses, its value as an instrument of exchange and where the conditions of flux imply conditions of reflex, giving the infinite debt its capitalist form. It is here that Deleuze and Guattari predict the impact of credit money: 'bank credit effects a demonetisation or dematerialization of money, and is based on the circulation of drafts instead of the circulation of money' (Deleuze and Guattari 2000: 229). 'Drafts' here correspond only in part to the 97% bank-issued money identified by Positive Money; in reality they include the trillions of dollars conjured up by the shadow banking system. In short: the 'capitalist field of immanence' is sustained by the circulation of credit money (Kerslake 2009), and through credit 'the archetype of violence and savagery is forcibly built into the nature of money, and money is a precondition for existence in any part of the globe' (Shaviro 2011). This credit-and-exchange-money binary solves a residual problem with the Marxist theory of money.

It is unfortunate that Marxist economists too often dwell on the mode of production, and on the theory of money as the general equivalent as found in the first section of *Capital*, without attaching enough importance to banking practice, to financial operations, and the specific circulation of credit money (Deleuze and Guattari 2000: 230).

At this stage of the argument, it should be clear that trying to establish the essence or truth of money, trying to pinpoint its role and function, should give way to the problem of forces. What counts is less the essential nature of money than what it does. Capitalism is sustained by the great paradoxes between its dynamism and destructiveness; invention and despotism, freedom and servitude, the implacability of its axioms and demand to constantly revolutionize them, these can be understood in terms of this essential dualism and how the irrepressible creative charge and rhizomic flow of capital is essentially underpinned by credit money, or more importantly, how exchange money comes into existence as credit money:

> [Deleuze] underscores the impossibility of considering a market economy in itself, since the latter derives from and is always subordinate to the money economy and to the debt economy, which distribute power, subjection, and domination. ... The asymmetry of power, the differentials of power expressed in debt-money, hold for every society – primitive society, ancient society, feudal society, and capitalism. (Lazzarato 2012: 37–8)

At this point we can return to the earlier semi-orthodox economic theories of Positive Money, their fellow travellers, Steven Keen, Margrit Kennedy and the longer tail represented by the likes of Frederick Soddy, Irving Fisher et al. We can see more clearly now what Deleuze and Guattari mean when they say that 'the circulation of money – *is the means of rendering the debt infinite.*' Money is not issued, as it should be, like oil to smooth the system of trade, investment and exchange. Instead it is deployed as an opportunity to charge rent and to sustain the entire system of the production and circulation of commodities. Financial institutions and banks 'create a debt spontaneously to themselves' that releases 'a flow possessing a power of mutation' determining the planning of investment in technology and labor (Deleuze and Guattari 2000: 237).

It is essential to retain all the subtleties and nuances outlined above; capitalism *is* sustained by a virtuous circle of customer demand, freedom of choice, and an astonishingly productive power underpinned by the invisible hand of the inescapable market. Exchange is liberatory but only within the conditions set by the market that have to be accepted. Capitalism's first principle is the encouragement and release of flows that lead in unexpected directions and the constant revolutionizing of the instruments and relations of production, yet it must also limit and block these lines of flight.

The value of trading and the market and cannot be denied – it is the circularly system of libidinal and social production – but here we are discussing a very distorted market. Its lines of flight, rhizomic potential and accumulative charge are blocked by its own axioms and credit money. As Graeber has recently pointed out, the policies of the G20, G8, International Monetary Fund, World Trade Organization and the World Bank have singularly failed to foster wellbeing for the world's population;

where success is to be found where their policies have been ignored, yet all the while they have magnificently convinced the world that capitalism – and not just capitalism, but exactly the financialized, semi-feudal capitalism we happen to have right now – is the only viable economic system (Graeber 2013). Thus banks not only have the capacity to control investment and interest, most importantly they control the relationship between credit and exchange money that becomes the principal feature of the capitalist mode of production itself.

This is Deleuze's first axiomatic of capitalism – that it must be presented as common sense, irrefragable and transcendental in its immanence; that it insists there is no other way of controlling the schiz/flow, credit money/exchange money, credit/debt whilst concealing its chronic wastefulness and iniquity and the inherent power relations: therein; and that it inhibits human creativity largely through the issuance of money.

> Through the system of debts, money imposes an immense and irresistible system of social control on individuals, corporations, and governments, each of whom are threatened by economic failure if they refuse their obligations to the money system. (Kerslake 2009)

In this way, neoliberalism is the *control society* – we are controlled by and submit to its values as it insists that alternatives to its immanence are crushed. Kerslake is right, *Anti-Oedipus* was prophetic:

> There is always a monotheism on the horizon of despotism: the debt becomes a debt of existence, a debt of the existence of the subjects themselves. A time will come when the creditor has not yet lent while the debtor never quits repaying. (Deleuze and Guattari 2000: 197)

Here we can recognize the phenomenological struggle of the mind to take in the colossal sums of bank credit, the quadrillions produced by the financial services industry as assets, securities and virtual credit, that exist *alongside* the flows and intimacies of everyday life facilitated by exchange money. Whilst they may be expressed in the same coin their functions are so dissimilar as to make it impossible to conceive of them as the same thing. Today, consumption, production and the production of subjectivity are geared to provide the surplus value needed to give these inestimable virtual sums some 'objective' attachment to the 'real' world: an attachment that was stretched beyond breaking point in the crash of 2008. Indeed, far from a purely cash driven nexus we find that primitive, industrial, Fordist and post-Fordist forms of capital are required to produce leverageable assets in order that finance capital can continue to reproduce itself. Indeed, exchange (as the swapping of debts and promises creating a form of sociality and mutuality) far from being an antidote to credit is now, as a new form of feudal capitalism emerges, a kind of capture as all flows are permitted as long as they are quantified and circulated through the system of exchange.

How this dynamic process provides the historical material origins for systems that are in equal measure cognitive *and* social (the philosophical holy grail) is outlined perceptively by Goodchild in his paper 'Philosophy as a Way of Life: Deleuze on Thinking and Money,' where he argues that the exchange/credit money differential, the flow of the one into the other, is absolutely fundamental to the structure of human thought:

> Exchange money and credit money, segmented line and quantum flow: this unique self differentiation and re-conjugation is the schiz-flow that structures the capitalist social field, generating all the dualisms of Capitalism and Schizophrenia – representation or production, molar or molecular, striated or smooth, State or war-machine, neurosis or psychosis, extensive or intensive multiplicities, being or becoming, organization or consistency, transcendence or immanence – in each case, we are informed that it is not an exclusive disjunction or a value judgment, but that one term is continually passing into the other. Capitalism, a purely machinic process of segmentation, can only function alongside such intensifications of experience. (Goodchild 2010: 30 and 35)

To conclude, we have at hand a way of thinking that captures the intense contradictions that are inherent to the nature of money and how these contradictions subtend the oppositions and disjunctions inherent to the development of thought and social relations.

Although he does not use such combinative terms, Matthew Tiessen's statement could possible be laid atop of a Positive Money working paper:

> Today's money has become the primary agent of capital accumulation and an aggressive catalyst of dispossession that, in order to feed itself, uses enormous leverage to parasitically prey on life and energy in general, insatiably consuming emergent, biological and processual forms of life and matter in order to feed that which both keeps it alive and expanding: debt. (Tiessen 2012)

In the meeting of Positive Money, and Deleuze and Guattari there is no need to posit contradictions between philosophical and anthropological speculations and the objective political policies and programs of political economy. Controlling the bank's issuance of money is a specific weapon, perhaps the most urgently needed of our age. A range of currencies serving different purposes is also needed. Such a range already exists.[9] The coexistence of a range of currencies with a state-issued currency may be the first of a series of experiments wherein the philosophical work of Deleuze and Guattari might find practical concrete application. As would a combination of reforms that piece-by-piece may gain the consistency of a counter-aggregate sufficient to cause the capitalist abstract machine to lose its potency. Like much of the Occupy movement worldwide, the OccupyLSX Economics Working Group (EWG), of which the author is a member, is discussing a range of specific policy initiatives and reforms to the monetary system. The three main foci of these discussions for the EWG in London are thus: reform of the issuance of money; reform of the structure of land ownership and rent; and reform of wage structures along the lines of guaranteeing a minimum income to all citizens regardless of status or employment. It is striking how much of this chimes with Deleuze's description of the three main decodings that came together to create the capitalist system:

> These decodings of all kinds consisted in the decoding of land flows, under the form of the constitution of large private properties, the decoding of monetary flows, under the form of the development of merchant fortunes, the decoding of a flow of workers under the form of expropriation, of the deterritorialisation of serfs and peasant landholders. (Deleuze 1971)

Finally, what must be borne in mind, as the Occupy Economics Working Group and Positive Money do, is that credit is not an evil in and of itself, credit is a fact of life, and we measure people and ourselves by our capacity to repay debts. Credit is a requisite of non-simultaneous exchange, provided the charge behind the industrial revolution, and is the way in which production can be released from the shackles of time and space. The problem then is not credit or debt *per se* but who issues it and who controls it to what end. In this respect we have at hand a potential consilience between the highest level of philosophy – which is philosophy at its most concrete – and concrete proposals that in aggregate can create a revolution against what is now being commonly called despotic or feudal capitalism without tearing down society and creating chaos.

> *The modern banking system manufactures money out of nothing. The process is perhaps the most astounding piece of sleight of hand that was ever invented. Banking was conceived in inequity and born in sin …. Bankers own the earth. Take it away from them but leave them the power to create money, and, with a flick of a pen, they will create enough money to buy it back again. Take this great power away from them and all great fortunes like mine will disappear, for then this would be a better and happier world to live in. But, if you want to continue to be the slaves of bankers and pay the cost of your own slavery, then let bankers continue to create money and control credit.*
>
> Sir Josiah Stam, Director of the Bank of England 1927

Works Cited

Benes, Jaromir and Michael, Kumhof. 2012. *The Chicago Plan Revisited*. IMF Working Paper, WP/12/202. International Monetary Fund.

Coghlan, Andy and Debora Mackenzie. 2011. 'Revealed – The Capitalist Network that Runs the World'. *New Scientist* 2835. Accessed May 8, 2015 from: http://www.newscientist.com/article/mg21228354.500-revealed--the-capitalist-network-that-runs-the-world.html#.UidCblNvk0w

Colebrook, Claire. 2006. *Deleuze: A Guide for the Perplexed*. London: Continuum.

Deleuze, Gilles. 1971. 'Cours Vincennes 16/11/1971 (Deleuze / Anti-Oedipe et Mille Plateaux)'. Trans. Daniel W Smith. Accessed May 8 19, 2015 from: http://www.webdeleuze.com/php/texte.php?cle=116&groupe=anti+oedipe+et+mille+plateaux&langue=2

Deleuze, Gilles, and Félix Guattari. 1987. *A Thousand Plateaus: Capitalism and Schizophrenia.* Trans. by Brian Massumi. Minneapolis: University of Minnesota Press.

Deleuze, Gilles, and Félix Guattari. 1994. *What Is Philosophy?.* Trans by Hugh Tomlinson and Graham Burchell. New York: Columbia.

Deleuze, Gilles, and Félix Guattari. 2000. *Anti-Oedipus: Capitalism and Schizophrenia.* Trans. Robert Hurley, Mark Seem, and Helen R Lane. Minneapolis: University of Minnesota Press.

Deleuze, Gilles and Félix Guattari. 2001. 'Capitalism: A Very Special Delirium'. In *Hatred of Capitalism.* Ed. Chris Kraus and Sylvére Lotringer. New York: Semiotext(e): 215–21.

Boyle, David. 2002. *The Money Changers: Currency Reform from Aristotle to E-Cash.* London: Routledge.

Ferguson, Charles H. 2012. *Predator Nation: Corporate Criminals, Political Corruption, and the Hijacking of America.* New York: Crown Business.

Galbraith, John Kenneth. 1975. *Money, Whence It Came, Where It Went.* Boston: Houghton Mifflin.

Goodchild, Philip. 2010. 'Philosophy as a Way of Life: Deleuze on Thinking and Money'. *SubStance* 39 (1): 24–37.

Goodchild, Philip. 2013. 'Exposing Mammon: Devotion to Money in a Market Society'. *Dialog* 52 (1): 47–57.

Graeber David. 2012. *The History Of Debt: Slavery, Money, and the Crucial Role of Violence.* Accessed September 28, 2013 from: http://www.pubtheo.com/page.asp?PID=1745

Graeber, David. 'A Practical Utopian's Guide to the Coming Collapse'. *The Baffler* 22: 53–8.

Holland, EW. 1999. *Deleuze and Guattari's* Anti-Oedipus: *Introduction to Schizoanalysis.* London: Routledge.

Jackson, Ross. 2012. *Occupy World Street.* Cambridge: Green Books.

Keen, Steve. 2012. 'Instability in Financial Markets: Sources and Remedies'. *New Economic Thinking's Paradigm Lost Conference* (April 14). Berlin. Accessed May 6, 2015 from: at http://www.youtube.com/watch?v=js9WBi_ztvg

Kerslake, Christian. 2009. 'Deleuze and the Meanings of Immanence'. *'After 68' Conference* (June 16). Maastricht: Jan van Eyck Academy.

Lazzarato, Maurizio. 2011. *The Making of the Indebted Man: An Essay on the Neoliberal Condition*. Trans. by Joshua David Jordan. New York: Semiotext(e).

Lazzarato, Maurizio. 2012. *Deleuze and Guattari: A Short History of Debt*. Los Angeles: Semiotext(e).

Lofgren, Mike. 2012. 'Revolt of the Rich: Our Financial Elites are the New Secessionists'. *The American Conservative* (August 27). Accessed February 28, 2013 from: http://www.theamericanconservative.com/articles/revolt-of-the-rich/

Marx, Karl. 1973. *Grundrisse: Foundations of the Critique of Political Economy*. Trans. N Nicolaus. New York: Penguin.

Marx, Karl. 1887.*Capital: A Critique of Political Economy, vol. 1*. Ed. Friedrich Engels. Trans. Samuel Moore and Edward Aveling. Moscow: Progress Publishers.

Mattera, Philip and Kasia Tarczynska, et al. 2012. *Paying Taxes to the Boss*. Washington: Good Jobs First. Accessed September 19, 2013 from: http://www.goodjobsfirst.org/sites/default/files/docs/pdf/taxestotheboss.pdf

Nietzsche, Friedrich. 1988. *On the Genealogy of Morality*. Trans. Maudemarie Clark and Alan J Swensen. Indianapolis: Hackett.

Ryan-Collins, Josh, and CAE Goodhart. 2012. *Where Does Money Come From?: A Guide to the UK Monetary and Banking System*. London: New Economics Foundation.

Paul Fisher (Executive Director Bank of England). 2013. Speaking on the BBC Radio 4 programme *What is Money?*. Cited in Dyson, Ben. 2013. *Reforming the Monetary System*. Positive Money. Accessed 8 May, 2015 from: http://www.positivemoney.org/our-proposals/video-reforming-the-monetary-system/

Read, Jason. 2008. 'The Age of Cynicism'. In *Deleuze and Politics*. Ed. Ian Buchanan and Nicholas Thoburn. Edinburgh: Edinburgh University Press.

Rowbotham, Michael. 2011. 'The Significance of Monetary Reform: The Disaster of Debt Based Economics'. Paper presented to The Committee on Monetary and Economic Reform (April 13). London: House of Parliament. Accessed May 8, 2015 from: http://www.youtube.com/watch?v=XcCbGGlX8as

Steven Shaviro. 2011. 'The Bitter Necessity of Debt: Neoliberal Finance and the Society of Control'. *Concentric: Literacy & Cultural Studies* 37 (1): 73–82.

Tiessen, Mathew. 2012. 'Infinite Debt and the Mechanics of Dispossession'. In *Revisiting Normativity with Deleuze*. Ed. Rosi Braidotti and Patricia Pisters. London: Bloomsbury.

Venn, Couze. Forthcoming. *Protocols for a Post-Capitalist World*. Cited with permission.

Vogl Josef. 2012. 'Sovereignty Effects'. *INET Conference* (April 12). Berlin. Accessed July 19, 2013 from: http://ineteconomics.org/sites/inet.civicactions.net/files/Vogl%20Paper.pdf

Notes

1. I am grateful to the Occupy London Economics Working Group for the opportunity to discuss this paper on more than one occasion. I am particularly grateful to Clive Menzies, Dave Dewhirst and Tim Flitcroft for their comments.
2. Over 600,000 YouTube views of their video '97% Owned' (as of March 4, 2014); 30,000 visits per month to http://www.positivemoney.org
3. Including Prof. Herman Edward Daly; Dr Martin Harrison Martin Harrison (formerly Chief Investment Strategist with Deutsche Asset Management); Prof. Joseph Huber; Paul Moore (one of the UK's leading specialists in risk management, regulatory affairs and corporate governance in the financial sector with twenty-seven years experience of UK and other regulatory regimes); James Robertson (British-born political and economic thinker and activist, publisher of 14 books); Gordon Styles; and Prof. Richard Werner; in addition to advisors (who wish to remain anonymous) at the Bank of England, RBS and Lloyds Banking Group, the International Monetary Fund, and the BBC.
4. Mortgage, company, government, student and credit card debt is a massive dead weight on economy activity.
5. For Irving Fisher this refers to 200BC–500AD, for Graeber 800BC–600AD.
6. Deleuze and Guattari identify three different social machines: The primitive territorial machine of savage society; the imperial despotic machine of barbarian society; and the capitalist immanent machine of civilized society.
7. For Graeber, 2000BC–800AD.
8. A recent study of financial power by researchers at the Swiss Federal Institute of Technology shows how this structurally embedded form of power works in practice. Analysing the degree of connectivity amongst networks of transnational companies, the findings reveal a web of ownership linking the largest transnational corporations (TNCs), whereby a 'super-entity' formed through interlocking ownerships involving just 147 of them controls 40% of the entire network of 43,060 TNCs. Most of this 'tightly knit' entity were financial institutions, and the connections include shared ownership in

each other. The map of power also uncovers a wider set consisting of a core group of 1,318 companies which controlled 60% of global revenues (Coghlan and Mackenzie 2011). This concentration is the result of both preferential connectiveness motivated by existing power relations (players gravitate towards the most powerful groups, networks or individuals) and 'naturally' occurring structures relating to systems characterized by complexity.

So, the architecture of the network of power – showing the characteristics associated with small-world networks – together with the kind of business companies do, and the shared assumptions about the economy that unite decision-makers into a coherent hub, combine to establish the 'super-entity' determining the fate of the global economy. It means a small elite – the 1%? – wields enormous power which can by-pass democratic control and regulations.

9. In the form of: time banks; air miles (United Airlines in the USA used to pay their entire worldwide PR account in frequent flyer points); electronic barter currencies (Trade Dollars Northwest) and international currency (universal); herocards in Minneapolis, Local Economic Trading Schemes; and, loyalty cards (Boots loyalty card has space on it for various different loyalty currencies).

Bios

Ian Buchanan is Professor of Cultural Studies at the University of Wollongong. He is the author of the *Dictionary of Critical Theory* (OUP) and the editor of *Deleuze Studies* (EUP).

David Burrows is an artist, writer and lecturer based in London and working at Slade School of Fine Art, UCL. He exhibits and presents performances in the UK and abroad, working independently and in collaboration to produce the performance fiction Plastique Fantastique.

Claire Colebrook is Edwin Erle Sparks Professor of English at Penn State University. She has written books and articles on Literary Theory, Feminist Theory, Queer Theory, Contemporary European Philosophy and the visual culture. Her most recent books are the two-volume *Essays on Extinction* (Open Humanities Press, 2013). She is currently completing *Fragility: Species, Planet, Earth* for Duke University Press.

Andrew Conio is an artist, writer and activist. He organised public debates and gatherings at Occupy St Paul's in London, worked on the information tent and served as a member of the Occupy Economic Working Group until 2014. Andrew teaches at the School of Music and Fine Art, Kent University, and has published on a range of subjects including language, the moving image, architecture, painting, institutional critique and creativity.

Verena Andermatt Conley teaches in Comparative Literature and Romance Languages and Literature at Harvard University. She writes on issues of ecology and technology. Her recent publications include *Spatial Ecologies* (Liverpool, 2012) and *Nancy Now* (Polity, 2013), co-edited with Irving Goh.

Eugene W. Holland is the author of *Deleuze and Guattari's 'A Thousand Plateaus': A Reader's Guide* (Bloomsbury 2013), *Nomad Citizenship: Free-Market Communism and the Slow-Motion General Strike* (University of Minnesota Press 2011), Deleuze and Guattari's *Anti-Oedipus: Introduction to Schizoanalysis* (Routledge 1999), and *Baudelaire and Schizoanalysis: The Socio-Poetics of Modernism* (Cambridge 1993). He has published widely on the work of Deleuze and Guattari, on Western Marxism, and on French poststructuralism in anthologies and in journals such as *Angelaki*, *South Atlantic Quarterly*, and *SubStance*. Dr. Holland is Professor of Comparative Studies at the Ohio State University.

Giuseppina Mecchia is Associate Professor of French and Italian and Director of French Graduate Studies at the University of Pittsburgh. She has co-edited a special issue of the journal *SubStance* on Italian Post-workerist Thought (*SubStance*, 112, v. 36, n.1, 2007). She is the co-editor of *The Futures of Empire*, a special issue of *Theory and Event* about the legacy of Hardt and Negri *Empire* trilogy (forthcoming 2015). She has co-translated, edited and introduced the book by Franco Berardi Bifo *Félix Guattari: Thought, Friendship and Visionary Cartography* (Palgrave, 2008). For Semiotext(e), she has translated, edited and introduced one other monograph by Franco Berardi Bifo (*The Soul at Work*, 2009), one monograph by the Swiss-Italian political economist Christian Marazzi (*Capital and Affects*, 2011) and one book of philosophy of language by Paolo Virno (*When the Verb becomes Flesh*, forthcoming 2015). She has published numerous essays covering matters such as the political thought of Jacques Rancière, the esthetics and politics of Marcel Proust, the terrorist esthetics of Jean Baudrillard, the biopolitical concept in Antonin Artaud, the political thought of Gilles Deleuze and Félix Guattari, the philosophical grounding of Elsa Morante's esthetics, Paolo Virno's politics of language and the political implications of the Italian Post-Modern novel.

Rodrigo Nunes is a lecturer in modern and contemporary philosophy at the Catholic University of Rio de Janeiro (PUC-Rio), Brazil. He is the author of Organisation of the Organisationless. Collective Action After Networks (Mute/PML Books, 2014) and has recently edited a dossier on the Brazilian protests of 2013 for *Les Temps Modernes*.

John Protevi is Phyllis M. Taylor Professor of French Studies and Professor of Philosophy at Louisiana State University. He is the author of *Life, War, Earth: Deleuze and the Sciences* (Minnesota, 2013), *Political Affect: Connecting the Social and the Somatic* (Minnesota, 2009), *Political Physics: Deleuze, Derrida, and the Body Politic* (Athlone, 2001), *Time and Exteriority: Aristotle, Heidegger, Derrida* (Bucknell, 1994), and co-author, with Mark Bonta, of *Deleuze and Geophilosophy* (Edinburgh, 2004). He is also the editor of *A Dictionary of Continental Philosophy* (Yale, 2006). His research and teaching materials can be found at www.protevi.com/john and he blogs at http://proteviblog.typepad.com/protevi/.

Nicholas Thoburn is a Senior Lecturer in Sociology at the University of Manchester. He has published on media aesthetics, political theory, and social movements. He is author of *Deleuze, Marx and Politics* (Routledge, 2003) and co-editor of *Deleuze and Politics* (Edinburgh UP, 2008) and *Objects and Materials* (Routledge, 2013). His monograph, *Anti-Book: Material Text and the Art of Political Publishing* is forthcoming with University of Minnesota Press.

www.ingramcontent.com/pod-product-compliance
Lightning Source LLC
Chambersburg PA
CBHW031137160426
43193CB00008B/175